More than Munitions

WOMEN AND MEN IN HISTORY

This series, published for students, scholars and interested general readers, will tackle themes in gender history from the early medieval period through to the present day. Gender issues are now an integral part of all history courses and yet many traditional texts do not reflect this change. Much exciting work is now being done to redress the gender imbalances of the past, and we hope that these books will make their own substantial contribution to that process. This is an open-ended series, which means that many new titles can be included. We hope that these will both synthesise and shape future developments in gender studies.

The General Editors of the series are *Patricia Skinner* (University of Southampton) for the medieval period; *Pamela Sharpe* (University of Bristol) for the early modern period; and *Penny Summerfield* (University of Lancaster) for the modern period. *Margaret Walsh* (University of Nottingham) was the Founding Editor of the series.

Published books:

Masculinity in Medieval Europe
D.M. Hadley (ed.)
Gender and Society in Renaissance Italy
Judith C. Brown and Robert C. Davis (eds)
Gender, Church and State in Early Modern Germany: Essays by Merry E. Wiesner
Merry E. Wiesner
Manhood in Early Modern England: Honour, Sex and Marriage
Elizabeth W. Foyster
Disorderly Women in Eighteenth-Century London: Prostitution in the Metropolis, 1730–1830
Tony Henderson
Gender, Power and the Unitarians in England, 1760–1860
Ruth Watts
Women and Work in Russia, 1880–1930: A Study in Continuity through Change
Jane McDermid and Anna Hillyar
The Family Story: Blood, Contract and Intimacy, 1830–1960
Leonore Davidoff, Megan Doolittle, Janet Fink and Katherine Holden
More than Munitions: Women, Work and the Engineering Industries, 1900–1950
Clare Wightman

More than Munitions

Women, Work and the Engineering Industries,
1900–1950

CLARE WIGHTMAN

Longman
London and New York

Addison Wesley Longman Limited
Edinburgh Gate,
Harlow, Essex CM20 2JE, United Kingdom
and Associated Companies throughout the world.

Published in the United States of America by Addison Wesley Longman, New York.

© Addison Wesley Longman Limited 1999

First published 1999

ISBN 0-582-41435-0 PPR

Visit Addison Wesley Longman on the world wide web at http://www.awl-he.com

British Library Cataloguing in Publication Data

A catalogue entry for this title is available from the British Library

Library of Congress Cataloging-in-Publication Data

A catalogue entry for this title is available from the Library of Congress

Set by 35 in 10/12pt Baskerville
Printed in Malaysia

Contents

List of Figures and Tables

List of Abbreviations

AEU   Amalgamated Engineering Union
ASE   Amalgamated Society of Engineers
ASI   Amalgamated Society of Instrument Makers
BSA   Birmingham Small Arms
BTH   British Thomson-Houston
EEF   Engineering Employers' Federation
ETU   Electrical Trades Union
GEC   General Electric Company
GMWU   General and Municipal Workers' Union
GPO   General Post Office
GWR   Great Western Railway
NFWW   National Federation of Women Workers
NUFW   National Union of Foundry Workers
NUGMW   National Union of General and Municipal Workers
NUGW   National Union of General Workers
NUVB   National Union of Vehicle Builders
TGWU   Transport and General Workers' Union
TUC   Trades Union Congress
WU   Workers' Union

Acknowledgements

It is both a relief and a pleasure to be able to acknowledge publicly those who have helped to bring a piece of research to fruition. First among my archival debts is the Modern Records Centre at the University of Warwick, a unique and important repository whose staff were supportive in many ways. They are probably as relieved as I am at this book's completion. The following archives also deserve thanks: British Motor Industry Heritage Trust Archive and Library, Coventry City Archives, Local Studies Department, Coventry City Library, Birmingham Reference Library and Birmingham City Archives, the Institution of Electrical Engineers, Manchester City Archives and the Public Record Office. I am very grateful to several firms for making their records available to me, including GEC-Alsthom (Electro-mechanical) Trafford Park, Manchester and Lucas Industries, Plc, Solihull. Thanks are also due to all those former employees of GEC, Lucas and Metropolitan-Vickers who offered recollections of the engineering industry and help in locating records. The Engineering Employers' Federation, The Transport and General Workers' Union and the Amalgamated Engineering and Electrical Trades Union also allowed me access to their archives.

Jim Obelkevich has always provided kind hospitality. For their intellectual guidance and help I am especially indebted to Joanna Bourke, Michael Dintenfass and Jonathan Zeitlin. For support of the most valuable kind, however, my final debt is to my husband, Tony Mason.

Introduction

'The engineering industry is, and must always be, primarily an industry for men.'[1]

The authors of a report made to the Engineering Employers' Federation (EEF) in 1934 were right – the industry predominantly employed men and it continued to do so. At its peacetime height in 1946, only a fifth of the workforce was female. In terms of women's employment as a whole, engineering accounted for only a minority of workers. In 1900 most women worked in either domestic service, textiles or garment making. Later they worked mainly in the white collar and service industries. No more than 3 per cent of all women in the major occupational groups worked in the engineering industry.[2] Numerically small, female employment was not insignificant however. After 1919, women and girls made up an increasing share of the workforce in the industry's fastest growing and most productive sector – the 'new' industries of electrical goods, light engineering and vehicles.

This book is about women's employment in the engineering industry between 1900 and 1950. The time span was chosen in order to avoid over-emphasis on the role of both world wars. In spite of popular conceptions, the growth in women's employment was not mainly associated with wartime engineering. An increase in female engineering employment was recorded by the 1911 census and confirmed a decade later. After the sharp fluctuation of both wars, the main

---

1. Engineering Employers' Federation (EEF), *Report to the Administration Committee by the Sub-Committee of the Administration Committee in regard to Female Labour* (Jun. 1934), p. 9, para 39. MRC MSS.237/3/1/89, F(6)56.
2. Jane Lewis, *Women in England 1870–1950. Sexual Divisions and Social Change* (1984), p. 156, Table 10.

source for female employment was the normal peacetime expansion of electrical engineering and motor vehicle manufacture.

In spite of the importance of women to new and growing areas of engineering production, very little has been written about female employment in the industry since the Fabian socialist, Barbara Drake, published *Women in the Engineering Trades* in 1918.[3] Two recent books, however, do include examinations of women's engineering work between 1918 and 1939. The authors of these studies, Laura Lee Downs and Miriam Glucksmann, are both concerned with an epoch-marking shift from craft to mass production, in which women played a central role. They build on and adapt (though neither makes this explicit) Harry Braverman's account of the progressive erosion of workers' skills in the transition to the modern era of scientific management.[4] But while Braverman mostly neglects women workers, Glucksmann and Downs bring them to the forefront of the history of deskilling. In both their accounts it is women, subjected to extensive subdivision of tasks and time and motion study in new mass production industries, who first experience the most advanced expression of capitalist control over the industrial workforce.

In the first of these histories, Miriam Glucksmann focuses on food processing and electrical engineering. *Women Assemble* looks at female employment in the context of the restructuring of the inter-war economy during a period of depression. She claims that 'the large increase in women's industrial employment between the wars can be explained neither as an extension of trends already apparent before 1914 nor as an effect of the First World War'.[5] Instead, fundamental changes in the structure and organisation of production and the development of new consumer goods industries lay at the centre of women's changing occupational distribution.

Glucksmann is not concerned with arguments between economic historians over definitions of new industries and their significance to economic recovery. She identifies them simply as 'those sectors of British industry whose realisation of profit rested on the adoption of mass production methods and a new type of labour process'.[6] They mostly produced new products or products intended for a much wider market than before. They depended on the home

---

3. Barbara Drake, *Women in the Engineering Trades. A Problem, a Solution and Some Criticism: Being a Report based on an Enquiry by a Joint Committee of the Labour Research Department and the Fabian Women's Group* (1918).

4. But Glucksmann also makes criticisms similar to those below, p. 8.

5. Miriam Glucksmann, *Women Assemble. Women Workers and the New Industries in Inter-war Britain* (1990), p. 10.

6. Ibid., p. 77.

rather than the export market. The relevant point for her is that in new industries a close link was established between the employment of women and a particular type of production process (mass production) and the manufacture of particular kinds of goods (consumer goods).

New commodities and markets were accompanied by innovations in technology and work organisation aimed at ensuring rapid and steady output of large numbers of goods. 'Continuous flow' manufacture – organising production into a progressive sequence of operations – was the significant new development of the period and the assembly line its most advanced expression. Cheap women workers, tolerant of monotony, became the assembly line workers of the new industries. As such, they were subject to unprecedented degrees of capitalist exploitation and subordination. Through the conveyor belt employers were able to predetermine their level of output, work intensity and pay. Men serviced the line, working as machine setters, repairers and electricians. They also worked as rate fixers, bonus clerks and in supervisory grades. New specialisms were created among such workers but these posed no problem for employers. There was therefore little or no basis for resistance to the new work methods, especially in recently established factories. The organised labour movement played a negligible role and male trade unionists shared the view of employers that women were 'temporary, uncommitted and unreliable workers'.[7]

The other modern account of women's employment in engineering is found in Laura Lee Downs's comparative study of the French and British metals industries.[8] Like Glucksmann, Downs has two ambitious themes: the genesis of the modern factory through the shift from craft-based to mass production and the centrality of women workers and ideas about gender to the construction of the modern factory world.[9] According to Downs, engineering employers held what she calls an 'Aristotelian presumption' that 'social being dictates differential and complementary productive capacities'.[10] Effective use of labour therefore depended on recognising that men and women were 'in every way distinct and complementary beings'.[11] This belief, together with a shift in the nature of production hastened by the First World War, shape Downs's account of how women were employed. Technological and organisational change accelerated in

7. Ibid., p. 194.
8. Laura Lee Downs, *Manufacturing Inequality. Gender Division in the French and British Metal-working Industries, 1914–1939* (1995).
9. Ibid., p. 10.   10. Ibid., p. 223.   11. Ibid., pp. 105–6.

order to meet the demand for munitions. The processes of production were simplified and subdivided and female labour was narrowly employed on a few rapid, repetitive tasks, often streamlined to the mass production of standardised commodities like shells and fuses. After the war, employers' reasoning in the light of this experience, together with their conviction that women represented a specific and limited form of labour power, prevented them absorbing women into the existing categories of skill or employing them beyond the realm of light repetitive taskwork. Thus, during the inter-war period, women emerged as especially suited to the work of new mass production industries.[12] Ideas about gender also drove employers to adopt methods of work organisation specifically designed to accommodate and to discipline female workers, especially assembly lines and the 'Bedaux' system, an inter-war system of work study pioneered by the French engineer and industrialist Charles Bedaux which aimed to extract maximum effort from a workforce. 'Aristotelian' reasoning extended to wage payment too. It followed that, if women were a unique form of labour, they were deserving of a separate level of wages based on their needs as a gender not as individuals or as workers in a particular industry with specific skills or experience. In brief, gender ideology shaped how women were employed and paid between the wars.

Innovative as these two books are, each has important shortcomings. Downs's use of the notion of Aristotelian ideas about social being shaping the minds of employers seems an unnecessarily complicated restatement of what is already known: that employers saw male and female labour differently. It can describe but does not satisfactorily explain why they used that labour differently, which in her account is reduced to constricting, irrational, ideology-driven choices. She neglects other influences on employers' use of labour, among them the role of demand, the market for engineering goods and the nature of engineering production as well as factors that have nothing to do with ideology but which shield employers from the need to minimise labour costs.

The role of organised labour is another unresolved issue in Downs's book. She concentrates almost wholly on the ideology of employers and does not demonstrate her claim that the new gender division of labour can usefully be understood as 'the outcome of bitter struggles with [organised] men'.[13]

12. Ibid., pp. 104–5.   13. Ibid., p. 8.

Glucksmann ties women's employment too closely to assembly line work. This study will question the primacy she gives to the experience of women who worked under the newest and most advanced conditions of mass production, rewarding employers with unprecedented degrees of control and confining women to routinised, machine-paced assembly jobs. The need for flexibility and novelty in the products of the new industries tended to inhibit comprehensive technological and organisational change, even among the most advanced engineering firms. These factors in turn influenced the nature of female and male employment, leading away from comprehensive deskilling and tightening managerial control. This was not, as Glucksmann might argue, evidence of an inevitable tendency maturing unevenly among firms which would, sooner or later, be forced to conform to new standards or 'go to the wall'.[14] Instead, it indicates that, given the nature of the market, mass production, as described by Glucksmann, was neither inevitable nor attainable.

Some of the criticisms that have been levelled at Braverman, which are examined in more detail below, can also be applied to Downs and Glucksmann. In brief his critics have suggested that increased deskilling and tightened managerial control is not the inevitable result of certain forms of work organisation. They point to the unevenness of change in the nature of work caused, for example, by pressure of competition between firms, the nature of product markets and the bargaining power of the workforce. There is recognition too that historical developments in the organisation of work can lead employers to collaborate with workers and to harness the variability and flexibility of labour power rather than to suppress it.[15] Downs either ignores or leaves little scope for contingent outcomes or unevenness of change. Both she and Glucksmann neglect, either as non-existent or as insignificant, women's employment which does not conform to the full-blown stereotype of work under mass production.[16]

Some theoretical issues

No history of women's employment can ignore the complex and sometimes impenetrable series of theoretical debates which centres on the continued segregation of women in low paid and low skilled

14. Glucksmann, *Women Assemble*, pp. 153–4.   15. See below, pp. 7–8.
16. Glucksmann, *Women Assemble*, pp. 153–4.

jobs. A necessary starting point is Harry Braverman's *Labor and Monopoly Capital*, which, since its publication in 1974, has sparked off new approaches to the problem of deskilling and female labour. Braverman offered a modern Marxist industrial history in which Taylorist scientific management had a new and vital role to play. In his view, this new system of production management, first described by American F.W. Taylor in the last decades of the nineteenth century, marked the culmination of capitalism's drive to accumulate capital and to mechanise, of the 'purposive and systematic application of science to production' which would inevitably displace craft expertise. Through scientific management and its 'dictation to the worker of the precise manner in which work is to be performed' control over the labour process passed, for the first time, into the hands of management – not just a general control but a detailed control over each step of the process.[17] With Taylor's methods managerial power reached unprecedented dimensions. In consequence, Braverman claimed that most jobs were now empty of skill and of meaning to those who did them. Women were included in this increasingly deskilled workforce as a supplement to the 'industrial reserve army' displaced by technological change. This reserve army supplies both the poorly paid labour intensive areas which have not yet been, or cannot be, automated and the clerical, sales and service fields, the only occupational sectors to grow in the modern era of high technology.[18]

In the decade following the publication of *Labor and Monopoly Capital*, two main objections to Braverman's work emerged. Both have consequences (indirectly) for the occupational segregation of women. The first objection is to his view of Taylorism as the essential capitalist practice which all firms will inevitably adopt. The second is to his neglect of class struggle or organised resistance in the workplace as shaping the labour process.[19] There was no simple transition, his critics argue, from craft control to deskilled and Taylorist forms of work organisation. Braverman, they argue, moves too hastily

17. Harry Braverman, *Labor and Monopoly Capital* (1974), p. 100, p. 90.
18. Ibid., chs 15, 16, 17.
19. A general guide to the debate about Braverman's work is provided in S. Wood (ed.), *The Degradation of Work? Deskilling and the Labour Process* (1982). For a discussion of subsequent contributions see J. Zeitlin's review article, 'Social theory and the history of work', *Social History*, 8 (1983), pp. 365–74. For defences of Braverman see P. Armstrong, 'Labour and monopoly capital, the degradation of debate', in R. Hyman and W. Streeck (eds), *New Technology and Industrial Relations* (1988) and Kevin Whitson, 'Scientific Management and production management practice in Britain between the wars', *Historical Studies in Industrial Relations*, 1 (Mar. 1996).

from an abstract capitalist impulsion to control to the practice of deskilling, ignoring the unevenness of capital accumulation and mechanisation, and the way both may have contradictory and unintended effects upon control in the workplace.[20] These observations lead to the second main criticism made of Braverman's work – the passive role he attributes to the workforce. Technological change and new methods of work organisation may create new, narrower skills, new forms of expertise, acceptable to employers because they increase labour productivity. Workers are thus able to gain a bargaining lever and to resist or shape future changes.[21] The progress of labour control under capitalism then is not predictable and uncomplicated but the outcome of a number of factors, like the conditions which affect capital accumulation, competition between firms, and organised resistance from the workforce.

This last point is especially relevant for feminist critiques of Braverman which have argued that women's entry into paid work is determined not only by the demands of capital but by the attempts of male trade unionists to 'sex-type' jobs and thereby restrict the range of occupations open to women.[22]

Other writing on the labour process continues to move away from the inevitability of deskilling and resistance to it. There is a new focus on how the exercise of skill and workers' co-operation or consent are central features of labour processes. This revision of labour process thought is partly informed by 'flexible specialisation' theory. The work of its proponents, including Jonathan Zeitlin and Steven Tolliday, has emphasised the potential of new technology to increase skills and offer more rewarding work.[23] Writers now accept that historical developments in the way work is organised can lead to new skills and collaborative relationships between employers and workers. In a similar vein, recent feminist criticism has focused on the failure of Braverman and the labour process debate

20. This objection is not confined to Marxist critics. See, for example, Craig Littler, 'Deskilling and changing structures of control', in Wood (ed.), *Degradation of Work?*. From a different standpoint see, for example, S. Berger and M.J. Piore, *Dualism and Discontinuity in Industrial Societies* (1980), ch. 2.
21. For instance, see J. Rubery, 'Structured labour markets, worker organisation, and low pay', in A.H. Amsden (ed.), *The Economics of Women and Work* (1980); C. Craig, J. Rubery, R. Tarling and F. Wilkinson, *Labour Market Structure, Industrial Organisation and Low Pay* (1982).
22. For example, Veronica Beechey, 'The sexual division of labour and the labour process', in Wood (ed.), *Degradation of Work*.
23. Proponents include M.J. Piore and C.F. Sabel, *The Second Industrial Divide. Possibilities for Prosperity* (1984); J. Zeitlin and S. Tolliday (eds), *The Automobile Industry and its Workers* (1986), 'Introduction: between Fordism and flexibility'.

to take account of the changing gender structure that accompanied historical developments in the labour process. Deskilling has been seen too much from the perspective of the displaced craft worker, overlooking the many other workers who were upgraded or moved on to new work as a result of new technology. It says that if skill is no longer a workable concept then neither is deskilling and that the role of technological change in women's employment has to be understood in some other way. The impact of new technology and work methods on women is instead determined by the power of the dominant workforce (male or female) to prevent or to control innovation. Once labelled, the gender definition of new work is relatively inflexible.[24]

To sum up, the labour process debate has restored recognition of a degree of skill or job control to the history of work. The implication of much of this writing is that occupational segregation is caused by the exclusion of women by male workforces.[25]

Feminist writers have typically believed that sexual divisions at work cannot be explained simply in terms of the workings of the economy. They emphasise instead the influence of an ideology which prescribes certain sorts of work as suitable for women. Thus the actions of employers, male trade unionists, and often women too are explained by reference to normative ideas about gender roles. Domestic ideology, for instance, defines women's work as subordinate or auxiliary to that of men with a subordinate or supplementary wage as its corollary. Its consequences are lower pay and exclusion from skilled work by male trade unionists and or by employers.[26]

The exclusionary practices of male trade unionists form an important strand of this approach, particularly since, for Marxist feminist authors, the interests of capitalist employers point not to segregation but to treating all labour equally.[27] Fearing that their wages will be undercut, men seek to exclude cheaper female workers and draw on notions of what is 'suitable' work as justification. Two

---

24. Gertjan de Groot and Marlou Schrover, *Women Workers and Technological Change in Europe in the Nineteenth and Twentieth Centuries* (1995), General Introduction.

25. For more detail on developments in labour-process writing and how it relates to women see A. Sturdy, D. Knights and H. Wilmott (eds), *Skill and Consent. Contemporary Studies in the Labour Process* (1992) and D. Knights and H. Wilmott (eds), *Gender and the Labour Process* (1986).

26. For example, Felicity Hunt, 'Opportunities lost and gained: mechanisation and women's work in the London bookbinding and printing trades', in A.V. John (ed.), *Unequal Opportunities. Women's Employment in England 1800–1918* (1986).

27. Ben Fine, *Women's Employment and the Capitalist Family* (1992), p. 76.

significant assumptions behind this approach are that, whenever possible, employers attempt to hire women instead of men or to create new technology intended to be operated by women. Where they fail it is because of strong trade union organisation and bargaining power. A typical example of this approach is the work of Sonya Rose in which she relates the exclusionary strategies of male trade unionists in nineteenth-century Britain to an emerging masculine identity as the primary or sole source of the family income.[28] A similar approach has recently been applied to the history of female employment in new industries in inter-war Holland. According to Gertjan de Groot and Marlou Schrover, 'employers could not tamper with the gender-based labels of these jobs without running the risk of coming up against union or general resistance'.[29]

Other authors accept that trade unions were generally too weak to control entry into their trades. They claim that if employers did not employ women more widely while male union control was weak it was because of their own adherence to gender ideology. Believing women's wage earning capacity to be secondary to their reproductive function, they channelled women into accordingly 'suitable' occupations. Here male solidarity in the workplace and wider society is the key. Ellen Jordan, for example, shows how in the late nineteenth century vertical segregation by sex in clerical work occurred in the interests of male solidarity to preserve the male career ladder in the face of a vast expansion of routine office work. This development was acceptable because it conformed to the 'gendered' lives and expectations of the mid-Victorian middle class. The implication is that gender ideology at work and in the household and community restricts female employment and prevents employers from seeing the possibility that some of the tasks within their industries could be performed just as well and more cheaply by women.[30] This

28. Sonya O. Rose, *Limited Livelihoods. Gender and Class in Nineteenth Century England* (1992), ch. 6; and 'Gender antagonism and class conflict: exclusionary strategies of male trade unionists in nineteenth century Britain', *Social History*, 13. 2 (May 1988). Also Harriet Bradley, *Men's Work, Women's Work. A Sociological History of the Sexual Division of Labour in Employment* (1989), p. 115.

29. Gertjan de Groot and Marlou Schrover, 'Between men and machines: women workers in new industries 1870–1940', *Social History*, 20. 3 (Oct. 1995), p. 296.

30. Ellen Jordan, 'The lady clerks at the Prudential: the beginning of vertical segregation by sex in clerical work in nineteenth-century Britain', *Gender and History*, 8. 1 (Apr. 1996); and 'The exclusion of women from industry in nineteenth century Britain', *Comparative Studies in Society and History*, 31. 2 (Apr. 1989). For a sophisticated use of the concept of domestic ideology see N. Grey-Osterud, 'Gender divisions and the organisation of work in the Leicester hosiery industry', in John (ed.), *Unequal Opportunities.*

approach often involves a view of skill as an artificial concept determined not by the content of the job but by the sex of the worker.[31]

Feminist and Marxist feminist authors have generally paid more
attention than other writers to the role of organised labour in
affecting the direction taken by industry. The difficulty with theories which underline 'exclusion' explanations, though, is that they
imply that female workers can always be substituted by male workers
and that employers are prevented from following the economically
rational course of employing women more widely only by the threat
of industrial disruption. As we have seen, one objection to this is
that trade unions, where they existed, have not always been strong
enough to control entry to their trades. A second is that where
unions have been strong enough to exclude, they have done so when
skills and crafts were under threat, as a defensive response against
all potential competitors, not simply women.

As Ben Fine points out, it is normally the patriarchal ideology of
workers that is underlined in 'exclusion' explanations of women's
work.[32] The interest of capitalist employers is usually seen to lie with
treating all labour equally, breaking down restrictions in the labour
market. Therefore when employers' actions are given a role to play,
they become 'economically irrational' and shaped by 'gendered'
ideology. The following examples underline the inadequacy of this
view in explaining women's employment. In the new industries of
Slough in the inter-war period, Savage has shown, trade unionism
was weak but employers still opted for a predominantly male workforce.[33] The explanation does not lie, however, with the 'domestic
ideology' of employers causing them to prefer men to women but
with their search for the cheapest labour available, in this case
juvenile male labour. Ruth Milkman uses management strategy
determined by the nature of production to explain the unequal
share of female employment between two apparently comparable
US industries between the wars. Both auto and electrical engineering were unionised but many more women worked in the latter
than the former. The difference in employment was the result of
wage-cutting by management in labour-intensive electrical engineering. Thus it was employers' response to the nature of production
which affected the sexual division of labour, not exclusion by

31. For example, A. Phillips and B. Taylor, 'Sex and skill: notes towards a feminist
economics', *Feminist Review*, 6 (1980).
32. Fine, *Women's Employment*, ch. 2, esp. pp. 76–86.
33. Mike Savage, 'Trade unionism, sex segregation and the State: women's employment in new industries in inter-war Britain', *Social History*, 13. 2 (May 1988).

unionised workforces or irrational sex-typing of work.[34] These two examples suggest that the reason for employers' actions may be economically comprehensible and contingent on circumstances such as, in the example of Slough, the nature of the local labour market, or, as in the case of American electrical engineering, the labour-intensive nature of production. In both there was no initial role for either exclusion by trade unions or the sex typing of work by employers on the grounds of ideology.

Samuel Cohn compares the markedly different entry of women clerks into the General Post Office (GPO) and the Great Western Railway (GWR), again giving a negligible role to legitimating ideologies of gender.[35] He looked at the firms' financial structure. In the case of the railway firm, labour accounted for a lower percentage of total production costs than capital, in other words machinery, buildings and stock. This capital-intensive nature of the GWR protected it from the need to minimise labour costs by employing more women clerical workers. Not only were labour costs a smaller portion of its overall budget but the preponderance of blue-collar labour meant that savings, if needed, could be made among these workers and the smaller number of male clerical workers left relatively untouched. For the labour-intensive GPO such options were not available. The employment of more female clerks not only allowed them to make significant savings but also provided, through women's propensity to marry, a form of artificial labour turnover which preserved male career ladders and therefore continued to ensure a supply of well-educated male labour. Cohn further shows how within both firms gendered policies like the exclusion of women from night work and the sex segregation of offices were only maintained while they were compatible with the efficient working of the firm. Cohn's innovative study of female clerical labour probes beyond discrimination based on ideology. Instead he relates the employment or non-employment of women to the capacity of employers to tolerate discrimination which in turn depended on a number of economic factors including, most obviously, the capital structure of the firm.

Savage, in his examination of Slough, also applied Cohn's reasoning to the motor industry. Why were car firms overwhelmingly male, even where there were no unions to promote and defend male

34. Ruth Milkman, 'Female factory labor and industrial structure: control and conflict over "Woman's Place" in automobile and electrical manufacturing', *Politics and Society*, 12. 2 (1983).
35. Samuel Cohn, *The Process of Occupational Sex-typing. The Feminization of Clerical Labour in Great Britain* (1985).

employment? The industry was capital-intensive and used incentive payment systems to drive productivity. Its employers, he suggests, were therefore relatively uninterested in cheap (female) labour, preferring instead reliable (male) labour.[36]

Another more recent American study also shows how employers, in bringing about change, were faced with a complicated set of factors of which gender was only one. In his sophisticated study of work, technology and gender in the American telephone industry, Kenneth Lipartito argues against explanations of technical change (and attendant changes to the labour process) that rely on generalised single causes. Innovation, in his view, is a complex process in which many factors and influences are implicated. It is only by looking at the process of change as part of a system embracing the specifics of labour, gender, technology, company structure, business strategy and the political moment, that variations and differences between firms, the apparent lags in development and failures in innovation can be properly understood.[37]

Lipartito argues that innovators target critical problems such as bottlenecks and breakdowns which threaten the smooth working of the system of production. In this way innovation is both focused and constrained. Firms concentrate resources on making only incremental improvements to existing technology. They 'build systems that follow historically determined patterns of change derived from previous events and choices'.[38] Added to this are the interests of workers, consumers and others which gather round the evolving system and reinforce still further a tendency to follow an existing trajectory. Such systems can become closed, resistant to radical change even in the face of strong incentives. It can take a long time to move the system in a new direction. In this way, the failure to innovate, introducing deskilling and labour-saving automation or changing the gender make-up of a workforce, for example, becomes economically comprehensible.

Lipartito uses this analysis to explain why the largest US telephone company was slow in adopting automatic switching, a new technology which removed skilled workers from production. In spite of increased competition and labour conflict it was not until after

36. Savage, 'Trade unionism', p. 226.
37. Kenneth Lipartito, 'When women were switches: technology, work and gender in the telephone industry, 1890–1920', *American Historical Review* (Oct. 1994). Lipartito draws on systems analysis and the work of American historian Thomas Hughes and economist Nathan Rosenberg.
38. Lipartito, 'When women were switches', p. 1081.

1913 that AT&T finally adopted automated switching. A new combination of technology, business strategy, politics and labour issues at last made the risk viable, indeed essential.

The labour process debate has remained tied to Marxist theory and the task of reworking it. Feminist theories which draw on the concepts of patriarchy and domestic ideology generally offer explanations that cannot account for the varied choices and motives of employers and trade unions. Their single theme of male dominance through exclusion and job segregation neglects the other factors which structure labour markets and decide change, as the examples taken from Savage, Milkman, Cohn and Lipartito show. One of the aims of what follows is to question further the decisive importance attributed to the 'gender ideology' of employers and male trade unionists in shaping the history of women's work by looking at the complexity of their employment in the engineering industry.

Male workers were the 'mainstay' of the engineering industry. Women, however, formed an increasing share of its workforce in new and growing areas of production. Their rising numbers reflected a shift in women's employment in general, away from domestic service and the textile and clothing industries towards new, 'lighter' employment in factories, shops and offices. After the First World War, more women began to work in the fields of engineering, chemicals, food processing, drink and tobacco, clerical and distributive service than in the traditional industries of clothing, textiles and domestic service. Between 1900 and 1950, female employment in the engineering industry's most prosperous trades of electrical engineering and motor vehicle manufacture increased fourfold. The present study examines the factors which determined how and why such growth occurred. In doing so, it challenges the singular importance given to male dominance – whether through gender ideology or through job exclusion – which pervades most historical explanations of women's work. This book deliberately highlights other influences on employers' use of labour. It demonstrates the complexity of female employment which was determined not only by ideology but also by market circumstances, the nature of engineering production, the need for flexibility in work organisation and a continuing reliance on skilled male workforces. This is most clearly shown in electrical engineering and motor vehicle manufacture between the wars. A study of demarcation disputes also questions the decisive role of ideology. These show that engineering employers responded to a number of influences in their decision to employ women, such as cheapness, volume of work, competition, labour supply and opposition from unions. In the absence of union power during the decade following the 1922 lock-out they did not automatically opt for female labour. Instead there had to be a range of factors in place for women to seem a profitable alternative to male workers. As well as broadening the explanation of women's work beyond male dominance in order to take account of other influences and factors, this book re-evaluates the role and attitudes of trade unions. An examination of their approach to female labour challenges the view that it was an unambiguous gender struggle, in which unions (like employers) sought to promote the interests of men over women.

CHAPTER ONE

Women's Employment, 1900–1950

Between 1900 and 1950 women flocked into an industry of huge importance to the society and economy of the twentieth century. They made the shells of the First World War and the weapons and telecommunications systems of the Second. They also manufactured the light bulbs, refrigerators, televisions, radios, telephones, windscreen wipers and car ignition gear consumed for the first time this century. This new employment of women within engineering was part of a broader shift in women's employment in general, away from traditional occupations and towards new areas of work in food processing, artificial fibres and modern shops and offices. This chapter places women's growing importance to the engineering industry within the changing pattern of women's work more generally.

In the twentieth century women have been concentrated in those sectors of employment that have grown most rapidly, those at the forefront of the transition from a mature industrial economy whose wealth was founded on primary and manufacturing industry to one founded on mass consumption and the provision of services. The most significant changes occurred after 1950, though the broad shifts in employment patterns were underway before then.

Accompanying these changes was a growth in the employment rates of women. In other words, of all women aged 15 to 59 the percentage who were in paid work rose. Between 1901 and 1931 the figure was fairly constant at 38 per cent. By 1951, though, it had risen to 43 per cent. The corresponding figures for men were always higher and relatively unchanging. The largest increases in female employment rates date from the 1970s. These figures conceal other, more dramatic rises, however. For example, the participation of married women in paid work leapt up from 10 per cent in both 1911 and 1931 to 22 per cent in 1951. In the following twenty years the figure more than doubled again.[1] In practice, the employment of married women often exceeded these national rates. In certain industries and regions it was traditional or acceptable for married women to work, the textile trade of the North West for example and, Miriam Glucksmann has suggested, London and the South East. Many married women may also have worked at times of labour shortage in seasonal new trades like food processing, motor and radio components. These women, because they were not continuously employed throughout the year, were not included in official statistics.[2]

Previously most working women – more than three-quarters in 1901 – had been under 35. Higher participation rates for married women, however, also meant that a greater percentage of women aged 35 to 59 were working between 1931 and 1951 than ever before, although the female workforce as a whole remained a relatively young one. Even so, the census recorded a significant increase from 26 per cent of over-35s working in 1931 to 43 per cent in 1951. A declining birth rate from the inter-war period allowed women to spend longer in the workforce, before or after child rearing.[3] Thus, in the first half of the century the trend to greater levels of female employment and more employment of older and married women was already underway.

Attitudes among women to work did not change, however. It was almost certainly a necessity rather than an ideal for most of the married women who took it. There was ambivalence among women, especially perhaps single women, as well as men about the propriety of women's work after marriage and a presumption by both sexes that the main duty of wives was the care of their husbands and children.[4] As Joanna Bourke points out, the attractions of work for working-class wives were meagre. Employment doubled their workload.[5] Elizabeth Roberts adds that women in this period rarely complained of having wanted to be in full-time work and of somehow having been prevented.[6]

1. T.J. Hatton and R.E. Bailey, 'Female labour force participation in interwar Britain', *Oxford Economic Papers*, 40 (1988).
2. Miriam Glucksmann, *Women Assemble. Women Workers and the New Industries in Inter-war Britain* (1990), pp. 42–3.
3. Glucksmann, *Women Assemble*, p. 42.
4. Joanna Bourke, *Working-class Cultures in Britain. Gender, Class and Ethnicity* (1994), pp. 126–7.
5. See Bourke, *Working-Class Cultures*, p. 127.
6. Elizabeth Roberts, *Women's Work, 1840–1940* (1995 edn), p. 64.

The most pronounced characteristic of twentieth-century work, for men and for women, has been the move away from manual occupations and towards professional, technical and white-collar employment. In 1900 in Britain, private domestic service was the largest female occupation and accounted for over a third of total employment. It was followed by textiles, clothing and footwear which gave employment to a further third of all females in paid work. Meanwhile only a tiny 3 per cent of working women were found in clerical employment.[7] By 1951 this pattern had been completely and dramatically overturned with women and girls turning away from those traditional fields of work and towards shops and offices as well as the metals, paper, chemicals, food, drink and tobacco trades. It is true that there was some recovery of employment in domestic service between the wars but it declined finally and irreversibly after 1939. The 'personal services' category of work recorded in the government's census was now increasingly made up of cleaning in hotels and offices and work within catering and hairdressing. Daily cleaning, not live-in private domestic service, was the norm. Meanwhile women's opportunities in clerical work were increased with the growth of modern banking, insurance and communications and the rise of the public service sector. Already by 1911 women had become a fifth of the clerical workforce and the proportion of employed women who did clerical and typing work almost doubled between 1930 and 1950.[8] In shops the employment of women was facilitated by the expansion of department stores and the growing association of shopping with glamour and luxury, especially in women's footwear and clothing. New products like cosmetics and toiletries were sold by women to women. Modernisation also created new jobs, such as cashier, which women filled.

The employment of men too broadly shifted away from primary and manufacturing industry, though many of them continued to fill these areas up to 1951. The move from manual work towards white-collar employment occurred more slowly for men than for women.[9] However, men were more likely to be found in managerial, administrative or lower professional and technical occupations

7. A.T. Mallier and M.J. Rosser, *Women and the Economy. A Comparative Study of Britain and the USA* (1987), ch. 3.

8. Glucksmann, *Women Assemble*, p. 54; Pat Thane, 'The social, economic and political status of women', in Paul Johnson (ed.), *Twentieth Century Britain. Economic, Social and Cultural Change* (1994), p. 100.

9. Bourke, *Working-Class Cultures*, p. 99, Table 4.1.

than women.[10] Within retail, men remained in areas with a craft element – as dispensers in chemists, in meat trades and fishmongery, 'where processing as well as selling was still part of the job'.[11]

Women predominated over men in some, though clearly not all, the new sources of work. In the clerical and service sectors particularly women have been over-represented. This means that the female percentage of these workforces has been far higher than the female percentage of the total labour force available in the economy. In other words, given the proportion of women available for work generally, more of them have worked in these two fields of employment than might have been expected.

In industry, women have generally been under-represented. Before the Second World War, however, manufacturing jobs accounted for roughly half of women's total employment. It was mainly after the war that manufacturing industry significantly lost ground to the service sector as an area of female employment.[12] It is also the case that women have been over-represented within certain manufacturing sub-sectors and occupations. Plastics-moulding, biscuit making, telephone and lamp manufacture for example, were overwhelmingly staffed by women and girls.

In addition, even where women did not predominate, they formed an increasing proportion of the workforce in new industries. A third of workers in the new rayon industry were female by 1936.[13] A fifth of food and drink workers had been women in 1901 and by 1931 the proportion had risen to more than a third. In electrical engineering, between the wars, at almost three times the male increase, women's employment rose much faster than men's.

These patterns clearly show, as other historians have pointed out, an important link between women's employment and the emergence of significant new fields of work like clerical and retail services and of new industries like artificial fibres, food processing and electrical engineering.[14] But they also indicate that, in spite of the huge changes in the economy of the twentieth century, certain

10. Jane Lewis, *Women in England 1870–1950. Sexual Divisions and Social Change* (1984), p. 163.

11. Harriet Bradley, *Men's Work, Women's Work. A Sociological History of the Sexual Division of Labour in Employment* (1989), p. 182.

12. Mallier and Rosser, *Women and the Economy*, p. 49.

13. Lewis, *Women in England*, p. 158.

14. Glucksmann, *Women Assemble*; Gertjan de Groot and Marlou Schrover, 'Between men and machines: women workers in new industries 1870–1940', *Social History*, 20. 3 (Oct. 1995).

industries and sectors had an above average proportion of females (or males) and that men and women often continued to do different work, with women concentrated in 'women's' occupations.

Changing women's work?

The introduction examined some of the theories and histories which have attempted to account for the occupational segregation of women. The rest of this chapter will look at studies of the sexual division of labour in new industries in particular and the reasons authors have put forward for the employment of women and their apparent concentration in the least-favoured jobs.

One of the reasons historians are interested in new industries is the opportunity they seem to offer of finding out how and why jobs are given either to men or to women in the absence of the dead hand of tradition or custom or union power. Savage, as we saw, showed how the availability of other low paid groups such as young males operated against the employment of women in new industries. In addition, attempts by employers in capital-intensive industries like motor manufacture to reduce the turnover of labour by offering high wages to 'reliable' workers led employers to favour men over women. Ruth Milkman has stressed the capital-/labour-intensive divide in new industries but also suggested that the factors which account for the patterns of female employment vary from case to case. In her view ideology – the idioms which distinguish women's work from men's work – has a role to play in perpetuating the sex definition of jobs once they have emerged in a particular labour market. Ellen Jordan suggested employers in new industries were held back from employing women more widely by middle-class ideas about what work was suitable for women. In Harriet Bradley's sociological study, the gender label of new work was decided by analogy with the gender label of existing work, and in her words, 'the allocation of jobs mirrored stereotypes of men's and women's work which had been constructed in the older industries'.[15] Finally, the Dutch economic historians Schrover and de Groot suggest that opportunities for female employment in new industries have been exaggerated. With technological advance and the growth of very large, capital-intensive business the proportion of women workers shrank.

15. Bradley, *Men's Work, Women's Work*, p. 116.

The following sections look at what hindered and what promoted female employment in three important new industries, namely food processing, the production of electrical consumer goods and artificial fibres, in Britain and abroad.

Food processing

The food processing industry has become a major twentieth-century employer of women and the rise in the number and proportion of women has been associated with an unprecedented expansion of the industry in terms of its range of products, methods of production and scale.

In Britain female employment grew by 20 per cent between 1890 and 1930. More than a third of these workers at that date were girls aged under 18. In the expanding and more mechanised sections of the industry, biscuit production for example, women workers far outnumbered men.[16] According to Bradley, women were attractive to employers in the food industries because of their cheapness, and so-called natural attributes of dexterity, neatness and cleanliness. They were employed in all processes except those needing physical strength and skill, for example mixing and transportation. In biscuit production, men mixed dough and tended ovens, said to be skilled work on the grounds that it required training and experience and involved the use of dangerous machinery, while women stamped out biscuits, took them to be baked and decorated them. With the adoption of mass production methods, men's work tended to be displaced by machines but women's increased because of the growth of unskilled or semi-skilled repetitive machining tasks for which cheap female labour was deemed suitable.[17]

In Holland the food processing industry included some of the largest and most significant world producers of new products but the relation between mechanisation, deskilling and female employment was not as straightforward as that described for Britain. In 1928 the world's largest margarine producer, a Dutch firm called Margarine Unie, merged with the British company Lever Brothers to form Unilever. The development of margarine production into a one firm, multinational industry, employing thousands of workers per plant, was accompanied by a pattern of female employment

16. Glucksmann, *Women Assemble*, p. 63.
17. Bradley, *Men's Work, Women's Work*, p. 165.

which failed to follow the expected path of inexorable rises accompanied by the displacement of male workers.

Before 1900 most Dutch margarine factories were small and staffed by men. Pre-wrapping of margarine, which allowed producers to market particular brands, created openings first for boys and then, as boy labour became in short supply, girls. As with many other food industries the main trigger of female employment was the advent of wrapped products. Female employment grew further with the introduction in 1915 of machines which sliced the slabs of margarine into similar shaped pieces. These were operated by women and because the process was still labour-intensive, attention was paid to speeding up the pace of work through competing teams of female workers. In addition, women operators were cheap. They were never paid more than half the wages paid to men.[18] The introduction of more sophisticated wrapping machines in the 1920s and 1930s severely reduced the number of women and girls in the industry, however. Thus, in this industry, female employment did not grow at the expense of men – mechanised wrapping was a newly created job for which women were recruited from the outset. The impact of new technology also, at a later stage, led to female unemployment, prompting Marlou Schrover to conclude that 'mechanisation can create and destroy women's work without affecting male workers'.[19]

The example of margarine manufacture also shows that the effects of skill and deskilling on the 'gendering' of work are not straightforward. The work women did required training and experience. They could be promoted, according to their experience and speed, from simple packing to being the main operator of the packing machine in charge of a small team. Their work was not less skilled than most of the production jobs carried out by men. Male jobs like churning and oil refinery work were unskilled, with perhaps even fewer prospects of promotion or progression than female ones. This suggests in turn that the gender label of work cannot always be related to the career prospects carried by the job: these were very limited for most of the men who worked in the industry too. Schrover and de Groot conclude that the pattern of female employment was influenced by shortages in the supply of

18. De Groot and Schrover, 'Between men and machines', p. 287.
19. Marlou Schrover, 'Cooking up women's work: women workers in the Dutch food industries 1889–1960', in G. de Groot and M. Schrover (eds), *Women Workers and Technological Change in Europe in the Nineteenth and Twentieth Centuries* (1995), p. 190.

female labour which speeded up automation and eventually reduced both the female and male workforces.

In other Dutch food industries, however, lack of career prospects is seen as the key reason behind employers' choice of labour. In 1900 the country's largest cocoa producer replaced the boys who assisted skilled male cocoa roasters with girls, contrary to the practice of most other firms at that time. Wage differences between boys and girls were insignificant and cannot explain the firm's preference for female labour. The youngest girls earned the same wage as their boy counterparts and sometimes more. Nor were girls more readily available than boys. They commuted from a distance of up to an hour's train journey away and competition for their labour drove up wages. Instead their employment can be explained by a preference for youth. The Dutch cocoa firm only wanted to employ young workers and their tendency to marry made girls the best choice of labour. Any women who did not marry and leave were sacked at the age of 30.[20]

The trend to increased female employment was even more pronounced in chocolate factories where the introduction of machinery deskilled the work of male chocolatiers. At the same time the expansion of the market for cheap chocolate bars promoted women's employment as it was they who attended the machines that made the bars and wrapped them. As the demand for chocolate bars increased so did the employment of women.

In Britain's mass-produced confectionery industry men made the sweets and chocolate centres while women performed ancillary tasks. They dipped them in chocolate either by hand or by machine and also decorated, inspected and packed, an allocation of work which Bradley says was once again justified in terms of natural attributes like neatness.

The food canning industry underwent rapid growth in the late 1920s, though there were difficulties in sustaining this early impetus into the next decade. The market for canned food was already dominated by popular imported products and canning factories had uncertain and unsatisfactory relationships with food suppliers, causing wide seasonal price fluctuations and variable quality. However, the growth in demand can be measured by the output of just one manufacturer of cans, Metal Box in Worcester. From 23,000,000 in 1930 production rose to 100,000,000 cans only two years later. Like other firms, this company benefited from the expertise of

American machine makers with whom exclusive contracts were agreed.[21] Women had always outnumbered men in food preservation and the introduction of food canning between the wars reinforced the trend, boosting female employment. They formed 70 per cent of the total workforce in 1935.[22]

In common with Holland, youth may have been an important element of female employment in the food industries in Britain. These industries always employed more young women than young men and the youthfulness of the workforce became more pronounced during the 1930s. More than a third of the workforce between 1930 and 1935 consisted of girls aged under 18. There were 36,000 under-16s employed in the British food, drink and tobacco trades in 1936. A fifth of female workers in food canning were under 19 in 1935.[23]

Electrical consumer goods

In Britain, Holland and America, female labour was closely associated with the rise of the electrical industry. In America in 1910, over a third of the workforce in the new electrical consumer industry was female. In Britain women moved rapidly into the electrical goods field where their numbers rose by 123 per cent between 1921 and 1931.[24]

The division of labour between men and women was similar in all three countries. Women predominated in lamp manufacture, which had been mechanised and subdivided. They made sockets, wound and mounted filaments, tested lamps, made switches and fuses. During the 1920s and 1930s, as the consumer side grew, women worked in radio assembly, making speakers, transmitters, receivers and condensers. They worked in battery production and motor accessories in Britain. In general women performed light, repetitious work on automatic and semi-automatic machines, assembly tasks and hand operations including inspecting and testing.

The sale of American radios boomed during the 1920s and from being a competitve and volatile industry, by the early 1930s, it had become dominated by a few large producers. Philco was a Philadelphia battery manufacturer which switched to radio in 1928 and very

21. J.P. Johnston, 'The development of the food-canning industry in Britain during the inter-war period', in D. Oddy and D. Miller (eds), *The Making of the Modern British Diet* (1976).

22. Glucksmann, *Women Assemble*, p. 65.   23. Ibid., p. 65.   24. Ibid., p. 58.

soon made most of the industry's output. As the leading producer
it used new technology and assembly lines in a huge factory employing thousands of unskilled and semi-skilled workers of whom
half were female, many of them young and single. In Holland the
largest producer was Phillips, initially a lamp manufacturer which
took over competitor firms, moved into radio production and by
the inter-war years had come to dominate the electrical industry
with a wide range of products. It also had plants in Britain. However, the employment of women at these firms did not follow a
predictable pattern. Neither Philco nor Phillips was as 'female' as
might have been expected and each had a high proportion of male
workers.

Throughout the 1930s, Philco had a higher share of male workers
than comparable radio firms elsewhere. While other firms classed all
assembly jobs together and employed women to do them, Philco
divided assembly into final or heavy, for which it hired men, and
sub or light assembly, performed by women. Testing of products
was similarly divided, with women doing small equipment only.
Patricia Cooper, in her study of the firm, puts forward two explanations for this allocation of work. The first is that it perpetuated a
pattern established when the firm was a battery maker and almost
all employees were men doing heavy, dirty work. The employment
of men continued into the period of radio manufacture unexamined
because of personal and gender loyalty among managers and workers.
The second is that the sexual division of labour at Philco 'was a
social construction of sexual difference. It was in part related to the
desire to cut wage expenses, but given the high proportion of men
in the plant, it was based also on other assumptions about what
men and women ought to do.'[25] The company's resistance to innovation might also be explained by early market domination coupled
with the existence of alternative solutions to the problem of changing the established division of labour. Cooper describes, for instance,
how fears that unionisation would sweep through the industry
prompted the firm to agree to a contract with a trade union which
prevented other unions at other firms from agreeing lower wage
rates than Philco and which allowed wage increases only if another
radio firm introduced them first. In this way Philco expected to
force its competitors to pay the same high wages as it paid. It was
only when the predicted spread of trade unionism failed to occur

25. P. Cooper, 'The faces of gender: sex segregation and work relations at Philco, 1928–38', in Ava Baron (ed.), *Work Engendered. Toward a New History of American Labor* (1991), p. 327.

that managers at Philco were made to rationalise job classifications and introduce wage cuts. Even so, it is hard to understand fully from this account why a predominantly male, high wage firm like Philco was so much more successful than its low wage women-employing competitors.

Phillips in Holland was initially a female factory. After the First World War, however, it employed more men than women, in spite of increased mechanisation and automation and in spite of the fact that on average women's wages were a third lower than those of unskilled men.[26] Why? As in the case of the Dutch food industry, technological changes actually reduced the number of women needed by the firm. Women were the core of the production workers, and it was therefore typically women who were replaced by machines, not men. They moved out of automated departments and into those 'in a take-off phase', until eventually technological change reduced the female share of the workforce.[27]

While women were being displaced by automation, for example in lamp making, the amount of non-production work was expanding as the firm began to build its own machinery and produce its own glass, board and paper. In doing so the firm branched out into work that was not new and already had gender labels. This move restricted the percentage of women workers and the scope for their employment.[28]

Rayon

Like electrical appliances and processed food, rayon, or artificial silk, was a new product of great economic and social significance. It enjoyed one of the longest industrial booms of the twentieth century and aided a social revolution in clothing, bringing a fashion for lighter, less formal and shorter clothing to all classes. It became a new source of female employment and most of the customers for new rayon goods, including underwear, stockings, blouses and dresses, were women.[29]

While artificial fibres failed to overtake the natural fibres, for example, cotton, which in 1939 still accounted for the largest share of textiles consumption, the growth rates achieved by the rayon industry

26. De Groot and Shrover, 'Between men and machines', p. 293.
27. Ibid., p. 295.   28. Ibid., p. 296.
29. D.C. Coleman, *Courtauld's. A Social and Economic History*, vol. 2 (1969), pp. 171, 198; J. Harrop, 'Rayon', in N.K. Buxton and D.H. Aldcroft (eds), *British Industry Between the Wars. Instability and Industrial Development 1919–1939* (1979), pp. 283–4.

were astonishing. Output soared by 8,700 per cent between 1920 and 1941.

In the early 1920s Britain was the largest producer in Europe. Output during that decade increased by 500 per cent and 60 per cent of it came from just one firm. Given the costs of patents on technology, specialised machinery and technical expertise, rayon production lent itself to large-scale, capital-intensive business.[30] Thus, two main companies were responsible for most of the country's rayon output: Courtaulds followed by British Celanese.

Over the inter-war period the numbers employed on rayon manufacture at Courtaulds rose sixfold. There was a very rapid increase in employment after the war and throughout the 1920s followed by a much slower expansion of employment in the 1930s, by which time the proportion of female workers had fallen off and the firm employed more men than women. The pattern was repeated for the Dutch firm ENKA and, as in the examples taken from food processing and electrical goods above, the reason lay with women's concentration in labour-intensive areas of production, liable to be mechanised or reorganised with reduced scope for female employment.

The sexual division of labour at both ENKA and Courtaulds in Coventry was similar. Work involving heavy machinery and dangerous chemicals was allocated to men. In practice this meant that only men worked on the actual production of rayon yarn. Women's work was always clean or required cleanliness. Half of it required no machinery at all – sorting, checking, dispatching – and where machines were used, as in the case of reeling, they were light and relatively simple.[31]

Pressure to produce more and better quality yarn in the early 1930s led to technical developments which removed female jobs from production. Instead of the 'cake' of rayon yarn being washed, bleached, put onto reels and dried, as formerly, a process which often caused the rayon filament to break, it was wound directly onto cones ready for dispatch from the factory. The labour-intensive female tasks of reeling and sorting disappeared. At a time when the world market price for rayon was beginning to fall, costs were lowered and the quality of yarn and its range of uses improved.[32]

30. Harrop, 'Rayon', pp. 286–9.
31. J. Castle, 'Factory work for women: Courtaulds and GEC between the wars', in B. Lancaster and T. Mason (eds), *Life and Labour in a Twentieth Century City. The Experience of Coventry* (1986), p. 140.
32. De Groot and Schrover, 'Between men and machines', pp. 289–90; Coleman, *Courtauld's*, pp. 187–8.

ENKA was faster to adopt the new process, known as cake-washing, than Courtaulds. The latter suffered an intensely personal style of factory management at the hands of Harry Johnson, who was slow to accept the worth of the new method, and the firm's competitive ability and profits were reduced as a result.[33] But between 1935 and 1947 the employment of women at the Coventry works had fallen too and male employment was rising. By 1947 almost twice as many men as women worked at a factory which twenty years before had employed roughly equal numbers of both.[34]

Another cause of the reduction in numbers and proportion of women workers was the development and growing commercial importance of staple fibre, a kind of viscose made originally from rayon waste which could substitute for cotton or wool just as earlier fibres had substituted for silk. Less labour was now required in a new factory purpose built for the production of this fibre.

In common with many of the firms described earlier, Courtaulds only employed young and single women and girls. Thirty per cent of the females who worked there were under 18 between the wars compared with just 6 per cent of the males. The firm employed girls as soon as they left school at 14 and the operation of a marriage bar ensured that most left at around 20.[35]

In both the margarine industry and the rayon industry in Holland, the pace of women's work was speeded up either through competitive team working or through the use of the Bedaux system, both of which related earnings to output and the intensity of work. At Courtaulds women workers enjoyed day wages that were not dependent on how much they produced. They were also comparatively high, as were those paid to girls in the Dutch food industries. Rates of pay in the 1920s for unskilled female juveniles were well above those of other local employers and even when wage cuts were introduced in 1931 (a 20 per cent drop for females compared with 10 per cent for males) the wages paid by Courtaulds were still high in comparison with British Celanese and other employers in the district. This may have been because of the unpleasant nature of the work – hot, eye-straining, steeped in chemical odours. One worker recalled the acrid dust released during the sorting of rayon yarn: 'It was like peeling onions. Your eyes would be streaming.'[36] Another was forbidden from working for Courtaulds by her mother 'because of the fumes'.[37] Difficulties in recruiting women and girls

33. Coleman, *Courtauld's*, p. 188.
34. Castle, 'Factory work for women', p. 137.
35. Ibid., p. 147.   36. Ibid., p. 150.   37. Ibid., p. 145.

to such work also help to explain the firm's deliberate cultivation
of a reputation for genteel employment. But in return for the
cachet of being a 'Courtaulds girl' and high wages workers faced
harsh discipline and intrusive attention to their cleanliness and
respectability.

Women workers were important to new and growing areas of
work before 1950. But the examples of food processing, electrical
consumer goods and rayon raise questions about the central link
between female employment and new industries. Why, given their
cheapness and the absence of craft barriers, weren't more women
employed in new industries? Why, in some cases, did firms swap a
mainly female workforce for a mainly male one? Why did mechanisation and automation, the typical tools by which work is deskilled,
lead in some cases to less rather than, as might be expected, more
female employment?

The examples given above showed how mechanisation and
deskilling did not always promote female employment. The reason
lay with women's concentration in labour-intensive areas of production, liable to be mechanised or reorganised with reduced scope
for female employment. In the rayon industry female tasks which
typically required either light and simple machines or no machines
at all simply disappeared. In the Dutch electrical industry women
who were displaced by automation in areas like lamp making moved
on to newer areas until they too were more fully automated. Eventually technological change reduced the relative proportion of
women workers. They continued to form a significant proportion
of workers in radio production because, in spite of technological
change, it remained labour-intensive, employing a large number
of workers in checking, testing and inspecting. While none of the
tasks in new industries could be labelled male or female by analogy
with existing jobs, firms like Phillips branched out into ancillary
work (in the case of Phillips, building its own factories, producing
its own glass) – work which was labelled male. This development
also lowered the proportion of women workers relative to men.
Patricia Cooper explained the failure of a leading US electrical
firm to catch up with the practice of its rivals and employ more
women in terms of ideology and gender loyalty. But other factors
inhibiting innovation, which might have explained why a firm with
a high wages bill could be more successful than low wage competitors, were not examined.

Was youth as significant as gender? Much emphasis has been
placed on the youthfulness of the female workforce in new industries

but it is unclear how important that was. The examples from Holland suggested that employers had an explicit preference for young females over young males even where wages were comparable. Savage, in his case study of Slough, showed on the other hand that youth could be more significant than gender in employers' choice of labour. In engineering, as we shall see, the vast majority of female workers were adults in receipt of adult rates of pay and employers favoured experienced workers, particularly in seasonal trades. They did not have marriage bars. Young, 'green' workers slowed up production. This contrasts with Glucksmann's conclusion that it was specifically young, single and industrially inexperienced girls who were sought as the most suitable workers for new industries.

* * *

This chapter has described the changing areas of women's employment up to 1950 and looked in detail at how and why the employment of women and girls was hindered or promoted in three important new industries. The experience of producers in Europe described here supports the need for a broader range of reasons, not confined to ideological prescriptions, deskilling and mechanisation, or trade union opposition, to explain the history of women's work.

CHAPTER TWO

The Engineering Industry, 1900–1950

Engineering has never been a single industry. The Engineering Employers' Federation, the national representative body for employers in the industry, was obliged to divide its membership into thirty different 'sections' or trades. Their products ranged from capital equipment for other industries like agricultural and textile machinery, transport like aircraft, ships, locomotives and motor vehicles, to consumer goods like radios, lamps and telephones. They included producers geared mainly to domestic markets as well as those geared mostly for export. Further divisions could be drawn between 'old' and 'new' engineering trades and their regional concentrations. The older sector produced capital equipment like textile, agricultural and mining machinery, steam engines and ships. Electrical equipment and goods, aircraft, motor cars and cycles, on the other hand, were products of the newer sector. Manufacture within these two divisions was often highly localised. Between the wars, marine engineering was centred in Scotland and the North East, textile machinery in the North West, motors, vehicles and allied trades in the Midlands and electrical engineering in the South East. A simple underlying characteristic gave some unity and definition to the industry, however. All branches of engineering made 'highly composite articles of which the main constituents are metal', and they used 'the finished or semi-finished products of many different industries'.[1]

The years with which this book is concerned saw a far-reaching redistribution of employment, output and sources of growth among the engineering trades. In 1907 the most important sectors of the industry were still those like mechanical engineering, producing

1. G.C. Allen, *British Industries and Their Organisation* (1959), p. 135.

capital equipment for other industries or for transport. The most significant centres of engineering production were therefore the North, the North East Coast, the West Coast and Scotland, where the industries served by textile and marine engineering were located. By 1935, however, the share of mechanical engineering in the gross output of the industry had been halved. The newer trades of electrical engineering, motor vehicle and cycle manufacture, meanwhile, doubled and trebled their share.[2] The annual rate of growth in electrical engineering was at least twice that of mechanical engineering between 1920 and 1938 and the industry as a whole was, for the first time, turning away from the production of capital goods towards goods to be used directly by the consumer.[3]

These changes were reflected in a shift in the balance of employment too. In 1907 producers of electrical goods, aircraft, motor vehicles and cycles together employed about a tenth of engineering workers. By the mid-1930s that figure had risen to half. London and the Midlands rivalled Lancashire and Yorkshire as centres for engineering employment as both became sites for the fastest growing trades of motor vehicle manufacture and electrical goods.[4]

A simple division between new and old, light and heavy sectors, with their corresponding images of growth and stagnation, is misleading, however. Many electrical goods, for example, were neither new nor light. Some old staple trades like machine tool manufacture and agricultural machinery held or increased their share of output during the years of decline.[5] The rearmament drive and the Second World War further complicated the division between the two by reviving branches of the industry that had been in recession. In the late 1930s shipbuilding employment improved dramatically and employment in mechanical engineering stopped falling and began to rise so that by 1948 it was the largest single employer within the engineering group of trades. Both were to benefit from a post-war boom which lasted for most of the 1950s. A backlog of repair and maintenance work on capital equipment, significant government-sponsored investment in re-equipment and the development of new industries like oil refining and synthetic textiles all stimulated demand for machinery and plant. Electrical engineering

2. Mechanical engineering here includes textile machinery.
3. R.E. Catterall, 'Electrical engineering', in N.K. Buxton and D.H. Aldcroft (eds), *British Industry Between the Wars. Instability and Industrial Development 1919–1939* (1979), p. 241 and J.B. Jefferys, *The Story of the Engineers 1800–1945* (1945), p. 199.
4. Jefferys, *Story of the Engineers*, pp. 198–9.
5. T.R. Gourvish, 'Mechanical engineering', in Buxton and Aldcroft (eds), *British Industry Between the Wars*, pp. 142–3.

TABLE 2.1   *Engineering employment (in thousands), 1907–54*

Industry	1907	1924	1930	1935	1948	1954
Mechanical engineering	408	386	385	360	486	599
Shipbuilding	178	131	124	75	250	221
Railway carriage & wagon building	27	26	20	18	90	88
Motors & cycles	48	167	207	242	322	380
Aircraft		10	18	29	139	242
Electrical engineering	14	121	152	193	537	671
Radio & telecomm. components					269	358

Source: Census of Production 1907–54

now accounted for a fifth of the total number of workers, about the same as in 1935.[6] Heavy expenditure on armaments after 1950 brought renewed expansion to several branches of the industry.[7] General mechanical engineering had therefore regained its ground in terms of output by the 1950s. It remained one of the largest producers throughout the period.

Table 2.1 shows a pattern of rapid expansion in employment among the new trades between 1907 and 1935, with a growing proportion of the total workforce claimed by them. After the Second World War they continued to account for a significant proportion of employees – about a third excluding vehicle workers. But the core of the industry was still general mechanical engineering, with approximately the same proportion of workers as in the 1930s. Employment in this trade had stopped falling and was rising between 1948 and 1954. It rose faster than employment in general electrical engineering and kept pace with increases in radio and telecommunications.

Collective bargaining

Despite being a diverse grouping of trades, engineering had an industry-wide collective bargaining procedure. The 'Provisions for Avoiding Disputes' were first agreed after the lock-out of 1896 between the EEF and the Amalgamated Society of Engineers (ASE). The immediate cause of that dispute was the demand in London

6. The 1948 Census of Production reduced the size of the electrical engineering category. Electric wires and cables, batteries and accumulators, electric lighting accessories and fittings, radio and telecommunication formed a new group.
7. See Allen, *British Industries*, pp. 142–3.

for a forty-eight hour week, but its wider context was attempts by unions to control 'machine manning' and a conviction among employers that 'managerial freedom' in the workplace needed to be re-established. The resulting terms of settlement laid down provisions for avoiding disputes in the future. Negotiations were to take place at works, local and finally national level while the disputed change of practice remained in place until agreement was reached. The intended effect of this was to prevent the ASE from sanctioning a strike until all stages of the procedure had been exhausted, in other words, forcing it to discipline its own members and choking off unofficial local action.[8]

The subsequent history of the procedure was dogged by the internal difficulties of the ASE and by periods of trade depression with short-time working, unemployment and some business failure during which conflicts over machine manning, overtime, the closed shop, new payment systems and the terms of settlement in general resurfaced. When the First World War broke out there was no longer a formal agreed procedure on bargaining between the unions and employers. The terms of settlement of 1898, revised in 1907, had been rejected by the ASE in 1914 and an interim agreement – with no reference to managerial prerogatives – had been reached. Attempts after 1917 to negotiate a revived disputes procedure and relaxation of craft restrictions failed. Disputes about overtime working and machine manning brought matters to a head in 1922. The subsequent lock-out was a devastating failure for the ASE (now Amalgamated Engineering Union or AEU). It enabled employers to reassert the 'rights of management' and to establish a more complete collective bargaining system in which all unions were now included. However, the divisions within the industry in terms of employment, growth and location undermined the effectiveness and cohesion of its collective bargaining. An industry composed of different sectors exposed to different variations in profitability, competition and market stability, as engineering was, made it difficult for the EEF to expand its central principle, 'managerial prerogative', into a code of practice for all firms to follow.[9] Instead of national

8. Jonathan Zeitlin, 'The triumph of adversarial bargaining: industrial relations in British engineering 1880–1939', *Politics and Society*, 18. 3 (1990), p. 413.

9. J. Zeitlin and A. Mckinlay, 'The meanings of managerial prerogative: industrial relations and the organisation of work in British engineering, 1880–1939', *Business History*, 31. 2 (Apr. 1989), pp. 33–4; J. Zeitlin, 'The internal politics of employer organisation: the Engineering Employers' Federation 1896–1939', in J. Zeitlin and S. Tolliday (eds), *The Power to Manage? Employers and Industrial Relations in Comparative Historical Perspective* (1990), p. 57.

agreements on important issues like machine manning, therefore, it had an elaborate grievance procedure designed to contain disputes at their source – the workplace. The EEF was still able to influence industrial practice, though. In the field of female labour it often told member firms how to proceed and, as we shall see, had the last say in the settlement of long run disputes.

National and special conferences during disputes with trade unions were presided over by Sir Allan Smith, a former lawyer from Glasgow. As the EEF's chief officer from 1910 to 1935, he was domineering and dour. Walter Citrine, leader of the Trades Union Congress (TUC), later recalled Smith as 'an expert in procrastination whose icy cold speeches were enough to freeze to death any warm impulses towards progress which his members might feel'.[10] He was, Citrine said, loathed by trade union leaders. According to the EEF's official historian and industrial relations journalist, Eric Wigham, he was regarded with a mixture of hate and awe by most of his staff. It is difficult to reconcile this picture of Smith's bearing and personality with the role described for him by Jonathan Zeitlin of far-sighted conciliator, only provoked into the 1922 lock-out by weakened trade union authority.[11] Indeed, under his leadership, the EEF, in the words of Wigham, 'never hesitated to use the threat' of lock-out and did so several times in 1924 and in 1926.[12] In 1935 Allan Smith was carefully persuaded to resign on the grounds of health and make way for Alexander Ramsay, director of the EEF until 1953. A former works manager, full-time chairman of the Birmingham Association Board since 1921, Ramsay had also been elected Conservative MP for West Bromwich in 1931. He gave up his political career on appointment to his new post. In spite of an imposing and formal manner, he was regarded as more 'human' than Smith and more conciliatory.[13]

Six main trade unions negotiated with the EEF on behalf of engineering workers. They were the Amalgamated Engineering Union, the National Union of Foundry Workers (NUFW), the Electrical Trades Union (ETU), the National Union of Vehicle Builders (NUVB), the United Patternmakers' Association and the Boiler-makers' and Iron and Steel Shipbuilders' Society. By far the largest was the ASE, a craft union of skilled male workers. Its name was changed to the Amalgamated Engineering Union in 1921 following

10. Eric Wigham, *The Power to Manage. A History of the Engineering Employers' Federation,* (1973), pp. 112–13.
11. Zeitlin, 'Triumph of adversarial bargaining', pp. 415–17.
12. Wigham, *Power to Manage,* pp. 126–7.   13. Ibid., p. 138.

its merger with several smaller unions, apparently opening up the craft union to new trades and grades of skill. In practice, Tim Claydon has shown, there were no significant shifts in the composition of the membership or in the recruitment strategies of the new AEU.[14] Its male members were not joined by women engineering workers until 1943, when for the first time they were admitted to a special category of membership.

The other unions which made up the collective bargaining partnership were relatively small. The Electrical Trades Union was formed in 1889 and had a relatively low membership until 1920. It grew slowly at first but doubled in size in the five years after 1935. It more than doubled in the following decade and it was, at that time, only about a quarter of the size of the AEU. The National Union of Vehicle Builders, founded in 1919 from the merger of a handful of craft unions of the nineteenth century, lost members in the 1930s but more than doubled in size between 1940 and 1950. The TUC first recorded its female members in 1955 when there were just 1,590 of them. These unions – the AEU, ETU and NUVB – most often featured in disputes and negotiations over female labour.

More significant from the point of view of female membership were the two large general unions also party to the EEF's industrial relations procedure. These were the Transport and General Workers' Union (TGWU) and the General and Municipal Workers' Union (GMWU). The latter was formed in 1924 from an amalgamation of unions, one of which had already absorbed, in 1921, the National Federation of Women Workers (NFWW), a significant organiser of women during the First World War. The TGWU was formed in 1922 from the joining of fourteen separate unions. In 1929 it absorbed the Workers' Union (WU) which had recruited women workers among the light metal trades of the Midlands. Its membership grew throughout the period 1920 to 1950 and only began to fall slightly in the mid-1950s. In 1950 membership stood at 1,250,000 including 130,000 women.

All of these unions combined to meet the EEF on 'questions of common interest' through the Engineering Joint Trades Movement and the Federation of Engineering and Shipbuilding Trades. The latter became the Confederation of Engineering and Shipbuilding Unions in 1936 and the workers represented by its affiliated trade unions rose from 80,000 to 175,000. By 1939 all the main engineering

14. T.J. Claydon, 'The Development of Trade Unionism among British Automobile and Aircraft Workers, c.1914–1946' (Ph.D. thesis, University of Kent, 1981), pp. 352–3; p. 357.

unions were affiliated except the foundry workers and the AEU, who joined in 1942 and 1947. They also met at local, special and central conferences, generally to settle disputes that had arisen in the workplace. Negotiations relating to wage claims and working conditions took place at special conferences.

Many men did not belong to engineering trade unions. The density of union membership in the industry was roughly the same in 1950 as it had been in 1921, about 55 per cent. Its lowest point was in 1933 when only 24 per cent of potential recruits were unionised. From 1926 to 1938 the figure was about a third.[15] Nevertheless, these five trade unions – the AEU, ETU, NUVB, TGWU and GMWU – were significant in negotiating the wages and working conditions of the whole engineering workforce, organised and unorganised, male and female, within a rigorously structured collective bargaining system.

This overview of the main developments within the engineering industry has shown a growth of new industries, products and sources of employment during the 1920s and 1930s, later balanced by a revival among the traditional sector generated by the Second World War and the boom in demand for capital equipment which followed it. A divided industry, it nevertheless had a nationally agreed framework for collective bargaining in which all the relevant trade unions took part. Disputes over the introduction or extension of female labour were discussed and settled through its grievance procedure. It was potentially an important influence on the employment of women in federated firms, though its effectiveness was undermined by the diversity of the industry it represented.

Women's employment

None of the above descriptions of the changes in the industry has taken account of the rise in women's employment with which these changes were so much associated. What follows is an account of the general patterns of female employment over the period, their wages, earnings and trade union membership. It shows that female employment was highly segregated, being clearly associated with the rapid inter-war growth of the newer industries of electrical goods and motor vehicles. Theirs was an adult workforce with its own schedule of wages, prescribing much lower rates of pay than for men.

15. G.S. Bain and R. Price, *Profiles of Union Growth. A Comparative Statistical Portrait of Eight Countries* (1980), p. 50, Table, 2. 11.

FIGURE 2.1   *Average numbers employed in engineering, 1924–35 (in thousands)*

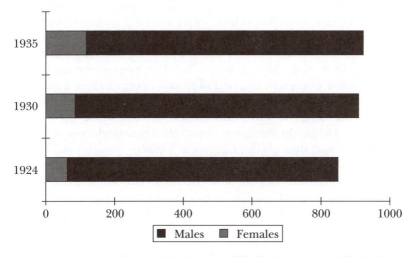

Source: based on the Census of Production 1935, Engineering and Shipbuilding Trades, Table XB

Census figures show women forming a small but rising percentage of engineering workers, growing very slowly from 6 per cent in 1921 to 8 per cent in 1931, peaking at around 30 per cent in 1945 and remaining at 25 per cent throughout the 1950s.[16] Between the wars a large and growing share of employment in engineering's most prosperous trades was taken by women workers. In 1924 the electrical engineering, motor, cycle and aircraft trades together accounted for three-quarters of the total number of women workers, but only one-third of the men. Women formed nearly a third of the workforce in electrical engineering and a tenth of the motors, cycle and aircraft workforces. In shipbuilding, railway carriage and wagon building, on the other hand, their numbers were negligible and in mechanical engineering women formed just 3 per cent of the total.[17]

Expansion in the electrical goods and the motor and cycle trades led to more women being employed in engineering by the end of the 1920s. By the mid-1930s, male employment was declining while female employment grew. Women now made up almost a fifth of

16. Fourteen per cent of vehicle workers were women, but these were listed separately.
17. *Final Report on the Third Census of Production of the UK* (1924); *The Iron and Steel Trades, the Engineering Trades and the Non-Ferrous Metals Trades* (1931), p. 210.

the total workforce, concentrated in electrical engineering (36 per cent) and motor and cycle manufacture (13 per cent). Clearly, it was in those industries which were growing fastest, the newer industries of electrical goods, vehicles and aircraft, that an increasing number of women were employed.

Women continued to form a fifth of the engineering workforce between 1948 and 1954. Almost a third of electrical engineering workers were women in this period as well as over half of a new and large category – radio and telecommunications. In much smaller sections like electric wires and cables, women made up a third of the workforce. In batteries, accumulators and electric lighting, accessories and fittings, the figure was higher – roughly half.[18]

Detailed workforce statistics compiled by the EEF show more precisely the distribution of women workers across the engineering trades and even between firms. The numbers and proportions of women in given trades and firms are shown in tables 2.2 and 2.3 below.

As we can see, most women throughout the period worked in electrical and motor vehicle manufacture. Within the EEF's category of motors, cycles and accessories, women were disproportionately concentrated in Joseph Lucas Ltd and its subsidiaries, who specialised in accessories and components manufacture for cars. Until the Second World War more than half the total number of women in the trade worked at these firms. The remainder was spread fairly evenly if thinly between car manufacturers, the largest employers being Austin Motors Ltd and BSA where women were largely confined to trim operations. Within electrical engineering the spread of female employment appears more even, though three large employers stand out: Siemens Bros (London), Ferranti and Metropolitan-Vickers (Manchester). Within these firms women's employment was concentrated in telephone manufacture and in the machining, assembly, testing and finishing of coils, meters, mica, cores and fuses.

In other electrical firms women were generally employed in the production of electrical appliances and accessories, including lamps, telephones and radios, though they also worked in the manufacture of larger, heavier equipment like telephone exchanges while men were concentrated in the heavy sections of the trade, producing electrical machinery and plant.

The percentage of women in these two sections remained fairly constant between the wars. Both were given a sudden boost from

18. *The Report on the Census of Production for 1954*, Table 11, 4/k/20, 4/m/18, 4/l/10, 4/n/9, 4/o/9 (larger establishments only during a specified week).

TABLE 2.2 *Employment of women (in firms where over 500 women were employed) in engineering trades (federated firms), 1920–50. (Figures in italic refer to numbers of female workers as a percentage of the total workforce)*

Trade	1920	1926	1933	1939	1946	1950
Electrical	15,709	10,484	10,569	19,380	42,259	37,133
	23	*20*	*24*	*22*	*32*	*26*
Motors	6,226	7,872	11,254	9,790	22,393	22,922
	8	*11*	*16*	*12*	*19*	*15*
Lamps	570	2,447	4,229	5,382	7,155	7,314
	62	*72*	*70*	*65*	*54*	*47*
Telephones	2,700	5,146	4,429	10,354	11,048	10,691
	47	*45*	*44*	*45*	*48*	*38*
Instrument-makers	—	—	1,309	3,281	6,860	6,749
			24	*23*	*30*	*29*
Sheet-metal	619	346	393	1,076	—	—
	18	*19*	*12*	*18*		
General light	—	13,118	5,565	10,486	45,012	42,895
		6	*9*	*8*	*18*	*14*
General heavy	18,737	—	1,531	4,068	5,731	4,533
	6		*3*	*4*	*6*	*4*
Female employment all trades	58,320	44,279	43,944	75,138	190,946	167,403
	8	*9*	*11*	*11*	*17*	*14*
Total employment all trades	698,746	497,010	379,256	809,923	1,136,332	1,223,587

Source: EEF workforce statistics

TABLE 2.3   *Employment of women by firm, 1926–41*

	No.	% of total workforce	EEF section
1926			
Joseph Lucas	3,843	61	M
Siemens/Eng. Electric (London)	1,890	54	E
Osram GEC	1,582	73	L
Metropolitan-Vickers (Manchester)	1,224	18	E
Ferrantis	980	31	E
Edison Swan	778	47	E
Austin Motors	725	10	M
GEC (Witton)	539	18	E
BTH (Rugby)	496	16	E
Siemens/Eng. Electric (Preston)	466	84	T
1931			
Joseph Lucas	4,000	58	M
Siemens/Eng. Electric (London)	1,878	53	E
GEC/Peel-Conner	1,530	62	T
Osram GEC	1,517	72	T
Ferrantis	1,225	38	E
Metropolitan-Vickers (Manchester)	1,092	25	E
GEC (Witton)	1,384	25	E
BTH (Rugby)	765	19	E
BSA Motors	753	22	M
E.A. Hoffman & Co.	545	28	M
1936			
Joseph Lucas	5,933	48	M
Gramophone Co.	3,244	42	E
GEC/Peel-Conner	2,839	61	T
Siemens/Eng. Electric	2,570	55	E
Ferrantis	2,317	45	E
Osram GEC	1,998	69	L
Metropolitan-Vickers (Manchester)	1,622	15	E
GEC (Witton)	1,384	25	E
BSA Motors	1,347	28	M
Austin Motors	1,215	7	M
1941			
Joseph Lucas	7,067	45	M
Ferrantis	5,933	56	E
BSA Motors	3,836	25	M
Gramophone Co.	2,825	40	E
Metropolitan-Vickers (Manchester)	2,328	19	E

TABLE 2.3   *Cont'd*

	No.	*% of total workforce*	*EEF section*
E.A. Hoffman & Co.	2,129	36	M
Austin Motors	1,906	13	M
A.C. Cossor	1,874	52	L
Mullard Radio Valve	1,449	83	E
Metropolitan-Vickers (London)	1,397	54	E

Key: M = Motors, cycles & accessories
    E = Electrical
    L = Lamps
    T = Telephones
Source: EEF statistics

wartime demands, followed by an equally sudden drop between 1944 and 1946. By the beginning of the 1950s, female employment had returned to pre-war levels. In lamps and telephones, although the number of women employed was smaller, the percentage of the workforce composed of women was much higher. Up until the Second World War, two-thirds or more of such workers were women. By 1950 female employment in both had fallen below the pre-war average. In 1942 a new trade was added to the EEF's list, plastics or plastic moulding. Once again, although absolute numbers were quite small, the proportion of the workforce made up by women was high – two-thirds during the war, falling to approximately half in 1950. The only new industry where female employment remained small or declined was aircraft. From 10 per cent in 1920 the figure fell to 5 per cent by 1928 and 4 per cent by 1939. A year later the figure had doubled. It reached 34 per cent under the stimulus of war and abruptly collapsed when the war ended. By 1950, 8 per cent of the aircraft workforce was female.

In older trades the proportion of women employed continued to be very small. Only a tiny percentage of the workforce of the heavy general engineering and the founding sectors was female. These EEF figures confirm what is clear from census evidence – that women were not employed evenly throughout the industry but concentrated in a few trades and sectors. The figures suggest a highly segregated workforce.

It was also an adult workforce, although, given age specific patterns of women's employment generally, it probably comprised

mainly young women under 25.[19] Around two-thirds of the females
employed in engineering were adults between 1907 and 1935, compared with three-quarters of the male workforce. This pattern is
repeated for the largest employers of women – electrical engineering and motor vehicles, although by 1935 the proportion of women
over girls had risen further. Aircraft too had a much higher proportion of adult female workers.[20] From the end of the war to 1950
nearly all female employees in federated firms were women over
18.[21] The population censuses for 1931 and 1951 break down the
age make-up of women in engineering and metal manufacture into
a little more detail. In 1931 there were more or less even numbers
of women aged 16 to 17, 18 to 19 and 20 to 24 but by 1951, most of
the under 25s were aged 20 to 24. Overall these figures suggest that
many women left the industry on marriage, although formal marriage bars do not seem to have been a common practice.

This brief overview has shown that, though low, women's employment was not insignificant, nor was it associated mainly with
wartime engineering. The main sources for this employment were
the newest and fastest growing sections of the inter-war period:
electrical engineering and motor vehicle manufacture. Most of the
workers were adults.

Female wages, earnings and regularity of work

The payment of women engineering workers is a complicated issue
which will be looked at in more detail in later chapters. Increases
granted by the government's arbitration board in 1919 brought the
basic rate for women up to 43s. 3d. per week. Until June 1920,
women's wages were kept at wartime levels by the Wages Temporary Regulation Act (1918). When the act expired, general unions
prepared to petition the employers for wage increases but a decline
in trade ensured that requests were rejected. Wage cuts followed

19. Jane Lewis, *Women in England, 1870–1950, Sexual Divisions and Social Change*
(1984), pp. 148–9.
20. *Final Report on the Third Census of Production of the UK* (1924); *The Iron and Steel
Trades, the Engineering Trades and the Non-Ferrous Metals Trades* (1931), p. 211. *Final
Report of the Fifth Census of Production and the Import Duties Act Inquiry 1935 Part II*
(1939); *The Iron and Steel Trades, the Engineering and Shipbuilding and Vehicle Trades, the
Non-Ferrous Metals Trades* (1939), p. 221.
21. In 1920 and 1923 the EEF used the definition of 21 and over. No figures
about age were then collected until 1932 when the definition had changed to 18
and over. In 1943 the classification by age is 21 and over.

in the spring of 1921. Unable to come to an agreement with the general unions, EEF employers imposed a new schedule of wage rates for women. It described a basic time rate of 12s. at 18 and 16s. at 21, with a sliding scale cost of living bonus. A time rate was a flat rate of pay for a full working week. A modified lower rate was later introduced, Schedule B, but some employers continued to pay the old rates or alternatively negotiated their own. In practice, by 1935 the time rate paid at 21 varied between 24s. and 28s. The average provincial pay rate for skilled men at that time was around three times higher. Subsequent national advances meant that by 1942 the minimum time rate for women of 21 and over was 50s., 75s. by 1950 and 105s. by 1958 for a forty-four-hour week.[22]

Earnings are harder to discover than wage rates. There is evidence from the EEF that many women were on piecework, a system which related pay to output and so would not have been tied to the time rate wages described here. Some, especially in trades like plastic moulding, were only part-time workers. Others, it was suggested, routinely worked on short-time, that is, less than a full working week. At other periods they may have worked overtime. The numbers of full- and part-time workers of both sexes were only calculated by the EEF from 1944. At that time, 12 per cent of women employed by federated firms were working part-time. The figure rose to 16 per cent by 1950. The highest concentrations of part-time women workers were in plastic moulding, telephone and lamp manufacture, with approximately a fifth of women employees working part-time between 1944 and 1950. Light engineering, instrument makers and motors also employed approximately a fifth of their female workers on part-time work.[23]

There is some evidence about short-time working. In 1928 the Balfour Committee on Trade and Industry noted that, in the motor cycle trade, it had been usual for workers to be out of work for five or six months a year.[24] The number in steady employment was about 80 per cent, and in some firms only 60 per cent. During a special conference with the EEF on women's wages in 1935, general unions claimed that numbers of women were routinely employed on a casual basis. In Lancashire, for instance, the electric fires and wireless sections of the electrical industry were noted for dismissing

22. TGWU, *Record*, 1937. MRC MSS.126/T&G/4/2/11.

23. EEF, workforce statistics, 1944–50. MRC MSS.237/13/3/51–56.

24. *The Committee on Industry and Trade, Iron and Steel Trades, Engineering, Electrical Manufacture, Shipbuilding, being Part IV of a Survey of Industry* Cmnd 3282 (1928), p. 227.

women workers for three or four months a year. In London and elsewhere the manufacture of gramophones and domestic electrical appliances involved seasonal lay-offs that kept the workforce young and therefore cheap. One official claimed:

> It is becoming the custom of firms to work for a portion of the year and, when they have a slack time, to dismiss wholesale both the young and very often a considerable portion of the older girls. When the busy time comes along the younger girls are taken on so that there is a complete cycle throughout the year of actually getting rid of the older girls and replacing them with younger girls when the busy time comes round again.[25]

It is hard to know how widespread this practice was. In 1934 the EEF put female labour turnover among member firms at 25 per cent. 'In other words,' reported its sub-committee, 'roughly seventy-five per cent of the women employed were constantly employed throughout the year.'[26]

In 1939 the average provincial rate of pay for a skilled man was £3 4s., around a pound a week less than it had been in 1919. For women the figure was £1 12s. Five years later women's earnings had doubled to reach a level approximately half that enjoyed by skilled men and two-thirds of that earned by unskilled labourers. By the end of the 1950s women's earnings had reached three-quarters of the earnings of a male labourer.[27]

Women's wages, then, fell dramatically after wartime regulation was withdrawn in 1920 and replaced by two gender-based, wage for age pay scales which remained in force – with small rises – until the Second World War. The problem of measuring women's earnings is complicated by insufficient evidence about the numbers employed on piecework and the average hours worked.

Female union membership

Low pay was associated with low levels of unionism. Only general unions, open to all types of workers, attempted to recruit women in engineering at first, often basing their campaigns on the offer of

25. EEF, proceedings at special conference 19 Jul. 1935, MRC MSS.237/1/13/39.

26. EEF, *Report to the Administration Committee by the Sub-Committee of the Administration Committee in regard to Female Labour* (Jun. 1934), p. 3, para 13. MRC MSS.237/3/1/89, F(6)56.

27. A. Marsh, *Industrial Relations in Engineering* (1965), pp. 191–5 and Jefferys, *Story of the Engineers*, pp. 214–15.

improved wages.[28] The AEU, a craft union, only began to admit women in 1943. Within the year it had acquired nearly 140,000 new members. But by 1950 it had lost 100,000 of them. The figure had risen again to around 80,000 a decade later, when women made up just 6 per cent of the membership. The ETU first admitted women in 1943. In 1950, only about 4,500 of its 186,000 members were women. The NUVB did not recruit women until 1955. It then had 55,000 men and less than 2,000 women.

The TGWU and the GMWU were open to membership regardless of sex or skill and both absorbed women's trade unions as they grew. In 1921, the NFWW joined the predecessor of the GMWU on the understanding that a separate women's section with a national women's officer would be created. Female membership fell between 1925 and 1930 and then rose dramatically, more than doubling between 1935 and 1940. Numbers trebled over the next decade to reach 150,000.

The TGWU amalgamated with the WU in 1929. Founded in 1898 as a union of all workers, skilled or unskilled, the WU had recruited widely among women and had several female organisers. Female membership grew from 18,500 in 1930 to 38,000 in 1940 and 130,000 by 1950. It is not clear how many of these unions' female members were engineering workers. According to Steven Tolliday, the TGWU did not sanction large-scale recruitment in engineering until the mid-1930s and its secretary, Ernest Bevin, was afraid of overstretching the union.[29] Thus female trade union membership overall, like male, was relatively low. It was concentrated in general unions like the GMWU and TGWU while craft unions only began to recruit women under the pressure of their wartime employment.

*   *   *.

This chapter has described significant shifts towards new industries and products in engineering employment and output. These changes were founded on the spread of electrification, technical innovations in radio and telecommunications and the growth of new markets, especially the home market. The old staple trades like mechanical engineering were not completely eclipsed, however, and both the war and post-war boom in demand revived and strengthened some traditional sectors. The nature and scope of women's employment

28. See below, p. 120.
29. Steve Tolliday, 'Militancy and organisation: women workers and trade unions in the motor trades in the 1930s', *Oral History*, 11. 2 (Autumn 1983), p. 45.

in engineering was related to these changes. As later chapters will show, employers sought out women workers for many of the processes involved in the manufacture of new products, while women's employment failed to grow in areas of traditional and heavy engineering, like shipbuilding. Women's employment was therefore highly segregated and linked with the fortunes of particular sectors. Mobilisation for war, meanwhile, had limited impact, producing sharp but short-term fluctuations, though it is munitions factories that have been popularly credited as the originators of women's engineering employment. The next chapter concerns the significance of the First World War and questions whether and in what ways the later patterns of segregation described here can be related to employers' wartime experience of female labour.

CHAPTER THREE

The First World War: Munitions Work and its Impact, 1914–1919

In the historiography of the First World War women's work is presented as revolutionary in potential but conservative in impact. On the one hand, war challenged the pre-war system of labour, revealing women's ability to do work previously closed to them. In this view, dilution, the process by which women were introduced to new jobs in wartime, threatened to expose skill as an empty concept used by craft unions to protect their livelihoods. The war also introduced new methods of production in which skill would not be called for. Both, on the face of it, might have led to a better future for female employment in which women worked in a broader range of jobs, enjoying pay related to their work rather than their gender. The fact that the Armistice did not bring about this improved working life is usually explained by the beliefs and prejudices of men, employers and workers alike.[1] Women were seen primarily as wives and mothers, not workers. The hold of domestic ideology was so strong that 'even the evidence of their war work failed to shake ideas about their "true role"'.[2] Peacetime inevitably brought a return to traditional patterns of pay and employment, with the war experience seen only as proof of female suitability for simplified, monotonous, repetitive tasks, work which would not distract women from their domestic role and responsibilities by being interesting or well paid.[3]

1. Laura Lee Downs, *Manufacturing Inequality. Gender Division in the French and British Metal-working Industries 1914–39* (1995), pp. 104–5.
2. Gail Braybon, *Women Workers in the First World War* (1989), p. 229.
3. Braybon, *Women Workers*, p. 88. See Susan Pederson, *Family, Dependence and the Origins of the Welfare State. Britain and France 1914–1945* (1993); Angela Woollacott, *On Her Their Lives Depend. Munition Workers and the Great War* (1994).

There is little or no discussion in this historiography about the nature of British engineering production before and after the First World War and the way it influenced the employment of women. This chapter aims to show economic reasons for the reluctance of employers to take up dilution, extend female employment and release skilled labour that the 'ideology' argument described above leaves out. It builds on a picture of British engineering on the eve of the First World War as a complex mix of craft and mass production in which employers were rarely able to break away completely from dependence on skill.[4] It also examines the extent to which male trade unions were opposed to women workers on ideological grounds and how far they were driven by fear of cheap labour.

Negotiating dilution

The persistent carnage of the Western Front from 1915 brought with it unforeseen demands for men and munitions. By the spring of that year the government's arsenals and established suppliers had failed to meet the demand for artillery shells and orders were in arrears. Munitions production had to be rapidly increased and men released for fighting.

The government intervened to meet this need in a way that was wholly new. Its first step was to negotiate directly with trade unions for the extension of women's employment into work previously done by men. Under discussion since the previous October, the introduction of women had so far been left to the industry's own collective bargaining processes. It very soon became clear to employers that these would not meet war needs and in February 1915 the government intervened, appointing the Committee on Production in the Engineering and Shipbuilding Trades to act as a court of arbitration between unions and the EEF and to consider the use of less skilled labour. The committee backed the employers, calling for the abolition of output restrictions, the use of female labour, and a ban on labour stoppages, all for the period of the war only. The Shells and Fuses Agreement, a national agreement between trade unions and employers, was the result. Women and boys were now allowed to work on semi- or fully automatic machines normally

4. I am indebted here to the work of Jonathan Zeitlin. On the idea of engineering as a mix of standardised and more flexible production with limited scope for automated, mass production see his *Between Flexibility and Mass Production. Strategic Debate and Industrial Reorganisation in British Engineering 1830–1990* (forthcoming).

operated by adult men. Only a month later, though, questions of rates of pay and interpretation caused the government to intervene directly. A conference at the Treasury between Lloyd George and thirty-three trade unions in March 1915 finally brought about an agreement in which unions gave up the right to strike, agreed to relax all customs which restricted the output of munitions and permitted dilution on government work. The agreement was mainly designed to deal with the substitution of semi-skilled for skilled workers. The safeguards Lloyd George offered in return were that the agreement would operate only in firms on war work, that it would only be for the duration of the war, and that dilutees including women would get the customary rate for the job. Profits of such firms would also be limited. It had taken six months for the government to intervene directly and even then it was in reaction to union protests. The fact that the agreement was a voluntary one shows how ambivalent the government remained towards intervention in industry.

Its second step was more decisive. In the summer of 1915 it set up the Ministry of Munitions, under the leadership of Lloyd George. The purpose of the new ministry was to increase munitions output through the creation of government-owned shell factories and by encouraging standardisation, specialisation and dilution in existing factories engaged on war work. The state now owned 250 'national' factories and controlled another 20,000.[5] It was also responsible for all aspects of the training, health and management of munitions workers. At the same time, the terms of the Treasury Agreement were incorporated into the Munitions of War Act of July 1915. Strikes were made illegal. Leaving certificates (which had to be obtained from an employer to show that a worker was genuinely not needed) were intended to control labour supply. From October 1915, circulars relating to the pay of female dilutees were issued by the ministry in an attempt to overcome problems in achieving the 'customary' rate of pay, a move designed to ease the acceptance of dilutees by organised labour.

The summer of 1915, then, was the turning point for women's employment in munitions. In the early months of war, women had experienced increased unemployment and few of the women who presented themselves for war work were being placed.[6] The Treasury Agreement had seen the beginning of a process of direct substitution,

---

5. Gail Braybon and Penny Summerfield, *Out of the Cage. Women's Experiences in Two World Wars* (1987), p. 37.
6. Ibid., p. 35.

with semi-skilled replacing skilled workers on certain machine operations, while the latter concentrated on work requiring higher degrees of skill. The whole process was further accelerated by the formation of the Ministry of Munitions's Central Munitions Labour Supply Committee. Its Dilution Scheme of October 1915 introduced women and unskilled men to semi-skilled types of machine operation and the less skilled portion of work previously done by skilled men, which was now sub-divided and rearranged. Female substitutes introduced to unskilled work at the earlier stage would have been upgraded. The scheme was carried through by dilution officers who advised and persuaded employers to increase their use of female labour, as well as through the subdivision of tasks, the introduction of automatic and special purpose machinery, the use of limit gauges and the upgrading of skilled men to work such as toolmaking and toolsetting. Technical advisers to the labour supply department of the Ministry of Munitions, ministry training schools and short employer training schemes also aimed at maximising the use of female labour. Together with the new powers of the Munitions of War Act and the ministry's 'L' circulars on women's pay which followed it, the scheme facilitated huge increases in female employment. In July 1915, 121,000 women worked on government or war work in the metals trades as a whole, rising to 534,000 by July 1918. In other words, women constituted 60 per cent of the total workforce in 1915, soaring to 90 per cent by 1918.[7] The employment of so many women made possible the introduction of conscription in January 1916 and the cancellation of exemption from military service for skilled men in April 1918. By the middle of 1916, the shell shortage had been overcome.

Historians of the First World War agree that in this process of negotiation, legislation, substitution and dilution women were seen, not as workers, but as wives and mothers. It was this bedrock of belief about women's 'proper role' that circumscribed the extent of dilution and its impact on the future of women's work. It accounts for the ambivalence of employers towards women in munitions employment, despite the opportunities which dilution appeared to offer them to rationalise and cheapen production, confining skilled men to work only they could do, reallocating their other work to more suitable semi-skilled, unskilled or female labour. As one employer said in 1915, '[T]he fact of the matter is really, not that

---

7. These figures included private firms as well as all government establishments.

women are paid too little or much too little – but that men are paid too much for work which can be done without previous training.'[8]

While there is obvious truth in these arguments, as we shall see, the question of dilution is more complicated. The critique just described relies too much on the notion that skilled work in engineering had been largely eroded before 1914, with dilution threatening to expose 'skill' as an empty concept used by craftsmen to protect their livelihoods. It also leads to ideology as the only explanation of why employers failed to overcome craft barriers in order to employ women more widely, both before and after the Armistice. If skill is reinstated, however, then the reasons for employers' conservatism during and after the war become more varied and rooted in economic as well as ideological concerns.

How far then did the employment of women in munitions go and what form did it take? In the first year of war, women are likely to have worked as unskilled machine minders, under the supervision of a skilled man who also ground tools for the machines and set them up. The ceaseless requirements of war urged the government to upgrade all workers and remove skilled men to fully skilled tasks such as toolroom work and the erection, maintenance and repair of machinery. Semi-skilled men who had previously operated semi-automatic machines like capstan lathes, used in munitions for turning the bodies of shells, would have moved up to supervision and toolsetting and women from unskilled to semi-skilled work. This process was taking place from the summer of 1915 onwards and was largely complete by the middle of 1918.

By the last year of war, most of the women working in national factories and admiralty dockyards, and on national work in controlled firms, were employed in the manufacture and filling of gun ammunition, where they made up 70 per cent of the workforce.[9] Many of them were on jobs which had been altered or subdivided to accommodate those with limited training or experience. The number of women directly replacing men in the metal trades was put at 194,200 at its peak in July 1918.[10] The remainder performed either a portion of a skilled man's job or work on which women had been employed before the war and which was classified now as 'women's work'. Between 1917 and 1918 dilution was at its

8. Braybon, *Women Workers*, p. 85.

9. *Official History of the Ministry of Munitions* (*OHMM*), vol. 6, part 4, p. 46, Table xiii (b), and p. 55, Table xix.

10. *OHMM*, vol. 6, part 4, p. 32, Table ix.

peak and in May of that year women were producing one-third of the total output of the munitions industries.

The process of upgrading during the course of a long war may have allowed women to pick up skills. However, the fully skilled woman was, in practice, rare. The emphasis of dilution was on narrow training directed at the most rapid production possible. It was most advanced in state-owned national factories engaged in the production of light, standardised products such as shells and small arms. According to Braybon, 'although as the war progressed more women did do skilled work, and became adept at using machines and setting them, they were confined to work on one or two processes only, and did not have the range of knowledge possessed by the pre-war craftsman'.[11]

Opposition from trade unions

The most obvious break on the nature and extent of dilution then was the needs of the war itself for a rapid increase in production of the same goods in large quantities, for example, shells. But opposition from trade unionists and conservatism from employers meant even this kind of dilution was not achieved easily or all at once.[12]

The strategy of skilled unions like the ASE in the face of an unprecedented influx of unskilled labour was naturally to protect its position as the mainstay of the industry, portraying other kinds of labour as peripheral to it and attempting to ensure that such labour was therefore confined to a narrow range of work. They also concentrated on securing promises that pre-war practices in the trade would be restored and that dilutees would be removed. The ASE succeeded in halting dilution outside the scope of the Munitions Act and into private firms where it had no promises that 'trade customs' would be restored. Strikes in Lancashire and the Midlands in May 1917, for instance, led the government to abandon its plan to extend dilution beyond its own factories and controlled establishments. Strikes also occurred at Coventry, Birmingham, Manchester and Leicester when, in 1918, the government limited the proportion of skilled labour in certain private firms, a move which therefore obliged employers to introduce dilution. It was

11. Braybon, *Women Workers*, p. 62.
12. Ben Morgan, 'The efficient utilisation of labour in engineering factories (with special reference to women's work)', *Proceedings of the Institution of Mechanical Engineers*, May 1918.

also successful in ensuring that male dilutees were conscripted before skilled men.

It is not clear the extent to which unions were opposing the withdrawal of customary rights or the introduction of women *per se.* There are many examples of skilled men opposing the introduction of other men, that is, the encroachment of the unskilled of either gender. A continued mistrust of restoration pledges by the government reinforced that opposition.[13] In her study of women munition workers, Marion Kozak points out that the ASE journal did not show a particularly anti-feminist bias, rather 'It was the craft bias of the ASE Journal that was far more evident in its pages than its anti-feminist comments; its craft orientation combined with a fear of cheap labour.'[14] Shop floor opposition to dilution may have centred on the refusal of managements to consult labour on the implementation of dilution schemes rather than on the issue of women as such.[15] Again, fear and a reluctance to pass on knowledge to a section of the labour force which might be used to undermine their position and privileges was a factor in refusals to supervise or train women.

So far this seems like a practical strategy motivated by concern to protect livelihoods. However, there were also many examples of male unionists who were opposed to the introduction of women and who resented their presence on the shop floor out of prejudice. The ASE treated male and female dilutees differently, indicating an especial hostility towards women. It still tried to limit the introduction of males and the scope of their work but was prepared to organise them within a special section of membership. A proposal in 1915 to admit women, however, was turned down. Instead of organising women the union made an alliance with the NFWW. In June that year the latter promised that in exchange for help with recruiting women munition workers it would withdraw its members from engineering at the end of the war. The same priority – that female dilutees should be removed at the end of the war – shaped ASE support for equal pay and will be examined later.

It is hard to disentangle the mix of motives among skilled trade unionists nationally and locally, but their opposition is hardly surprising given doubtful pledges of restoration and equal pay and the use by some employers of women dilutees to discipline the male workforce, for example, by introducing them following strikes in

13. See Marion Kozak, 'Women Munitions Workers During the First World War' (Ph.D. thesis, Hull University, 1976), p. 81.
14. Ibid., p. 83.   15. Ibid., p. 86.

order to curb further unrest.[16] But it seems that the craft unions (of which the ASE was the leader) opposed dilution first and foremost because it threatened the erosion of hard-won rights and privileges.

The response of the general unions to dilution was different and has been described as 'defensive incorporation'. Unions like the NUGW and the WU lacked the industrial strength to take the lead in negotiations with the government or to impose restrictions and demarcation rules in the way that skilled unions could. Their security lay in recruiting the new 'threat' to their own ranks. Here, too, the aim was to strengthen and defend the position of male workers. For these unions, the motive behind their drive to recruit new women workers was to establish a 'common front designed to protect male labour from the threat of a low paid, unorganised section of the workforce – the women'.[17]

The single most important general union for women was the NFWW, led by Mary Macarthur. It was founded in 1906 as an organisation for women excluded from male trade societies and grew hugely during the war. Numbers rose from 20,000 in October 1915 to nearly 80,000 by 1918. The success of the union was at least partly owed to its close co-operation with the ASE. In return for assistance with recruitment, the NFWW was pledged to protect men's wage standards and to support the restoration of trade union practices and in particular the reinstatement of ASE members. Its pledge acted as an additional guarantee to the ASE that what had been promised by the government in the Treasury Agreement would actually happen in the workplace. In her book on the origins of the welfare state, Susan Pederson blames the NFWW's agreement with the ASE for undermining its effectiveness as a vehicle for women dilutees' interests. In promising to withdraw its members from jobs claimed by the union at the end of the war, it had accepted the central importance of the male as breadwinner. It fatally linked women's wartime struggles 'not to their current interests as *workers* but to their presumed post-war roles as dependent wives and daughters'.[18] But Mary Macarthur's support for male reinstatement was consistent with the position of other important organising bodies like the Women's Trade Union League. In the circumstances of the time, it seemed right that, according to Violet Markham, then a member of the Central Committee on Women's Training and Employment, 'the position of workers who have voluntarily thrown

16. Ibid., p. 94.   17. Ibid., p. 309.
18. Pederson, *Family, Dependence*, p. 100.

up their employment to serve the nation in the field must not be prejudiced on their return'.[19] The impact of this policy on the NFWW's support for equal pay is discussed later.

The conservatism of employers

The response from employers towards the government's encouragement of dilution was mixed. The process was complicated in its early stages by the experimental nature of the scheme. It was difficult to make hard and fast rules about how far and in what circumstances women should be employed on engineering work previously done only by men. Even the Labour Supply Committee had assumed as one of its guiding principles that dilution could not be applied to all firms in the same degree. While it was applicable to repetition work (the manufacture of ammunition on which most women were employed is a good example), it was of more limited use to shipbuilding or repair works, where tasks were heavy and not easily subdivided.[20]

Kozak argues that, after an initial recoil, engineering employers seized eagerly on dilution, standardisation and improved technology as heralding the end of the skilled craftsmen and paving the way for a restructuring of the industry. However, the continued reluctance of some employers to experiment is reflected in the concentration of women's wartime employment in government controlled firms and national factories where dilution was compulsory. The employment of women on munitions had grown by 300 per cent in government controlled works by October 1916 but by just 36 per cent in uncontrolled establishments.[21]

Economic influences

Was ideology the only factor causing conservatism and reluctance among engineering employers, though? Before the war, shipbuilding and general engineering dominated the industry and the scope

19. Violet Markham, 'Women trade unionists and the war', in *Women's Trade Union Review*, July 1915, quoted by Kozak, 'Women Munitions Workers', p. 327.
20. Labour Supply Committee, quoted in Morgan, 'Efficient utilisation of labour', p. 242.
21. Martin Pugh, *Women and the Women's Movement in Britain 1914–1959* (1992), p. 25.

of female employment in both was very much limited by the nature of production as well as by custom and craft barriers. Both continued to depend on the skills acquired by time-served craftsmen.

Before 1914 the heavy capital equipment which dominated engineering output was generally produced to customer requirements. It is true that there were specialised firms and sectors, as in the case of textile and agricultural engineering, where firms were able to produce standard and interchangeable goods in large batches, for instance up to 100,000 for small parts like spindles, on special purpose machinery. But even a huge textile machinery manufacturer like the Lancashire firm of Platts had to offer a wide range of products. Special machines were not necessarily single purpose and were often capable of handling a variety of components. The speed of technological change and fluctuations in demand through the trade cycle discouraged such firms from stockpiling standard goods. The ideal seems to have been to cheapen certain phases of production, but without losing the ability to respond to changes in demand. For that, the versatility of skilled workers was important. In other trades producing capital equipment, like ships or heavy guns, work simply could not be produced in repetition using semi-skilled machinists.[22]

On the other hand, new sectors of engineering were emerging, among them motor vehicles, cycles and electrical goods, which aimed towards a mass market and did offer more scope for standardised production. In turn, they stimulated some standardisation in the machine tool trade. As the introductory chapter showed, these were precisely the areas where women were employed.[23]

An EEF enquiry of 1915 shows how women's pre-war work in the industry was concentrated in these new trades and the processes they involved: polishing, lacquering, assembling small parts for fuses and other electrical equipment, painting, operating coil-winding machines, operating small drill presses and light lathes, winding and assembling small motors, coremaking, acetylene welding, feeding semi-automatic machines, hand milling machines on repetition work, examining and packing light goods. Some of these are described as widespread in the given district, as having been carried on by the particular firm for many years or as having been established, for example in the electrical trade, since its earliest days. The electrical firm of British-Thomson-Houston in Willesden gave

22. Zeitlin, *Between Flexibility and Mass Production*, ch. 1, pp. 5–11.
23. Ibid., ch. 2, p. 15.

an example of its 'women's work' as 'any miscellaneous light work which is fairly clean and does not require great strength'. Linotype and Machinery Ltd of Manchester employed women in the handling of small machine tools, their tasks including milling, drilling and the filing of parts using a jig as well as other work 'made to special machines'. They explained to the EEF that their employment of women 'is very difficult to definitely explain, but anywhere where a special machine is made for the work it was invariably arranged for women labour. It has not been the practice for women to be engaged on heavy machine tools, but any light machine tool we have considered comes within the employment of women labour.'[24]

Women, then, were being used on automatic and semi-automatic machines before the war – in capstan operation, press milling, drilling, grinding, polishing, screwing and gear cutting. They performed both hand and machine operations of a light, repetitious kind. Sometimes these were operations requiring accuracy – that is, attention to fine detail in handling small parts – and speed. Repetitious work naturally tended to be associated with large orders. Women were considered to be too expensive when employed on shorter production runs, where experience of a variety of work would be needed.[25] In addition to their employment in certain processes of electrical and small arms production, there were trades already characterised as 'women's trades'. Before the war these included telephone making, surgical and other branches of scientific instrument making, sewing machine and typewriter making, and lamps.[26]

As we saw, the processes and trades described above were a small part of engineering before the First World War. In general, engineering was still a mix of standardised and more flexible production, with limited opportunity for highly automated machinery or 'repetition work' by hand or on machines. Even the electrical goods and motor components trades complained about the difficulties of imposing standardised products on their customers and the need to maintain flexibility.

Most engineering employers, therefore, came to dilution with little experience of employing women or of the mechanical and organisational changes through which they might have been introduced.

24. EEF archive kept at EEF Head Office, Broadway House, London: F6(8) *Enquiry as to Classes of Work Recognised as Women's Work Prior to the War* (1915).
25. *Report of the Committee on Women in Industry* (1919), Cmnd 167. Appendices: Summaries of Evidence, p. 51 (para. 1), p. 52 (para. 1).
26. Barbara Drake, *Women in the Engineering Trades. A Problem, a Solution and Some Criticism: Being a Report based on an Enquiry by a Joint Committee of the Labour Research Department and the Fabian Women's Group* (1918), p. 8.

From their point of view, women's employment disrupted production while they were trained and incurred extra expenditure in terms of accommodation, reorganisation, special lifting and conveyancing appliances, all in the face of an unproven ability. Moreover, employers brought with them firms which, though they might imitate mass production methods piecemeal as the market for their goods allowed, wanted to remain flexible. The skilled worker was needed to provide that flexibility and, as we shall see, employers would prove reluctant to sacrifice him for changes in production which were unlikely to be needed in peacetime.

Women's wages

If the wartime upheaval in gender and skill demarcations was limited it follows that the pre-war basis of wages – paying rates according to types or 'grades' of labour – was not fundamentally altered either, and here ideology and custom do have a clear part to play. Government, skilled unions and employers all shared a belief that women ought (normally) to receive lower rates of pay than men.

The Treasury Agreement set the framework for women's pay. It had allowed for the payment of 'customary rates' as trade restrictions were relaxed and semi-skilled and unskilled labour admitted to work previously done by skilled men. The aim of both government and unions was to protect the wages of skilled men and the agreement therefore proved too imprecise to protect the rates of pay given to women on semi-skilled and unskilled work, the kind of work most war workers actually did.

The skilled unions' insistence that women and other dilutee labour be treated as peripheral to the industry and limited therefore to only a narrow range of work left the way open for employers to argue that such workers were less valuable than the skilled men they (indirectly) replaced, a belief of course shared by the ASE. Within days of the Treasury Agreement, the EEF was telling its member firms to pay women the district rate for youths, not adult men, on the semi-skilled or unskilled work to which they were introduced.[27] In the six months that followed the Treasury Agreement, employers continued to resist its recommendation on pay.

Low rates of pay for women replacing men caused dissatisfaction, which rose as the cost of living increased, not merely among

27. M.L. Yates, *Wages and Labour in British Engineering* (1937), p. 150.

skilled unions but among bodies representing women also. From discussions between women's organisations and male trade unions came a proposal that all women over 18 on munitions work receive not less than £1 a week. The women's representatives wanted all munition workers included and were concerned with broader issues too, like proper training facilities and security against unemployment for women after the war. But the men's unions were not prepared to consider the future position of women and the proposals that were actually put to the Ministry of Munitions in August 1915 concerned only the wages of women engaged on work 'not recognised as women's before the war'.[28] Once more under pressure from organised labour, the government was forced to regulate wages in munitions. The new ministry's Labour Supply Committee was made responsible for the wages and conditions of dilutees, as well as for introducing dilution schemes. It drew up a series of circulars on wages designed to supplement the Munitions of War Act which provided that 'the relaxation of existing demarcation restrictions or admission of semi-skilled or female labour shall not affect adversely the rates customarily paid for the job'.[29] But these circulars were only recommendations and none addressed the wages of women who did not directly replace men but performed only a portion of a skilled man's job.

In February 1916, after an amendment to the Munitions of War Act, the ministry was at last empowered to fix rates of wages and conditions of labour in munitions. Recommendations now became statutory orders issued to all controlled establishments as well as the government's own national factories. But only later, with Order 49, did women performing subdivided or simplified tasks (the great majority of munitions workers, in other words) receive equal time and piece rates – and then only after a three month probation period.

In their opposition to equal pay rates, employers argued that work which had been subdivided was only a portion of a skilled man's work and therefore should not receive his customary rate. They argued that female labour was more costly to them because women who were inexperienced needed more supervision than the men they replaced and required new amenities. Their resistance to equal pay went beyond practical objections like these, however. For them it was simply customary for women to earn less than

28. Yates, *Wages and Labour*, p. 151.
29. Quoted in Kozak, 'Women Munitions Workers', p. 139.

men. Thus, they argued, any change in the labour process made to accommodate female labour, however slight, meant that a new job had been created to which customary rates of pay did not apply. Kozak gives an example of a Glasgow firm where the work done by women in finishing off the nose of 4.5" shells was identical to that done by men except that in the case of women the thread was milled by machine. This tiny change resulted in a piece rate for women far lower than that for men.[30] There are other examples of employers evading equal pay by cutting piece rates, so that earnings would not equal those of men. As one manager told the Fabian writer Barbara Drake in 1915, 'what can one do when a girl is earning as much as 15s a week but lower the piece rate?'[31] For employers, a shift of women into men's jobs did not undermine the custom of lower pay.

The ASE shared the view that women munition workers were less valuable than the men they replaced. Their strategy was to ensure that women would ultimately be dismissed from the industry and their pressure for equal pay was motivated by the same concern. In 1917 the ASE journal reported the outcome of an equal pay dispute which resulted in the removal of the women to other work as 'far more satisfactory than any award would have been'.[32] They supported equal pay, therefore, in order to make female labour expensive and unpopular and to protect their own future position in the industry. This policy was directed against the unskilled as a whole, however, and not merely women. In December 1915, for example, J.T. Brownlie, chairman of the ASE's executive committee, told Lloyd George: 'we are very anxious to see that the semi-skilled and unskilled men coming into the shops shall receive the rates of wages set out in the circular [L3], not so much in the interests of the semi-skilled and unskilled but in the interests of the highly skilled men.'[33] Equal pay policy and the insistence on the return of pre-war customs went together as part of the union's self defence against other sections of the workforce.

The general unions supported equal pay. But in the early part of the war the WU, which had a history of recruitment among women in the newer, lighter engineering trades of the Midlands, was not in a position to demand equal rates. It was a source of friction

30. Kozak, 'Women Munitions Workers', p. 163.
31. Quoted in Braybon, *Women Workers*, p. 86.
32. Braybon, *Women Workers*, p. 75.
33. PRO MUN 5/70/324/3: Deputation to Prime Minister, 31 Dec. 1915, p. 6; quoted by Kozak, 'Women Munitions Workers', p. 189.

between it and the NFWW that the union had fixed the minimum wage for women workers in the Midlands below the £1 minimum guaranteed by the government. This reflected not so much a lesser commitment to the ideal of equal pay as its lack of bargaining strength in areas where women's employment had been established in engineering at customary low rates of pay. From 1916, though, it became increasingly insistent on equal rates, notably the payment of equal war advances.[34] The motives of the general unions may have been less clear-cut than those of the ASE. Women were, after all, a source of membership that it was not in their interests to lose. But, given that the main aim of recruitment was to remove the threat to men's livelihoods posed by women workers, their support for equal pay is likely to have been cast in similar terms.

The position of the NFWW on equal pay was derived in part from their agreement with the ASE. This meant they were committed to pursuing a policy for women's pay specifically in order to protect the man's wage. In her evidence to the War Cabinet Committee, Mary Macarthur upheld 'the rate for the job' as the best path to equal pay. Women would only then be recruited for jobs for which they were suitable, a process involving a revaluation of the real worth of women's work. Her support for equal pay was not simply based on the need to protect the jobs of men. As Kozak points out, the new ingredient in this position is a preference to see women excluded from certain jobs sooner than accept unequal pay. But women's trade unionists like Macarthur do not seem to have foreseen that such a policy could result in deeper sex-based divisions of work.[35]

Government showed itself slow to tackle the core of the wages problem – how to settle the pay rates of women doing portions of a skilled man's work – and slow to make the solution enforceable. Eventually, women's wages were regulated by the state but only in its own factories and in controlled establishments. Even where wages were controlled, the concern of the ministry was not equity for women workers but an easing of the process of dilution whereby skilled trade unionists felt their livelihoods and standard of living were protected. As we saw, the steps they took in shaping women's pay only came in reaction to pressure from male trade unions. Their piecemeal, apparently reluctant intervention also reveals a fear of disrupting – by example – women's wage levels in other industries and a theoretical notion of women's wage earning needs

34. Kozak, 'Women Munitions Workers', p. 193.   35. Ibid., pp. 200–6.

which was unrelated to the work they did.[36] Especially relevant here is the government's refusal to extend existing orders for women's wage rates in engineering to the aircraft industry. Aircraft was a new industry ungoverned by trade union custom and tradition but involving woodworking and welding processes which would normally have been considered as skilled or semi-skilled men's work and for which women were in urgent demand. In spite of this, women were not paid the equivalent customary rates for men. Unlike the other engineering trades, in aircraft manufacture there was no pressure on the government from organised labour to relate female wage rates to the skilled male rates and instead they kept female wages down to what was called a 'fair' level.[37] The pay rate that women received in other munitions industries therefore was not so much a reflection of the work they did as of the value given to the male labour they replaced. The deciding factor in pay was often therefore not *what* job but *whose* job.

Gender and notions of suitable and proper roles did influence women's work and pay in munitions. Equally important, however, were employers' economic concerns about the viability of mass production and the defensive response of skilled trade unions in the face of cheap, unskilled labour. These factors also shaped the terms on which women were employed and their future prospects in the engineering industry.

Demobilisation and post-war prospects

Within a year of the Armistice, three-quarters of a million women had been dismissed. There was a natural contraction of those sectors, like munitions, which had employed women during the war. Three-quarters of those in private firms were employed on government work. The return of peace and the withdrawal of government intervention in the industry would inevitably reduce the permanent impact of the war on women's engineering work.[38] In 1919 government pledges to skilled unions that the pre-war position of their members would be restored were made statutory with the Restoration of Pre-War Practices Act and dilutees were accordingly dismissed. Little machinery appears to have been put in place to manage the

36. See *OHMM*, vol. 5, part 2, ch. 10.
37. Kozak, 'Women Munitions Workers', pp. 146–7; Downs, *Manufacturing Inequality*, p. 157.
38. Pugh, *Women and the Women's Movement*, p. 25 and Drake, *Women in the Engineering Trades*, p. 81.

demobilisation of so many workers, however. Wages were guaranteed for six months after the Armistice, followed by unemployment or 'out of work' donation which was administered so as to force women to return to 'appropriate' work. For instance, it was only to be given to women who could show that they had worked before the war. Those who had not were simply expected to return to their homes. No woman who had once been a domestic servant was considered eligible and no woman applicant was allowed to turn down a 'suitable vacancy'. Evidence from hearings before the Court of Referees, the body that heard appeals from those whose benefit had been withdrawn, suggests 'suitable' meant, in practice, low paid domestic service or employment in women's trades such as laundry work. By 1921 domestic service was the only job for which a retraining scheme was offered to the 900,000 women displaced at the end of the war.[39] The press, enthusiastic and sentimental in its praise for women war workers, now saw them as unpatriotic if they did not return to more traditional work both in and out of the home. In one press campaign they were portrayed as deceitful and selfish claimants of unemployment benefits. Deborah Thom says that the hostility of male workers and unionists discouraged women from perceiving their war experience as capable of leading to permanent employment. 'Addressed as a danger and always characterised as affecting men rather than themselves,' she writes, 'it is perhaps not surprising that women learned not to be workers . . . but women war workers, inherently temporary . . .'.[40] Only about 300,000 women out of the 1,200,000 who had gone into war work were still doing the same jobs by April 1920.[41]

The slump and unemployment of 1922 reinforced feeling against wage-earning women. It also narrowed the prospects for engineering employers who wished to continue with wartime experiments in labour and technology. For many more it confirmed their expectation that peacetime products and markets would not sustain wartime changes. Evidence from employers shows that not only ideological but economic concerns like these would shape their expectations about women's employment in engineering after the war.

39. Jane Lewis, *Women in England 1870–1950. Sexual Divisions and Social Change* (1984), pp. 189–91.

40. Deborah Thom, 'A revolution in the workplace? Women's work in munitions factories and technological change 1914–1918', in Gertjan de Groot and Marlou Schrover (eds), *Women Workers and Technological Change in Europe in the Nineteenth and Twentieth Centuries* (1995), p. 107.

41. Neal A. Ferguson, 'Women's work: employment opportunities and economic roles, 1918–1939', *Albion*, 7 (Spring 1975), p. 57.

Discussion among professional engineering circles after the war shows a mixture of unthinking prejudice which continually placed an upper limit on women's capabilities and suitability as workers, and caution about the economic prospects for the mass production with which they had been associated. In the opinion of Charles Wicksteed, a shell manufacturer employing 100 female workers, women were not engineers but only tool attendants:

> when it came to the question as to whether they ever would be suitable for the engineering trade, he had come to the conclusion that, although women would always be able to do the fringes of engineering work to advantage, such as duplicate work involving light inexpensive machinery or hand work, they were entirely unsuited for engineering proper.[42]

The reason for this was their inadaptability: wartime workers only had experience of a single operation on a special machine, they would require a long period of training and they were poor timekeepers. On average, he claimed, two girls were missing from every shift and their turnover was 50 per cent compared with 10 per cent for men. No allowance was made for the greater domestic responsibilities of women nor any consideration given to whether with training they would prove adaptable to other tasks. It is clear that, for this employer, women simply did not belong except as temporary machine minders. Taking their long term unsuitability as a fact, he had already set up a contributory unemployment benefit scheme for women to cover a period of unemployment after their dismissal at the end of the war.

Members of the Institution of Civil Engineers stressed female quickness, accuracy and 'much finer touch' and agreed that women were most efficient when employed on one operation only since 'a woman was generally less responsive to altered conditions than a man'. An expert on a fixed job, she was less adaptable and could not be moved about the shop as work demanded.[43] It was left to a woman factory welfare worker to point out some of the factors which affected the performance of women in industry. Many were unaccustomed to factory life and discipline. Men were not used to managing women, workshop conditions had been organised for men not women, they were not used to machinery, did not like long hours and did not have the physical strength of men. One could add, as Braybon does, that if women were not allowed to

42. Ibid. 43. From the *Woman Engineer*, Sept. 1921.

supervise or set tools, they could not reasonably be criticised for a lack of initiative or skill.[44] But these practical factors do not seem to have been taken into account by employers in their views of the suitability and success of women in engineering during the war.

There was evidence of a more liberal optimism from some employers who valued women for care, speed and accuracy and saw no limit to the use of women except that of physical strength. Richard Allen of Vickers in Kent, an employer of 900 women, also challenged the idea that women were suitable merely for repetition work. With proper training, they could do more. His firm promised to 'do everything possible to help the girls forward'. It would moreover be to their industrial advantage in competition with Germany after the war. But Allen's attitude was unusual.

More typically, a Board of Trade report in 1918 expected marriage to place a natural limit on women's future in the engineering industry, restricting their usefulness to a narrow range of work. 'As marriage will in most cases', its authors wrote, 'take them out of engineering work it is very little use for them to spend time acquiring all round knowledge at the expense of the increased output attained by confining them to one or two operations only.'[45]

The evidence of the EEF to the War Cabinet Committee on Women's Employment in 1919 repeated some of these views and saw the future of women's work in engineering as the extension of that work which had been more or less recognised as female before the war. Running through the evidence is a concern to strengthen the demarcations that had been emerging before the war rather than to challenge them. For example, they point out that men were often employed before the war on repetition work such as milling 'which was properly work for women' but the men themselves 'did not care for monotonous work' and apprentices objected to being kept on one operation.[46] One prominent employer linked this emerging redivision of labour in engineering with his notion of women's ability and social function. Alfred Herbert, machine tool manufacturer, in a statement submitted to the committee, saw the future of women's employment as to fill the places vacated by men, a role determined by the mentality of the woman worker and her social destiny as a wife and mother:

44. Braybon, *Women Workers*, p. 87.
45. *Report to the Board of Trade by the Committee Appointed to Consider the Position of Engineering Trades after the War* (1918). PRO BT 55/24 EIC 6.
46. *Report of the Committee on Women in Industry* (1919), Cmd 167, Appendices: Summaries of Evidence, p. 51.

the future of woman, therefore, in connection not only with the machine tool trade, but with mechanical industry generally, is to take over that work which is capable of being produced in quantities with the use of such machinery and appliances as reduce the work largely to a matter of routine . . . She will relieve the male worker from the drudgery of routine, to a large extent, and will give him that fuller scope for development in the higher branches of his trade which every keen and intelligent mechanic desires.[47]

In strengthening the evolving definition of women's work in engineering the EEF and employers like Herbert could justify a return to pre-war levels of payment and there was clearly a unanimous concern to point out that equal rates of the kind granted during the war would lead to the elimination of women from the industry. It was also claimed that supervision and accommodation made female labour more expensive than male.

The evidence of the ASE to the committee on the future employment of women is ambiguous. Its strategy remained to the end the complete removal of women from engineering. Thus, the work women were then doing on automatic machines and repetition processes was unsuitable for them. In contrast to the evidence given by the EEF, it stated that subdivided and standardised work was work men would be willing to do and could, at least, form part of the training of boy labour. Still mistrustful of promises that pre-war customs would be restored it also suggested that 'possibly some mutual arrangement might be made with the employers as to the classes of work on which women might subsequently be employed'.[48] In either event the ASE wanted only to safeguard the position of its members. It sought a complete removal of women – but failing that, a say in how women were to be employed.

Historians identify the experience of dilution by wartime employers as crucial in accounting for the nature of women's employment in engineering after the war. The wartime character of female labour – rapid and narrowly directed at a few repetitive tasks, often streamlined to the mass production of standardised commodities like shells and fuses, under simplified and subdivided conditions – is seen as shaping managerial practice on women's work and women's pay in inter-war light engineering. In Kozak's account, employers embraced wartime changes with enthusiasm and saw the war as the start of a restructuring of the industry whereby men would be upgraded and women slotted into the lower grades of

47. Ibid., p. 55 (para. 7).   48. Ibid., p. 59.

work vacated by them. She quotes the eagerness of motor manufacturer, Sir Herbert Austin: 'I am so impressed with the possibilities of standardisation that we shall build only one type of car . . . After the war . . . we shall organise as we do now with skilled labour directing a considerable proportion of women and unskilled workers.'[49] Other employers were more cautious, however. Their evidence suggests that the war had seen a suspension of the normal factors that influenced them and that when these returned, women's employment was likely to be confined to those sectors that had employed them before the war. They did not, in other words,. credit the war with a special influence or see it as an initiator of change. If there was to be restructuring it would have to be undertaken cautiously. Employers expected that the commercial use of wartime methods of munitions production would be restricted by the nature of the market for British engineering goods in peacetime.

From 1919, the engineering trade press began to discuss the disadvantages of large-scale and standardised production. It listed high initial capital expenditure in both special plant and stock-in-progress, problems of reorganisation and the balancing of machines of different abilities and speeds and a lack of versatility in response to demand. One mechanical engineer pinpointed the main anxiety in professional engineering circles about mass production in Britain – was there a market to sustain it? 'Engineers', he warned, 'must not run away with the idea that because during the War they had obtained mass production which was easily swallowed up, the same results would follow upon the mass production of commercial products in peacetime.'[50]

* * *

Neither individual employers nor the EEF and ASE could predict the scope for the employment of women even in those sections of the industry in which they had been employed before the war. Wartime demand for munitions had carried further and faster women's employment in engineering. There was no evidence, though, that in the more stable circumstances of peace continued simplification and rearrangement of work together with the widespread

---

49. Sir Herbert Austin, 'How I made substitution a success', *System*, May 1917, p. 320, quoted by Kozak, 'Women Munitions Workers', p. 126, see also pp. 130–1.

50. From discussion following H.C. Armitage, 'Jigs, tools and special machines with their relation to the production of standardised parts', *Proceedings of the Institution of Mechanical Engineers*, March 1919, p. 279; also quoted in Zeitlin, *Between Flexibility and Mass Production*, ch. 3.

employment of women would be necessary or profitable. Associated in wartime with special machinery, mass production and the absence of considerations of cost, female employment in engineering seemed to undergo an unnatural degree of development. It would be difficult to adapt wartime innovation to peacetime production, with its more gradual cost-conscious development and limited role for specialisation, particularly in the adverse economic conditions that were to follow.[51]

51. See, for example, G.D.H Cole, *Trade Unionism in the Munitions Industries* (1923), pp. 215–16, p. 218.

CHAPTER FOUR

Women's Employment between the Wars

In the newest and fastest growing trades of electrical engineering and motor component manufacture the core of the workforce was female. On average around 40,000 women worked in essential manufacturing and finishing processes, consistently accounting for two-thirds of the total employment.[1] In Miriam Glucksmann's study these women workers are elevated further to become the pioneers in a new relationship between labour and capital, subject, through their assembly line work, to unprecedented measures of exploitation and subordination.[2]

This chapter looks instead at the way women's employment in these two trades was shaped by the nature of mass production and the demand for mass produced goods. It argues that an uncertain market created a need for novelty and flexibility which in turn inhibited comprehensive technological and organisational change, even among the most advanced engineering firms. Flexible production influenced the nature of female and male employment, leading away from comprehensive deskilling and tightening managerial control.[3]

The following sections describe the expansion of two trades in which most women engineering workers were employed: electrical engineering and motor vehicle manufacture. Both the nature of their products and an expanding market encouraged investment in mass production methods which aimed at a rapid output of large

1. An average based on census of production figures, 1924, 1930, 1935.
2. Miriam Glucksmann, *Women Assemble. Women Workers and the New Industries in Inter-war Britain* (1990), pp. 3–4.
3. The emphasis within this chapter on the continuing importance of flexibility in British engineering between the wars supports the work of Jonathan Zeitlin. See his forthcoming book, *Between Flexibility and Mass Production. Strategic Debate and Industrial Reorganisation in British Engineering* (forthcoming).

numbers of goods. Here mass production means, as it did for contemporaries, the manufacture of standardised, parts or products,
using automatic or semi automatic machines, 'continuous processes'
and semi-skilled or unskilled labour.[4] In her study of women workers and new industries between the wars, Glucksmann identifies the
'continuous flow' method of work organisation aided by the moving assembly line as the defining characteristic of this new type
of production. Women in inter-war mass production industries
occupied a key position. As assembly line workers they were subject
to unprecedented degrees of exploitation and subordination as
managers controlled the pace and speed of the moving line. New
methods of organising work and the new technology of assembly
lines gave employers total control of the level of output, work intensity and pay. In short, the whole production process was now
more effectively controlled than ever before.[5] By contrast, what
follows suggests that, even in these industries, there was adaptation
and modification of 'pure' mass production methods and an uneven degree of deskilling which influenced both how women were
employed and the degree of control over the labour process gained
by employers.

One of the most significant surveys of women's employment in
the industry, so far overlooked, offers a more representative picture. In the summer of 1934 the EEF conducted an enquiry among
engineering employers into their use of female labour. In all, 170
federated firms replied, employing between them 31,000 women
and girls, or 75 per cent of the total female employment of federated firms. It found that, far from being associated with highly
mechanised production, most women in federated firms either
worked on hand operations or used non-automatic machinery. They
were certainly not limited to assembly work. Only a third of women
worked on assembly, viewing, testing and inspecting taken together.[6]
Together with evidence from GEC and Lucas (see pp. 72–91, below)

4. See *Engineering*, 3 Feb. 1922, p. 141; Sir Herbert Austin, 'The influence of mass
production on design', *Proceedings of the Institute of Production Engineers*, 14. 8 (Aug.
1935), pp. 429–30; T.P.N. Burness, 'Batch production and its effect on choice of
manufacturing plant', *Transactions of the Manchester Association of Engineers*, 6 (1944–
5), p. 123. For a critical approach to the definition of mass production see Dave
Lyddon, 'The myth of mass production and the mass production of myth' and Kevin
Whitson, 'Scientific Management and production management practice in Britain
between the wars', both in *Historical Studies in Industrial Relations*, 1 (Mar. 1996).
  5. Glucksmann, *Women Assemble*, pp. 3–4.
  6. EEF, *Report to the Administration Committee by the Sub-Committee of the Administration Committee in regard to Female Labour* (Jun. 1934), pp. 5–8 and Appendix I. MRC
MSS.237/3/1/89, F(6)56.

the EEF survey indicates that the uneven nature of mass production in British engineering limited and shaped women's work. Even leading firms in their field such as these were unable to implement fully mass production methods which might have given them exceptional control of production and labour.

Electrical engineering

The scope for the standardised, mass production predicted by enthusiasts of wartime changes was greater in some sections of the electrical trade than others. The lamp trade, where a standard product was produced in increasing numbers, drawing largely on women for its workforce, is an extreme example. Production there was almost entirely mechanised. A number of operations were carried out on machines with rotating tables, in some cases with young women working in teams and being paid on piecework according to the output of the whole group.[7] Other important consumer goods firms did not adopt the methods associated with mass production. Demand was relatively restricted – the most widely bought consumer goods at this time were radios and electric irons – and competition between producers was centred around innovations in the type of model offered. Both these factors tended to restrict the volume of production and modify mass production practice. One London electrical firm making a large variety of light parts in small numbers developed a flexible system of conveyorised assembly. It included a number of benches, each conveyorised and fed from a 'general purpose' conveyor running at right angles to the operators. Each bench was a general purpose bench with the necessary assembly tools and so on secured to it with movable clamps. This arrangement made it easy to set up any assembly in a very short time.[8]

The size of a firm also inhibited mass production practice. There were a large number of small producers in the industry who were unable or disinclined to spend money on the services of an efficiency expert to advise on mechanisation and reorganisation. As one production engineer observed in 1932, 'the small manufacturer is usually far too busy on production to spend the necessary

7. H. Llewellyn Smith, *The New Survey of London Life and Labour* (1931), vol. 2, p. 165.
8. G. Hurford, 'Mechanisation in a Works', *Proceedings of the Institute of Production Engineers*, 11. 8 (Nov. 1932).

time to make the studies which are so essential to bring and to keep his work up to date'.[9] Unlike the large firms such as English Electric, GEC or Joseph Lucas Ltd, they did not keep planning staffs of their own or design and manufacture special equipment for their own needs.

Even for larger firms the pattern is not straightforward. Many of the largest – who naturally employed most of the women in the industry – straddled both the 'heavy' and 'light' sections and large-scale standardised production co-existed with non-standard, small volume or 'batch' production. Metropolitan Vickers, for example, produced large and complex capital goods like turbines and generators in small batches. Here they depended on skilled use of general purpose machinery. But they also relied on simpler machines and operations for the production of components, employing large numbers of semi-skilled men and women whose operations were studied by a pioneering motion study department headed by the firm's chief supervisor of women, Miss A.G. Shaw.

There was then a spectrum of practice within engineering which did not just reach between the so-called old and new sectors, but existed within those trades, like electrical engineering, typically thought of as sources for the newest and most advanced techniques of mass production. The following case study of one of the largest electrical engineering firms producing both capital and consumer goods reveals a mixture of production and employment features, some typically associated with mass production, others adapted to suit the variable market for their products. It concludes that women were not so readily consigned to routine machine attendance and simple assembly under the newest and most advanced methods of mechanised production.

GEC and the Peel-Conner Telephone and Radio Works

GEC was a leading producer of standardised electrical goods, employing large numbers of women between the wars. Before the First World War, the firm had factories in Manchester, Birmingham, Lemington and London producing most types of electric lighting supplies. The main work of the decade before the war lay in

9. Ibid., p. 282. See also *Engineering*, Feb. 1918, p. 201 on the practical limitations of motion study.

extending the firm's business into heavy electrical engineering with the setting up of a factory at Witton in Birmingham and the erection of a large cable works at Southampton. Dynamos, motors and switchgear were transferred from Manchester to Witton and the Salford works began to specialise in telephone and telegraph work. A subsidiary company was set up to manage it, the Peel-Conner Telephone Works Ltd. Under the guidance of its American manager, M.S. Conner, the firm manufactured the first 10,000 line manual exchange, installed in Glasgow in 1910.[10]

As with the industry as a whole, the heavy engineering side of the firm was slow to prosper. In the early 1920s disappointing returns were blamed on low prices, irregular orders and insufficient demand for standard products. By 1930 the depression had further restricted the market for heavy industrial goods. Not until 1936 was there an increase in activity in all sections, with the heavy engineering works running to full capacity. Demand for telephone and wireless apparatus, lamps, switch gear, cables and general electrical goods, meanwhile, had steadily increased.[11]

Birmingham, traditional home of the brass trades, was chosen by GEC as the site for its production of electric fittings and motors because it was thought that the iron and steel and small metal trades of the district would be a good source of skilled and unskilled labour for a wide range of processes from foundry work to winding small motors. Labour supply – this time specifically 'skilful women workers' – was also behind the choice of Hammersmith in London as the centre for the manufacture of GEC-Osram lamps.[12] Early in the First World War the company established the Conner Magneto and Ignition Works on the Copsewood estate in Coventry. The previous year Conner had visited Coventry and decided that it would be a good place to expand the telephone works because of the supply of female labour. In 1921 the Peel-Conner Telephone Works were accordingly transferred from Salford to Coventry. Two years later, when Conner returned to America, the Conner Magneto Ignition Company was wound up and the factory turned over to the production of radios and absorbed into the existing telephone works.[13]

The Coventry telephone and radio factory was continually expanding. This growth was largely owed to the government's decision to

10. From *A Brief History of GEC Telecommunications Ltd produced by the Company* (1981), GEC-Plessey Telecommunications, Coventry.
11. GEC Annual Reports, 1930–6, The General Electric Company Plc, London.
12. *The Loudspeaker*, Jun. 1948, p. 93.
13. *A Brief History of GEC Telecommunications Ltd.*

purchase and operate the telephone system through the GPO. In the early 1920s GEC produced manual exchange equipment for the GPO in its Peel-Conner works and, from the mid-1920s, automatic exchanges. The first unattended rural automatic exchanges, adopted as standard by the GPO, were made in 1929. GEC also began in 1922 to develop transmission equipment in order to provide long distance telephone communication. The result was the thermionic-valve-amplifier repeaters which allowed rapid development of the trunk network. In the late 1920s, GEC supplied all stations in the UK south of Birmingham with repeaters. Both of these developments – the rural automatic exchange and long distance transmission equipment – opened up the export market for GEC. India, Australia, New Zealand and Egypt were the chief destinations for their equipment. When the Post Office wanted to improve the trunk telephone service, the Coventry works turned its attention to the production of carrier telephone apparatus which enabled several people to talk over one pair of wires.

In addition to exchange and transmission equipment the company produced telephone apparatus for private use throughout the 1920s and 1930s. The Coventry works also specialised in radio manufacture which was seasonal, geared, like motor cars, to an annual show. Competition at the show centred around novelty and improvements in design. However, in 1934 the Coventry Chamber of Commerce detected some attempts to avoid the practice of introducing new models at regular intervals: 'This practice has, in the past, made the radio industry "seasonal", with the attendant disadvantages of extremes in the rate of production. With a general desire to spread work evenly over the whole year, manufacturers are now introducing new models as development work permits'.[14] At its peak in 1936–7, output of GEC radios at Coventry reached the rate of one every half minute of the working day.[15]

GEC at Coventry was a significant mass producer contributing to the prosperity of the most buoyant section of electrical engineering – the manufacture of low voltage equipment and consumer goods. Yet even this firm lacked some of the typical organisational and employment features associated with mass production. It was obliged to deploy women workers within a semi-flexible work process in which they were not simply restricted to routine machine attendance and simple assembly under the most advanced conditions.

14. Coventry Chamber of Commerce, *Annual Report* 1933–4, p. 7.
15. Coventry Chamber of Commerce, *Annual Report* 1936–7, p. 6.

Instead of organising its work according to product, in line with American mass production practice, as might have been expected, GEC maintained an arrangement of work according to process, traditionally found in engineering's older, staple sectors. There were, for example, a press department, a drilling shop, an auto and capstan shop, milling and finishing departments. There were a number of specialist shops as well, like coil-winding and the cabling section.[16] The winding shop was decentralised in 1934 and work on coils for repeater equipment, an expanding part of the firm's telephone business, was transferred to a new department for repeaters.[17] Apart from these, there were few examples of GEC organising work according to product. Instead, from the early 1920s a chasing department existed to try to ensure a smooth flow of various products through the same shops at the same time. Speed of handling, speed of working and the balancing of speeds and machine capacities were its main concern.[18]

By the late 1930s a more elaborate system of work organisation seems to have been in operation, with master schedules being drawn up for each class of product to ensure that delivery times were met. Standard times were by then established for most work so that each department knew how much time was allowed to complete their particular operations. It was the job of shop planners and chasers to ensure that output was maintained at the rate according to the schedule. By 1938 each machine shop section, for instance, had its own planner with a detailed schedule of work for that section including the date by which each part had to be manufactured. The planner directed the progress of parts from incoming materials and through the various operations. Chasers looked after the orders for which parts were required. They told the schedule department the date by which subcomponents and components must be available for assembly in order to meet the delivery date.[19]

The fact that GEC in Coventry, a large employer of women and leading firm in the industry, lacked what is often taken to be one of the defining characteristics of mass production – line flow manufacture – is significant. It means that managerial control over levels of effort and output was exercised through an elaborate though

16. W.H. Malcolm, 'Our Works organisation', *The Loudspeaker*, Jan. 1925, p. 3, Feb. 1925, p. 3.

17. From profile of Mrs G. Hawkins, *The Loudspeaker*, Sept. 1936, p. 8.

18. W.H. Malcolm, 'Our Works organisation', *The Loudspeaker*, Mar. 1925, p. 4.

19. 'Scheduling, shop planners and chasing departments', *The Loudspeaker*, Dec. 1937, p. 14.

less intensive system of work schedules and progress chasers. Combined with uneven levels of mechanisation and automation, it also means that women's employment was not linked to the newest, most advanced work methods and technology, subjecting them to a peculiarly exploitative new form of control within the same routine tasks. As we shall see, the firm counted on using women with some flexibility across a range of operations and products in order to maintain quality and output during peaks of demand in an unstable market.

Between 1,000 and 3,000 women – about two-thirds of the workforce – were employed on most of the processes involved in the manufacture of the factory's products between the wars. Most were adult workers. In 1936 and 1941 only around 15 per cent of the female workforce was aged under 18. No marriage bar existed at the firm. One woman barred by marriage in 1932 from the other main factory employer of women in the town, Courtaulds, went straight to work at GEC.[20] Direct production jobs were frequently female while men were usually employed on indirect work, supervising, progress chasing and designing. In line with the EEF's findings, women's jobs were not confined to assembly tasks and included hand and machine operations, viewing, testing and other finishing work. Assembly itself was not always automated. With the exception of telephones, conveyors were not normally machine-driven, single purpose lines along which women worked but more often a means of transporting parts.

Winding coils for use in telephone and radio components was a female machining task at the factory, involving varying degrees of mechanisation and automation. At first, the process of coil-winding had involved placing layers of insulating material in by hand, but by the 1930s this had been mechanised.[21] In 1937 the coil-winding section had 180 machines of half a dozen different kinds from simple hand-operated spindles to machines that wound ten wires at once. Some of the machines were fitted with counters which could be preset to make a given number of turns. The machines were arranged in rows of nine and a conveyor belt running at right angles to the rows collected finished work and took it on to be inspected. A conveyor of this kind was known as 'general purpose' as it could be adapted to accommodate differing quantities. Coil-

20. J. Castle, 'Factory work for women: Courtaulds and GEC between the wars', in B. Lancaster and T. Mason, *Life and Labour in a Twentieth Century City. The Experience of Coventry* (1986), p. 149.
21. 'The coil-winding dept.', *The Loudspeaker*, Jul. 1938, pp. 7–8.

winding could be unpopular as workers were only paid for coils that registered correctly on the ampeter. If not, the work had to be done again.[22]

Women also worked in the cabling section attached to the wiring shop where cable was cut to length, formed and soldered ready for use in manual telephone exchanges. The function of the wiring shop itself was to assemble, equip and wire all apparatus needed in a telephone exchange.[23] By 1938 it was situated at the end of the telephone exchange manufacturing line and the cable department had become a small separate factory.[24] In the cable making and machine shops women operated presses set up for them by skilled men. The finishing shops employed women on buffing, plating and lacquering, using polishing machines, dips or sprays. By 1938 work was brought to the section on overhead conveyors.

Assembly shops were a further source of female employment within the factory. In 1924 they were described as being divided into product sections like exchange apparatus (relays and meters), subsidiary exchange apparatus (including fuse mountings and telephone apparatus), telephone sets and transmitters.[25] By the end of the 1930s general assembly had become the largest department, situated partly at Ford Street and partly at the main Stoke site. It was divided into seven subsections in which one and a half million parts were assembled each week by about 400 of the 2,600 women who worked in the factory as a whole. Assemblies then included bakelite telephones, meters, generators, fuse mountings, dials, contactor units and transmitters. The components for each operator were placed in racks or trays, some of which revolved in order to speed-up handling, and screwdrivers were suspended overhead so that time and bench space were saved.

As in the example above, conveyors were often, as their name suggests, both a means of transporting parts and finished goods and a tool for ensuring that work schedules (the time a given product was supposed to take to make) were met. Sometimes they formed a moving line on which women worked. In general assembly, by the end of the 1930s, for example, benches were in rows with operators about six feet apart, and a gangway for the foreman or inspector. The cases of bakelite telephones were first drilled to allow the cord through and then fed onto a manual conveyor, in fact a

22. Castle, 'Factory work for women', p. 157.
23. W.H. Malcolm, 'Our Works organisation', *The Loudspeaker* Feb. 1925, p. 3.
24. *The Loudspeaker*, Sept. 1938, p. 8 and Oct. 1938, p. 3.
25. W.H. Malcolm, 'Our Works organisation', *The Loudspeaker*, Jan. 1925, p. 3.

metal truck on wheels running between two iron rails. Each operator had a hopper containing the parts needed for their particular operation. The truck moved along the rails as each operation was carried out on the telephone case. At the end of the seventy-foot line each case was tested and taken via another conveyor to operators who assembled the base of the telephone. Unlike the first, this conveyor ran at right angles to the stationary assembly benches. The assembled telephone then had to be placed on a moving belt and transported to packing.[26]

For all the emphasis given to speed and timing, automated and even manual conveyors were still not the rule in general assembly. The author of the 'works' tour' published in the company magazine throughout 1938, for instance, assured readers that 'mechanised or manually operated conveyors *where practicable* provide transport without delay or fatigue' (my italics).[27] With operators six feet apart and a foreman or inspector nearby, talking must have been difficult, but singing is mentioned and music from the in-house radio. The work was in any case detailed and precise and demanded concentration. The qualifications for employment in assembly were, according to the same author, 'quick, supple fingers, care and "touch", which is an indefinable knack that transmits tone to the operator's work – an asset more pronounced in some individuals than others. When it is realised that a telephone dial – for example – has 102 distinct pieces within a circle 3 inches in diameter, there is not much margin for clumsy, thick fingers.'[28]

The male workforce was never employed on the machining, finishing and assembly tasks just described. Men worked in the engineering department which dealt with the development, design and technical aspects of products. It included a model room where samples of new designs were made and tested. The shop engineering department employed men in identifying the various processes involved in the manufacture of parts, in tool design and drafting and in rate fixing. They worked too in the chasing department, supervising the progress of parts through the works. Their job was to enable assemblies to be carried out with the minimum of delay and by the date needed. To do this they needed to maintain a balance of manufacture so that the assembly shops were not held up waiting for a particular component. Men also worked in the toolroom, producing all the press tools, drills, jigs and gauges that

26. 'General assembly', *The Loudspeaker*, Dec. 1938, pp. 6–7.
27. Ibid., p. 4.   28. Ibid., pp. 5–6.

were needed as products were introduced or modified, and in the jobbing department where small numbers of special articles were made.

Some direct production tasks were undertaken by men too. There were male fitters and setters up and semi-skilled male machine operators. The large, heavy metalworking of the frame shop was carried out entirely by men.[29] A description of the cabinet section suggests that cabinet manufacture was semi-skilled work akin to that performed by women. Elsewhere in the factory it was normal for women to be employed on construction and assemblies such as cabinets where jigs and templates had been used. It may be that men were employed there in preference to women because the work was likened to furniture making, a male craft with a strong history of trade unionism. The men who worked there were members of the furniture trades union. Timber for radio and television cabinets was cut on machines and where possible jigs, gauges and templates were used. Similarly, drilling and recessing of cabinet parts was done by the use of jigs and templates, as was their assembly. In the assembly and erection of sections and desks for exchanges men again worked with jigs and templates but a lot of hand work was still required. In contrast to the description of the natural, physical attributes described for assembly work, the company magazine noted that 'this work calls for operators who have had considerable experience and have become skilled in this particular work'.[30] In fairness, however, it was usual for women too to be described as competent, skilful or experienced.

Foremen and patrol inspectors were male but, unusually, women at GEC could become chargehands as well as 'key girls'. The company magazine carried a series of profiles of women workers in which the work histories and skills of some of the 'key girls' are described. Typically these workers had a sound knowledge of all the jobs in their department. One of them, Elizabeth Wootton, showed a particular ability for coil-winding, her skill 'causing her to be engaged on all manner of exacting work where difficult coils or resistances have to be handled'.

Other profiles show that women were moved about as need arose and could gain experience of more than one job. One profile describes five changes of job in five years, partly due to the boom in wireless sales. Another worked for five years on most of the

29. Castle, 'Factory work for women', p. 141.
30. 'Cabinet works', *The Loudspeaker*, Feb. 1938, p. 16.

assembly operations in the production of dials, selectors and bank entails. She was then transferred to the finishing department, dealing with enamelling, lacquering and cellulose spraying, where her skill was acknowledged: 'The variety and volume of work in this section calls for great care and skill on the part of those responsible for the high quality of finishes being maintained.'[31] A woman was put in charge of the cable forming shop in 1920. Miss Emily Wyatt, who had worked in the varnishing room of the cabinet works at Salford from 1904, was sent to Coventry in 1921 to become 'right hand man' to the foreman of the cabinet works there.[32] A few were promoted further. Miss Massey, who had joined the firm in 1902, was put in charge of the lacquering room in 1915. Ten years later she was made 'foremistress' of all finishing departments.[33] In 1930 the coil-winding section had a female chargehand, promoted after two years' service, as did relay and spring set assembly, condenser test and condenser winding.[34] Experienced women were used to train others. Miss Ella Smith, who worked on adjustment of relays, 'an operation calling for considerable skill and experience in the setting of springs and measurement of tension', took charge in 1936 of a learners' class in which new employees were instructed before they began work on the production benches.[35]

It seems then that GEC at Coventry did not adopt continuous flow lines of production in which work was organised according to a sequence of all the operations necessary for a given product. As we have seen, most production work was carried out in process shops instead and the firm relied on planning and chasing departments to ensure the smooth flow of various products through the same shops at the same time. Assembly lines were arranged with some flexibility to allow for a change over of work or variations in quantity. The highly seasonal demand for radios, for instance, would have made this arrangement more useful to the firm than fixed-quantity production. Mechanised handling and transportation – conveyors – were as important as assembly lines in making sure production schedules were met. As the profiles described above indicated, women were moved between sections in line with demand

31. 'Who's Who: Miss E. Murray', *The Loudspeaker*, Jan. 1936.
32. 'Who's Who No. 8', *The Loudspeaker*, Oct. 1926, p. 8.
33. 'Who's Who at Salford', *The Loudspeaker*, Mar. 1927, p. 8.
34. 'Who's Who: Miss Dot Strong', *The Loudspeaker*, Apr. 1930, p. 3; 'Who's Who: Miss H. Smith', *The Loudspeaker*, Aug. 1930, p. 5; 'Who's Who: Miss Dorothy Woods', *The Loudspeaker*, Sept. 1930, p. 7; 'Who's Who: Miss Suggate', *The Loudspeaker*, May 1935; 'Who's Who: Gladys Spicer', *The Loudspeaker*, Apr. 1935.
35. 'Who's Who: Miss Ella Smith', *The Loudspeaker*, Dec. 1936, p. 7.

and so picked up a range of experience and skill, allowing production to be maintained at a steady rate without the falling off of output associated with new labour. Some of these women were able to become chargehands and some undertook the training of other workers. The value of experienced women generally to production is suggested by the firm's preference for short-time working to redundancy as the seasonal peaks in demand for radios passed.[36]

This case study of GEC's Peel-Conner works shows one of the largest leading electrical engineering firms as having a range of characteristics, some typically associated with mass production, others adapted to suit the variable market for their products. Managerial control was exercised to some degree through organisational change, though it did not conform to the most advanced industrial practice and relied instead on work schedules implemented by planning and chasing departments. In spite of a need for efficient timing, mechanised handling and conveyorised assembly was not the rule. At the same time, the firm seems to have valued the experience and competencies of their female workforce, who were used with some flexibility across a range of operations as needed.

Motor vehicle manufacture

Motor vehicle manufacture was the second largest source of female employment, after electrical engineering, although women were typically employed only in the manufacture of components, not in making or assembling cars. As with the electrical industry, an unstable market produced a pattern of production and employment in which women were not merely confined to routine machine attendance and simple assembly under the newest and most advanced methods of mechanised production. The following case study of Joseph Lucas Ltd, one of the most significant suppliers and the largest single employer of women in the industry at this time shows how, under the pressure of a market centred on novelty and variability, employers were unable to implement fully mass production methods. In order to maintain output and quality, they still depended on skilled men and experienced female labour within a semi-flexible organisation of work.

36. J. Castle, 'Factory Work for Women in Inter-war Britain: the Experience of Women Workers at GEC and Courtauld's in Coventry 1919–39' (MA thesis, University of Warwick, 1984), ch. 4.

The British market for cars was narrower and more variable than the American.[37] Britain's was a luxury market where model and design counted for more than price. Larger producers were under constant pressure to maintain sales by multiplying the number of models offered and could therefore never gain complete control of the market. The main beneficiaries of the growing demand for cars in Britain were Morris and Austin, both of whom produced a wide range of well-equipped smaller cars. By 1930, Austin complained, the public had come to expect a new car model every year and profitability depended on bringing out the right model at the right time.[38] In practice, some standardisation did take place. By 1939 Morris had reduced its cars to seventeen types and its engines to ten. Meanwhile, manufacturers increasingly used common components across different models. However, there were no dramatic changes to the flexible methods of production which a wider range of cars demanded and constant changes in product design continued to influence the nature of production in the industry.[39]

The case study of Joseph Lucas Ltd, one of the main suppliers of components to car producers, shows how the variability of their needs and the seasonal nature of the car market scuppered attempts to take effective control of production. The firm was obliged to allow for flexibility in its use of advanced methods of work organisation and specialist machinery and it continued to depend on its supply of experienced female and male labour in order to meet peaks in demand. Women were therefore employed within a semi-flexible organisation of work. They acquired skills which their employer was concerned to retain in order to ensure even levels of output and quality throughout the season.

Joseph Lucas Ltd

Joseph Lucas Ltd was the largest single employer of women among federated engineering employers in the inter-war years. It drew on

37. In the motor-cycle industry too standardisation was limited and demand fragmented around a range of tastes. The success of the British motor cycle overseas was credited to the variety of types produced here. See the Committee on Industry and Trade, Part IV, p. 227.

38. H.C. Armitage, 'Machine tools from the manufacturing user's point of view', *Proceedings of the Institution of Automobile Engineers*, Dec. 1930.

39. Ibid., p. 432 and discussion on p. 441; C.R.F. Engelbach, Presidential Address, *PIAE* 1933–4, p. 17. See, for example, Steven Tolliday, 'Management and labour in Britain 1896–1939', in J. Zeitlin and S. Tolliday (eds), *The Automobile Industry and its Workers* (1986), pp. 37–8. For the general picture see J. Zeitlin and A. Mckinlay, 'The meanings of managerial prerogative: industrial relations and the organisation of work in British engineering 1880–1939', *Business History*, 31. 2 (Apr. 1989), p. 43.

a supply of female labour which had customarily worked in small metal wares and other metal goods made up of small parts. Before the First World War, women's work at Lucas itself included assembly of lamps and horns, weighing and boxing carbide for cycle lamps, and some processes of battery manufacture. Married women were probably barred from employment at this time. One pre-war worker felt that single women 'got a better chance' while married women were seen as unreliable. Wedding rings were hidden to escape the sack.[40] The firm supplied components and accessories to the motor industry, first for cycles and motor cycles and later for cars. Stimulated by the growth of the motor trade after the First World War, its business was increasingly taken up with the production of electrical components, car dynamos and batteries. Over the next few years, the firm established a strong position with Morris Motors, one of the largest car producers and a firm keen to use as many bought out components as possible. Expansion by acquisition, the manufacture of other companies' products under licence and market sharing agreements became the pattern of growth for Lucas between the wars.[41] In these ways Lucas was able to increase and then keep its share of a relatively small and fragmented market, allowing it to take advantage of the methods and economies of mass production. A programme of re-equipment and reorganisation had begun in 1924 and in 1927 a number of technical staff visited the USA to study American production methods. Continuous machining processes and conveyor assembly devised by a new production methods department were later introduced to the Birmingham factory.[42]

Between the wars, as the electrical side of its business came to dominate sales, Joseph Lucas became a leading employer of women, adopting, unlike GEC, American mass production methods. However, in terms of the nature of women's work and levels of control, the outcome was not very different to that at GEC's Coventry factory. The variable market for cars and therefore components continually undermined mass production at Lucas. In common with GEC, it was forced to deploy its female labour within a semi-flexible work process.

Lucas was quick to follow the advice and example of American motor components manufacturers in an attempt to benefit from

40. File 'women historical', Joseph Lucas Archive, the British Motor Industry Heritage Trust, notes on interview with Mrs Elsie Walker, addressed to Women's Employment Manager, Joseph Lucas Ltd, 1959.
41. Harold Nockolds, *Lucas. The First Hundred Years* (1976), vol. 1, p. 218.
42. Ibid., p. 244.

similar economies of scale. Switchbox and yoke (the outer casing of a dynamo) assembly and testing were the first operations to be mechanised following a visit by Lucas technical staff to the USA in 1927. By 1931 dynamo and starter assembly had been conveyorised too, with a whole floor of the Great King Street factory in Birmingham devoted to it. K5 for example – the fifth floor of the factory – was given over to dynamo and starter assembly. Conveyorised assembly and transport were widely used. Final sets of dynamos and starters were put together on a main assembly band or chain. The parts were placed on a slow moving band while women stood on either side and assembled them. An indicator at the end of the line showed the number of products being 'put through'. The work of testing, viewing and packing was again mainly carried out by women and girls. They also worked on secondary lines on which components made up of many parts and other small sub-assemblies were done. Both the lines were complemented by a new overhead conveyor consisting of a sequence of hooks from which women on the line could take whatever parts they needed. This had to be kept stocked.[43]

Three hundred people produced 20,000 motor lamps and other articles a week from the lamp assembly shop in 1931. The section had twelve modern conveyors for both assembly and transport. The longest was 380 feet long and carried lamp parts, after they had been sandblasted, to the spraying shop and on to the stores; from there they were sent to be polished and viewed. The stores acted as a junction for conveyors. Plated parts were taken from the plating works on a conveyor via tunnels beneath Farm Street and Great King Street and transferred to another conveyor to be delivered elsewhere. The company magazine, *Lucas Reflections,* boasted, 'the work is so highly organised and the operations so synchronised and dovetailed into one another that the smoothness of the working arrangements is very pronounced'.[44]

Assembly in the lamp shop was carried out on a band conveyor system. The parts travelled down the centre of the bench on a continually moving band and each operator took parts from it for their work. P100 lamps on the other hand were hand-made by 'craftsmen' described as having served on average twenty-three years with the company. No explanation is offered for male employment on what was typically 'female work'. In both cases the conveyor

43. Ibid., pp. 9–11.
44. 'Works tour with pen and camera III – lamp assembly (Department M 6)', *Lucas Reflections,* Jul. 1931, p. 9.

could be made more flexible using only one side of the band or bench. This would help to take care of variations in the amount of output needed. As we shall see, this was an important feature as Lucas remained very vulnerable to seasonal peaks and troughs in demand throughout the inter-war years.[45]

The Lucas Cable Works at Rocky Lane in Birmingham employed women on cable cutting either by hand using a lever operated guillotine or, where quantities justified it, by means of a motor driven automatic machine which cut the cable and stripped the ends. Women assembled cables into harness using special jig boards fitted with clips and pegs spaced so as to form the harness and checked to the dimensions of the drawing. They braided or covered the leads with cotton using a machine, bared the ends and fitted terminals and did the final tubing.[46]

In spite of comparatively advanced methods of production, there was some scope for women to develop competencies and to use their experience and judgment. Cyclometer assembly, for example, required an additional three months' training and women were allowed to use their own discretion about the parts they used for assembly as a form of quality control.[47] In general, women's experience in these jobs was important in maintaining quality at a time when large numbers of newcomers tended to lower quality and to increase inspection costs, as Lucas directors were constantly reminded.

Peter Bennett, the firm's managing director, continually complained in his monthly reports to the board of directors of being overwhelmed by the seasonal demands of the motor industry. A pattern established itself in the 1920s and mid-1930s of additional turnover induced by unexpectedly high demand being sapped by rises in labour costs as more workers were taken on and more overtime worked. Stocks were accumulated against future demand but only 'so far as is safe'.[48] The firm was always dependent on expanding its workforce to meet the new season's requirements for fear of losing custom.[49] The result was rising employment, overtime and weekend working during the season, followed by short-time

45. Ibid., p. 10; the advantages of a fixed assembly line of this kind are discussed by Hurford, 'Mechanisation in a Works', p. 288.

46. A.G. Anderson, 'The Lucas cable works, Rocky Lane, Birmingham', *Lucas Reflections*, Mar.–Apr. 1935, pp. 4–5.

47. 'The manufacture of Lucas cyclometers', *Lucas Reflections*, Jun. 1935, p. 5.

48. Joseph Lucas Ltd, Managing Director's Monthly Reports to the Board of Directors, Feb. 1937, Lucas Industries Plc, Brueton House, Solihull.

49. Ibid., Sept. 1932.

and lay-offs out of season. It was this kind of 'flexibility' in their use of labour which Lucas was keen to do without. Clearly Lucas management felt it lost control of production when pressurised into temporary expedients in order to satisfy an unpredictable demand.

Throughout the inter-war period, but especially in the 1930s, Lucas thus made attempts to curb its dependence on the manual labour force, all of which had an impact on women's employment at the factory. Women were used to try out the Bedaux method of work study, for example. They also worked under reorganised and more automated conditions, using specialised plant laid out for the first time on a flow line principle to produce standardised items. However, variable demand from the motor industry undermined the impact of these changes. Not all work could be fully automated or devoted to a single, standard product. Semi-flexible work organisation continued and the dependence of the firm on its ability to increase the supply of female labour and to attract and retain a nucleus of skilled men remained.

Profits lost through rising labour costs during periods of peak demand explain the firm's adoption and adaptation of the Bedaux system. As elsewhere in industry, women became the focus for this innovation in the firm's working. Bedaux was a popular or, among workers, notorious, inter-war management scheme aimed at extracting greater degrees of individual effort per unit of time. Details of the scheme were almost certainly learned from the American competitor, Autolite, with whom Lucas were negotiating during 1930. The firm tried to introduce it in November 1931 precisely so that it could be used to take advantage of the new season's increasing demand while maintaining and stabilising employment.[50] In common with its introduction in other firms, it was first tried on a group of 140 women in a section of the works. Lucas were optimistic but by January 1932 they had been forced to withdraw the system. It was strongly opposed, not only by the women themselves, but by male supervisors who until then had, according to Nockolds, 'enjoyed an excessive amount of control in their shops and they were consequently bitterly opposed to Bedaux engineers' recommendations for grouping machine tools'.[51] The women complained of stopwatch timing which had led to a speed-up of their jobs. A rank and file committee was set up and the National Unemployed Workers' Movement joined in the agitation. Meanwhile women workers at the Wolsey hosiery factory in Leicester had successfully

50. Ibid., Nov. 1931.   51. Nockolds, *Lucas*, vol. 1, p. 263.

struck against the introduction of Bedaux at their works. Lucas was forced to back down or risk a stoppage which it could not afford. However, this was by no means the last of the Lucas scheme for reorganisation. 'The Bedaux investigations have opened our eyes in many directions and we intend to profit by it', Bennett reported to the Lucas Board.[52] This was to be done quietly and gradually, reassuring the workers that it was now a Lucas scheme, operated by Lucas officials and not 'some outside policy imposed upon us by some unknown force operating from a mysterious quarter'.[53] The Lucas Points Plan was the result. Piecework rates were converted into 'points' and three years later this scheme was accepted 'gingerly' and almost without protest. That it was little more than the earlier scheme in disguise can be judged from the ten former Bedaux engineers who were still employed at Great King Street in 1938.

It is always assumed that Bedaux had a newly coercive impact on what had previously been, by implication, a relatively relaxed pace of work. Steven Tolliday, setting the scene for the introduction of Bedaux into Lucas in 1931, has described a familial pattern of workplace relations, a leisurely tempo of work and an authoritative and fairly autonomous role for supervisors.[54] In practice, the family element of recruitment must have proved increasingly inadequate, especially during recurrent periods of high demand after the mid-1920s. There also seems to be little evidence of a relaxed pace of work. Even before Bedaux, workers complained about the discipline of work at Lucas. Time keeping was strict and 'Polly Closet' was the name given to the unpopular woman who patrolled the toilets for lingerers. Those not in work by eight o'clock were locked out for the morning. Before 'clocking on' became the practice of the industry, operators were typically alloted numbered brass tags which were kept on a board at the gate house and transferred to a similar board in the workshop when they went in. Absentees were known by the tags still left hanging on the main board. If a worker's tag was removed from its usual hook in the workshop it usually meant she was sacked.[55] There was little, if any, talking to other operators and some claimed to be very much afraid of foremen and supervisors. A woman who began work at Lucas in 1910 described

52. Joseph Lucas Ltd, Managing Director's Monthly Reports to the Board of Directors, Feb. 1932.
53. Ibid.
54. S. Tolliday, 'Militancy and organisation: women workers and trade unions in the motor trades in the 1930s', *Oral History*, 11. 2 (Autumn 1983), pp. 48–9.
55. 'Half a century of memories', *English Electric and its People*, 9. 3 (Mar. 1954), p. 36.

the intimidating effect of the foreman continually walking up and down the shop. Girls were sent home for laughing or singing.[56] These reminiscences are an important reminder that, from the perspective of the worker, managerial control could be as deeply felt under old conditions as under new methods.

Training for women became part of the Lucas bid to control production more effectively, along with mechanised handling, wage incentive schemes and workshop reorganisation. Board minutes frequently refer to the costs incurred by on the job training and loss of quality when new labour was taken on during the season. This applied to women and girls as well as men. From 1935 there was a training school for young girls, mainly those, it seems, joining Lucas as their first employer. At the end of their last school term, girls, accompanied by their mothers, were interviewed by the works welfare supervisor. In 1935 there was accommodation for twenty-six such girls. In a quiet part of the factory at Shaftmoor Lane they were taught the care and use of tools such as screwdrivers and hammers and simple assembly tasks. Lectures on how to calculate wages, on factory rules, hygiene and safety were given. After a fortnight tests were taken to judge progress and aptitude and later on girls specialised in learning either machine, assembly or inspection operations. Towards the end of the course of instruction lectures dealt more specifically with the type of job the girls would be doing in the factory. After six weeks the girls were sent, as necessary, to one of the production departments but contact was kept up for about two months and their progress watched.[57]

Obviously, this school was catering for a tiny number of the women and girls employed by Lucas in the mid-1930s, including those who were newcomers. At the same time, Lucas must have regularly re-employed on a seasonal basis large numbers of women for whom such training was less necessary. In practice, young girls under 18 at whom such training was aimed rarely formed more than around a tenth of the female workforce.

Training schemes, changes in the system of wage payment and mechanisation of handling using conveyors were only part of the firm's attempt to control production more effectively. In the mid-1930s Lucas also began a new organisation of production with a

56. File 'women historical', Joseph Lucas Archive, British Motor Industry Heritage Trust, letter from Nellie Rowe to Women's Employment Manager, Joseph Lucas Ltd, 1959, also interview notes of Mrs Elsie Walker.

57. J.D. Maslin, 'The training of young girls in factory routine', *Lucas Reflections*, Dec. 1935.

new manufacturing layout. Instead of laying out shops by types of processes, placing all the press machines in one press shop as GEC in Coventry did, Lucas began to lay them out by product. At the same time they attempted to make only standardised items. The changes began with dynamos and starters. By 1936 one floor was devoted to the entire production of these articles and not just to their assembly as before. Special plant and tools were applied to their manufacture and the floor laid out to maintain a 'line' flow of work through its various stages. Women worked on the sub-assembly of end brackets for dynamos. This was carried out on a 'conveyor bench' with hoppers containing the necessary parts which were too small to be handled by overhead conveyors. A riveting machine was also used in this process and in order to enable it to be used continuously the operator was supplied with jigs on which other women on the same line had assembled all the parts that needed to be riveted. Insulating the core and armature winding were both automatic machine processes carried out by women. Male 'patrol' inspectors kept a check on quality at all stages. Final assembly of dynamos was done by men on a bench along which a twin rail track was placed. Above, a monorail conveyor carried the parts needed for assembly. These were removed as they were needed by the operator to carry out his own particular assembly operation. No explanation is offered as to why this assembly should have been carried out by men instead of women. It may have been because it involved the use of a heavy screwdriver operated by a large hand wheel.[58]

This and other attempts at reorganisation were meant to allow Lucas to take advantage of the economies of the high volume production demanded by the motor industry. They were hampered, though, by a continued insistence on variants of basic designs by their customers. Not all the manufacturing lines reorganised at this time were fully automated nor were they devoted to just one standard product. Albert Siddall, appointed in 1931 to help implement the Bedaux Plan and later head of the process planning department, recalls producing three different types of dynamo by making one sort one week, another the next week and so on.[59]

The high and unpredictable volume of the demand for Lucas products did not help either. The straight line manufacturing

---

58. L.P. Bullock, 'The Lucas dynamo and starter factory', *Lucas Reflections*, Oct. 1936, pp. 52–5.
59. Nockolds, *Lucas*, vol. 1, p. 313.

scheme described above did not lend itself easily to changes in capacity, either in providing more output or in remaining economical when output dropped. This meant that such schemes had to be semi-flexible and the alternate week working of the dynamo line was an example of this. It also meant new or changed models were, ideally, introduced only at predetermined intervals so that sufficient time was allowed for rearrangements.

Even so, the dependence of the firm on increasing its supply of mainly female but also male labour in order to meet demand was never completely removed. In spite of its attempts to stabilise production, employment at Lucas remained highly seasonal for both men and women in the 1920s and 1930s. The writer Joan Beauchamp claimed that from 1935 to 1937 between 3,000 and 5,000 women were dismissed by Lucas and most others were on a three-day week.[60] There is evidence that Lucas took a different attitude to women and men when making dismissals. As the season ended and stocks were replaced, Lucas generally relied on 'natural wastage' before dismissals began. Of the men and women who were still being regularly dismissed out of season by 1937, it was felt that 'good women will obtain new employment but it is not so easy for the unskilled men. We are making rearrangements in our Labour Department and are doing everything we possibly can to reduce this turnover of labour to an absolute minimum.'[61] There was nevertheless a core of semi-skilled women whose experience Lucas did not wish to lose through seasonal lay-offs. This would only result in lowered output and quality as new labour was taken on during the season. Surrounding its stable core of skilled men and semi-skilled women was a fluctuating pool of semi-skilled and unskilled men and women and it was they who were likely to have been most affected by attempts to standardise production and stabilise employment.

From the mid-1930s Lucas was also vulnerable to the loss of skilled men during its obligatory periods of short-time working. They never lost this dependence on a nucleus of skilled labour and there was no sign that this fundamental problem of gaining and shedding labour at the cost of profit as the periods of demand in the motor industry rose and fell had been overcome before the Second World War.[62]

60. Joan Beauchamp, *Women who Work* (1937), p. 30.
61. Joseph Lucas Ltd, Board Minutes, Feb. 1937.
62. Joseph Lucas Ltd, Managing Director's Monthly Reports to the Board of Directors, Jun. 1934. Ibid., Nov. 1936.

Lucas provides an example of a firm employing large numbers of women for whom mass production was a desirable but not quite attainable ideal. As a producer of large numbers of electrical components for the motor trade, the firm was always looking to take advantage of the methods and economies of mass production but was restricted by the unpredictable demands of its customers. Re-equipment or reorganisation schemes were undertaken in 1924, 1927, 1931–2 and 1936 but, in spite of advanced methods and some specialist machinery, the firm remained heavily dependent on labour, on a core of skilled men and a pool of 'good' (that is, experienced) women and a smaller number of semi-skilled and unskilled men and women which might be expanded or contracted seasonally. They also relied on overtime and short-time working.

* * *

These two accounts of the electrical and motor trades have tried to show that, in the modified British version of mass production, the use of male and female labour varied, as the ideals of production engineers were tempered by competition based on continuous innovation in products or models. Mass production in Britain retained a place for skilled men, even if their skill was appreciably narrowed and specialised. It is true that in both trades the employment of women tended to be on repetitious manufacture of standardised goods. They performed operations which, in the largest firms at least, were likely to have standardised costing, production planning and time and motion study applied to them. But the uneven nature of mass production in Britain limited and shaped women's work, suggesting that they may have been used with flexibility even if it was within a narrow range of tasks.

The two case studies showed how women were still used with some flexibility across a range of hand and machine operations, even by two of the most advanced employers of women, both of which depended on experienced female labour to maintain quality and output as demand for their goods peaked during its yearly cycle. In the supervisory structure of the industry women could reach chargehand and foremistress, as they did at GEC, though generally only in female departments. As we saw, both firms also relied on a core of skilled male labour as well as male production workers to maintain output. This in turn suggests that new levels of control over production associated with new technologies and methods may have narrowed but did not rule out the role of skilled male labour. Even would-be mass producers might have to compromise with labour, including organised labour, in their attempts to introduce change.

The significance of trade unions and the industrial relations of the industry to women's employment form the subject of the next chapter. Demarcation struggles over 'female' work help to reveal more about the circumstances under which women were introduced to engineering, the criteria that shaped employers' decisions and the limits which trade unionists tried to set on their employment. Chapter 5 will return to the question of the value of women workers – their experience, competencies and skills, and its effect on the outlook of the industry's non-craft unions.

CHAPTER FIVE

Disputes: The Significance of Collective Bargaining, 1919–1939

The last chapter revealed the complexity of women's employment even in advanced, mass production firms. In contrast to accounts based on the single theme of male dominance in a deskilled, tightly controlled labour process, it showed how women's employment was influenced by unstable markets, the variable nature of engineering production and a continuing need for a relatively experienced, versatile manual workforce. This chapter will consider disputes and negotiations between employers and unions as a further factor influencing how women engineering workers were employed. No other industry in which women worked had such an elaborate and well-established collective bargaining structure. What role did it play in shaping women's work and pay?

The 1922 lock-out

The 1922 lock-out was the most important event in engineering's industrial relations. The Managerial Functions Agreement that ended it reasserted what the employers called 'the rights of management', in other words, the right to alter working practice without prior consultation with the unions. It firmly re-established a framework for collective bargaining which had been abandoned (by the ASE) in 1914 and, for the first time, all the industry's unions were included in its scope. The following section examines the impact of the lock-out and the agreement which followed it in strengthening the influence of employers in the workplace and weakening the resistance of trade unions. It questions whether employers seeking to introduce women gained a significant advantage from the settlement's reassertion of 'the freedom to manage'.

The immediate background to the dispute was the failure of the ASE to keep to the terms of the recent Overtime and Nightshift Agreement and disputes over machine manning. These were the issues on which the EEF threatened a lock-out in April 1921. They were also demanding cuts in wages which had been increased by war bonuses, the Armistice boom and awards made by the Industrial Court in 1919 and 1920. An agreement on wages was reached in July but by the autumn of 1921 the EEF wanted not only the staged reduction that the union had already agreed to but a further cut. This was conceded in September. By November the AEU felt compelled to accept the EEF terms on the other issues as well. At that time the union had 90,000 unemployed members. But the proposed settlement, a memorandum on managerial functions, was rejected by a ballot of the membership. The lock-out then began in March 1922. In April it was extended to forty-six other unions in the industry, who were also told to sign the memorandum. Finally, a government court of inquiry found in favour of the employers, supporting their terms for ending the dispute. By June of 1922 union funds and morale were spent and, after thirteen weeks, the lock-out was over.[1]

On the face of it the lock-out and its conclusion helped to strengthen the hand of employers in the workplace. The 1922 Managerial Functions Agreement formally set down for the first time since April 1914 engineering employers' 'freedom to manage', including their right to introduce any class of labour they thought appropriate and to more or less freely alter working practices. As such it must have increased the optimism of employers who wanted to employ more women and the fears of those skilled unions which opposed them. For the first time, all engineering unions had been included in the agreement and compelled to accept 'managerial prerogatives'. The AEU had been reduced to bankruptcy. Its membership fell by 45 per cent between 1920 and 1923, and strength in the workplace was much reduced through unemployment and victimisation. As demand for skilled workers remained depressed for the next decade there could be little effective challenge from craft unions like the AEU.

In spite of overwhelming victory, however, the gains made by employers and the EEF as a result of the lock-out were not straightforward. Jonathan Zeitlin argues that engineering employers, given

---

1. For a narrative account of the lock-out see J.B. Jefferys, *The Story of the Engineers 1800–1945* (1945), pp. 220–6.

the nature of demand for their products, continued with a relatively labour-intensive style of production. Instead of rationalising production through comprehensive changes in methods and technology, those in the depressed sector turned to cost cutting, using more apprentices and downgrading skilled workers, and in the newer sectors to manipulating payment systems while production remained flexible and labour-intensive.[2]

The position of the EEF itself was in some respects weakened after the successful lock-out. Depression had opened up the differences between the fortunes of the light and heavy sectors of engineering, making it difficult for the EEF to devise national policies and agreements acceptable to both. At the same time, the quiescence of weakened trade unions made solidarity between employers and the functions of the EEF itself seem less important, a fact reflected in a declining membership. The numbers of affiliated firms fell from 2,690 in 1922 to 1,968 in 1931 and 1,806 in 1935.[3] The number of engineering employees covered was halved between 1922 and 1931.[4] In these circumstances, it was impossible for the EEF to pursue a strong line on female labour in its advice to firms, even if it wanted to. In spite of the success of the lock-out its advice throughout the period was always to act with caution. The EEF was consistently concerned to ensure that member firms did nothing without the knowledge and advice of the local Engineering Employers' Association, and did not antagonise the unions.

To firms which, because of the nature of their market, continued to depend on skilled and semi-skilled men, the gains after 1922 were therefore ambiguous. The EEF tended to encourage their caution or discourage plans too confrontational with skilled unions. This was especially noticeable after 1933, as we shall see. The assertion of 'freedom to manage' following the lock-out did not necessarily aid those who wanted to extend female employment, then. In the absence of union power, they did not automatically opt for female labour and, as the following discussion of demarcation disputes will show, there had to be a number of factors in place for women to seem a profitable alternative to male workers. These disputes also suggest that ideas of social and cultural suitability

2. J. Zeitlin, 'The internal politics of employer organisation: the Engineering Employers' Federation 1896–1939', in J. Zeitlin and S. Tolliday (eds), *The Power to Manage? Employers and Industrial Relations in Comparative Historical Perspective* (1990), p. 70.

3. Ibid., p. 71.

4. Eric Wigham, *The Power to Manage. A History of the Engineering Employers' Federation* (1973), p. 134.

were relatively unimportant in motivating union objections to women workers. The opposition of craft unions like the AEU to women's employment should instead be seen as a continuing defence of their standards and privileges.

Female labour disputes: employers' perspective

Laura Lee Downs argues that individual employers saw men and women as qualitatively distinct forms of labour. Efficient production relied on allotting the appropriate tasks to each class of labour. In that process, employers consistently adhered to a definition of 'women's work' as that suited to fragmented, repetitious tasks and modern production techniques.[5] It is true that employers divided labour into 'classes' with corresponding aptitudes and rates of pay. However, what follows shows that employers were also influenced by factors other than preconceived notions of women's suitability for certain kinds of work. A determination emerges on the part of employers to remain free to decide how work was to be allocated among the different 'classes of labour' and not to be tied too closely to definitions of 'suitable for women'.

Female labour was often associated with a move towards large volume production where women's cheapness became relevant. Thus, firms would attribute the introduction of women to the natural evolution of engineering work from an experimental stage where skilled labour might be employed to a commercial stage where the appropriate class of labour for the job would be required. The introduction of women or other unskilled labour was therefore described as 'one of the ordinary developments of engineering'.[6] In 1921 the Manchester electrical firm of Ferranti's extended its employment of women in a fuse shop – a wartime innovation for the firm – involving the displacement of some semi-skilled men. In its view the firm was belatedly bringing itself into line with correct commercial practice:

> We know there is a good deal of work carried out which in its initial stages and when the market has not been properly catered for or competed for may be carried out by craftsmen and skilled men but eventually when the market has been expanded, is dealt with on

5. Laura Lee Downs, *Manufacturing Inequality. Gender Divisions in the French and British Metal-working Industries, 1914–1939* (1995), pp. 104–6.
6. EEF, J. Stone and Co., Works Conference Proceedings, 21 Sept. 1925, p. 2. MRC MSS.237/3/1/89, F(6)41.

entirely different lines. Large sections of different forms of engineering work, by being laid out for manufacture on a large scale, is carried out under circumstances which allow quite legitimately of the employment of a different class of labour with its corresponding economic rate.[7]

Ferranti's argued that development along these lines would lead to more work for skilled men in toolmaking and development, would broaden the basis of a firm's products and help stabilise employment. The low cost of female labour was often central to employment disputes. A coremaking dispute ended with the firm offering to return to the former practice of splitting the work between men and apprentices, but only if they guaranteed to produce them at the same price per core as the women. In 1926 the textile engineers Fairbairn in Leeds extended the work of women in its bolt shop to drilling operations at a time when men were unemployed and on short-time. According to EEF figures, half the workers in federated textile firms had been on short-time in 1924. The firm, however, resisted pressure to employ any other than females on the grounds of cost and an inadequate supply of boy labour:

> The question arises of the class of labour to be employed when a firm has a great quantity of extremely simple repetition drilling work which is not work suitable for automatic machines where you can get over the difficulty by putting one really competent, smart man in charge . . . [instead] you have this kind of repetition drilling which is not automatic and which means one person for a machine and it is absolutely essential that you . . . have labour . . . not so costly as a grown man's.[8]

But boys had proved difficult to obtain and keep. When pressed to employ men, then on short-time, Ferranti's reply is more forthright: 'If the machines are such machines as the girls can work, and the work is of the simple jig character . . . then . . . all that work is work that is entirely suitable for girls and work that is absolutely unsuitable for grown men.'[9] This was work physically suited to women, too: 'no hole is big, no part is heavy'.[10] But clearly cost was the motivator.

7. EEF, Ferranti Ltd, Central Conference Proceedings with ETU, 13 May 1920, p. 3. MSS.237/3/1/243, R(6)14.

8. EEF, Fairbairn, Lawson, Combe, Barber Ltd, Local Conference Proceedings, 5 Jul. 1926, p. 5, Employers' Arguments. MRC MSS.237/3/1/89, F(6)43.

9. EEF, ibid.; Central Conference Proceedings with AEU, 15 Nov. 1927, p. 3.

10. Ibid., p. 2.

Yet the employment of women was often more than just a question of cheapness. Employers regarded girls or women as more productive than men or boys on work appropriate for them. In these
disputes, 'appropriate' work tended to mean work which was produced in large quantities and which was therefore repetitious and
monotonous. It might also mean work which called for patience, a
'sense of touch', 'light-fingered stuff'. When Platts introduced mechanised sorting of needles by girls in 1933, thereby displacing the boys
who had previously done the work, they explained that 'the girls
with their lighter touch were much more adaptable at the job than
boys could be . . . all the girls would have to do would be to grade
these needles into various sizes and then drop them into a jig'.[11]
Suitable work for women was also work which was considered to
be unskilled, typically expressed as 'the skill is in the machine and
the girl does the routine work' or 'The whole job is done to stops,
there is nothing but filling a fixture, starting the machine away and
operating it to stops. It is completely jigged from beginning to end.'[12]
In practice most work undertaken by women was not as automatic
as that described here but it was often claimed in disputes that the
work had been simplified or required little more than 'innate' female
attributes like patience or deft fingers even though, as the Birmingham District AEU said of women's employment in one dispute,
'There is nothing "sensitive" about a drilling machine that drills
$5/8$ and $3/4$ holes or a facing machine that faces castings weighing
hundredweights.'[13]

In spite of an unwillingness to define the boundaries of women's
work, engineering employers continued to think in terms of classes
or groups of labour with corresponding abilities or aptitudes and
corresponding rates of pay. As Downs argues, a mismatch between
class of labour and class of work was, in their view, uneconomic.
In 1921 a Preston firm refused a demand from the NUFW to sack
women coremakers and to take on some of the district's unemployed men instead, since 'to comply with the union would be to
increase the cost of production and to put skilled men on unskilled
and boys' work'.[14] J. Stone and Co., a London electrical firm, later

11. EEF, Platts and Co., memo to Sir Allan Smith from Mr W.R. Hall, 8 Sept.
1933. MRC MSS.237/3/1/89, F(6)53.
12. EEF, Vickers Armstrong Ltd, Central Conference Proceedings with AEU,
11–12 Jun. 1931. MRC MSS.237/3/1/165, M(9)78; EEF, Birmingham Small Arms
Co. Ltd, Central Conference Proceedings with AEU, 9 Oct. 1936, p. 7. MRC MSS.237/
3/1/89, F(6)65.
13. EEF, M(15)84, Union to Association, 30 Apr. 1921.
14. EEF, Preston Question, Women Employed on Coremaking, NUFW. Local Conference Notes, 7 Mar. 1921, Workmen's Arguments. MRC MSS.237/3/1/89, F(6)39.

insisted that the production of large quantities of goods should be 'taken away from the men and put into the hands of people who can deal with [it] far more suitably'.[15] 'Suitably' here refers to the ability to produce the same work at less cost, using machinery specially set up for a particular job, rather than to the physical or psychological suitability of women to quantity production. In this firm's view, skilled men who commanded higher rates of pay than women or girls were more productively employed on variable work calling for greater versatility and experience. What seems to have been at issue here was not the chance to employ women at the expense of men but the freedom to employ whatever class of labour could accomplish the job and at the rate of pay for that class. This meant that they were not always looking to introduce women simply because they were cheaper: 'I do not want you to run away with the idea that the Employers are arbitrarily turning everything upside down to the detriment of the skilled mechanic.' The firm wanted rather to insist 'on the right of using the labour which will give the skill and ability required for doing the work'.[16] In practice this meant the right to define the skills and abilities of the grades of engineering labour, broadening – or narrowing – the categories of what was 'appropriate' for each.

Why then did women's employment cluster, as we saw in previous chapters, around certain trades, firms and processes? Given women's cheapness, why not expand the category? In contrast to the conventional account, these disputes show that whether the category of 'suitable' work for women was expanded or not depended on a range of factors of which ideas about innate female attributes constituted only one. In some cases work became suitable for women when there was no alternative labour to be found. The state of the local labour market and difficulties in finding male workers featured as a factor shaping women's employment in several disputes. An electrical engineering firm in Bedfordshire in 1937, for instance, decided to employ women on capstan lathes and drilling machines because of the shortage of juvenile male labour. They had already employed boys from depressed areas but their turnover was high and 'we had quite an amount of trouble with them'. Meanwhile, there were better opportunities for boys in other industries in Bedford since 'the rate of pay offered even for messengers and dead end occupations is higher than that paid in the engineering

15. EEF, J. Stone and Co., Central Conference Proceedings, 9 Oct. 1925, p. 10. MRC MSS.237/3/1/89, F(6)41.
16. Ibid., p. 9.

industry'.[17] In 1921 the Midlands firm mentioned above had similarly argued that in their own district 'the Collieries rate of pay is better and so the supply of boy labour is short'.[18]

Periods of high demand could result in women being taken on for work normally given to youths. Gun manufacturer BSA claimed in 1936 that 'they had sufficient work only to maintain a nucleus of their people, and naturally when they were only able to do that they should prefer to retain the youths who were working in these machines rather than the women', suggesting that where there was no obvious commercial need to employ the cheapest labour they could afford a more 'moral' stance.[19] In other words limited demand 'buffered' this employer against the need to minimise labour costs by employing women.

The same EEF enquiry into women's employment which, in the last chapter, revealed the range of women's engineering work also showed the variety of criteria influencing employers' choice of female labour. The reasons they gave for employing women included aptitude for repetition work and for operations 'requiring delicacy of touch and quickness of movement' but also lower cost and 'environmental' factors like the local labour market, that is whether a surplus of male or female labour existed and competition from other local industries paying higher wages to women. Reasons given for not employing women were, as might be expected, trade union friction, heaviness of work and the length of the production run. One firm in Manchester stated that 'quantities are small and machines have to be continually reset'. Firms on the North East Coast and in the West of England cited a preference for boys or apprentices as being cheaper than female labour. These responses reveal a variety of issues determining the employment of women besides perceived suitability.[20]

It seems that firms drew on a stock of 'female' qualities to justify their allocation of labour which in practice was made on the basis of a number of factors. Together these factors were used to decide whether women would be more productive than men on a given job. Cheapness and perceived suitability, volume of work, speed

17. EEF, Ingranic Electric Co. Ltd, Letter from Firm to the Management Board, 24 Mar. 1937. MRC MSS.237/3/1/89, F(6)68.

18. EEF, H. Pooley and Son Ltd. Correspondence of AEU to Firm, 3 Feb. 1921. MRC MSS.237/3/1/169, M(15)84.

19. EEF, BSA Co., Central Conference Proceedings with AEU and TGWU, 9 Oct. 1936. MRC MSS.237/3/1/89, F(6)65.

20. EEF, Report to the Administration Committee by the Sub-committee in regard to Female Labour, Jun. 1934, Appendix A. MRC MSS.237/3/1/89, F(6)56.

and productivity, the practice of competitors, the available labour supply and opposition from trade unions were all part of the picture drawn during negotiations over the employment of women.

Female labour: trade-union perspective

Opposition to female labour within engineering came from craft unions, whose membership was concentrated in the depressed sectors of the trade where unemployment was highest. By the end of 1920 the Armistice boom had collapsed. One in every six workers was left without a job. The heavier, skill-intensive sectors of engineering were among the hardest hit by this severe economic downturn and for more than a decade the labour market would be glutted by out of work craftsmen.[21] Their wages had been reduced and union membership halved by the lock-out. These disputes reveal the craft union's attitude towards women workers as a defensive response to what it saw as the fragmentation of skilled work at a time of unemployment, wage cuts and weakened union authority.

Forty-six unions had been brought into the industry's bargaining procedure at the conclusion of the lock-out in 1922. By the mid-1920s the Managerial Functions Agreement covered nearly all the union membership in federated firms. With the exception of the TGWU and the GMWU, these were all craft unions. Of these, the AEU was the most important, with the largest engineering membership.

The AEU and other skilled unions wanted to control entry to the engineering trades as much as possible in order to protect the standard of living, wages and employment prospects of their members, and to protect their own financial stability as unions. They objected to the employment of women on the same grounds that they objected to the misuse of the apprenticeship system. In successive local and national disputes conferences after 1920 they argued, at first, that skilled work, when sectionalised, should remain skilled and not become semi-skilled and unskilled operations for women or boys. Their objection to women went hand in hand with their objection to the excessive employment of apprentices and to the narrow training they were then offered. The AEU wanted firms to employ only the number of apprentices it could later take on as

---

21. Jonathan Zeitlin, *The Sinews of Flexibility. Skills, Training and Technical Education in British Engineering, 1850–1980* (book manuscript in progress), ch. 3, p. 2.

fully qualified tradesmen. If more than that number was employed the fear was the apprentices would become just a form of cheap, dead-end labour. Both the employment of women and the excessive employment of apprentices were 'only another way of getting round the question of employing more boys'.[22] It is important to remember that until 1937 the unions had no say in or control over the wages or working conditions of junior male workers. As far as the EEF was concerned, until boys or apprentices came of age, 'they should be regarded as being *in statu pupillari* and not subject to the same industrial relationships as adult workers'.[23] Thus, young male workers, girls and women were all potential threats to skilled unions attempting to control access to jobs and protect their own standards of living.

At first, craft unions responded to the threat of new or changed work by attempting to exclude all potential competitors. Immediately after the First World War there were examples of skilled unions claiming that all work hitherto done by their members was *ipso facto* skilled work. The NUVB at Standard Motors in Coventry took an uncompromising line on the extension of women's employment in the trimming department there. The firm had begun to employ women on making cushions, seats and door pockets, including the cutting out of draught pieces. The union claimed all this work for skilled men, reasoning, 'if men cut the template it is men's work'. They refused an offer to define a schedule of women's work which the firm would abide by. In reply, the firm claimed that this was unskilled work which could not be economically produced by men. They were anxious, though, to get the agreement of the union. This was the time of the Armistice boom and when employers were meant to be returning to pre-war practices. 'The firm is as anxious as any other firm to employ male labour,' it said. 'In the Trimming business women are particularly suitable for the work . . . The firm are not out for cheap labour but for production. It is not skilled work to cut out draught pieces.'[24] The dispute ended when the union agreed to the employment of women in the firm's Leamington works on the same or similar operations to those they did at Coventry before the war, provided 'similar' was not interpreted too freely.

---

22. EEF, Central Conference Proceedings with AEU and ASI, 11 Jun. 1920, p. 3. MRC MSS.237/3/1/89, A(6)18.

23. A. Marsh, *Industrial Relations in Engineering* (1965), p. 105.

24. EEF, Women and Unskilled Workers on Trimming Motor Car Bodies, Abstract of Notes of Conference held on 25 Aug. 1919, between Coventry Engineering Employers' Association and NUVB, p. 3. MRC MSS.237/3/1/89, F(6)33.

Later on in the 1920s came an admission that some work was not skilled and did not properly belong to skilled men. It could be given to women without threatening the livelihoods of union members but they feared the 'thin end of the wedge' and therefore preferred beginners or apprentices to do the work. Thus, they argued that portions of formerly skilled men's work could usefully be given to apprentices for short periods as part of their training, as long as they were not kept exclusively on them. Such work would remain 'part and parcel' of the trade which apprentices entered.[25] Clearly, while this was not desirable, it at least gave them more control of the situation than the employment of women would have allowed.[26] It was also said that the work done by women was of a type that had formerly been offered to older and disabled male workers and that employers were morally bound to continue the practice.[27] As with the attempt to allot simplified work to apprentices, this was an attempt to control a shifting division of labour rather than an attempt to exclude women on ideological grounds.

Where they were forced to accept female labour (for example, where it was customary in other firms or districts) skilled unions tried to limit it to single purpose machinery as a way of ensuring that it would not be extended. At a Midlands firm in 1921, for example, the AEU objected to the employment of women on certain drilling, facing and screwing machines 'which are such as can be adapted to any class of work and not to one operation only and as such ought to be operated by male labour'.[28]

Short-time working, depression and unemployment often formed the background to female labour disputes. In this context, unions were concerned not just that the employment of women would actually displace men but that it would reduce their opportunities for work in the future as women became a permanent feature of the workforce, a concern voiced during a dispute at the textile engineers Fairbairns in Leeds in 1934.[29] In other words, mechanical and organisational changes allowing the employment of cheaper labour would irreversibly narrow the scope for male employment.

25. EEF, Dobson and Barlow Ltd, Local Conference Notes, 21 Mar. 1921, Workmen's Arguments. MRC MSS.237/3/1/89, F(6)38.
26. Apprentices were potentially future members of the union.
27. EEF, Central Conference Proceedings with AEU, 11 Jun. 1937, p. 10. MRC MSS.237/3/1/89, F(6)66.
28. EEF, Letter from AEU to Local Association, 30 Apr. 1921. MRC MSS.237/3/1/169, M(15)84.
29. EEF, Fairbairn, Lawson, Combe, Barber Ltd, Local Conference Notes, Apr. 1934, Workmen's Arguments. MRC MSS.237/3/1/89, F(6)57.

They would not even benefit from a revival of trade. They claimed that employers should take into account the depression and employ as many men as possible. One of the strongest examples of this approach came during a dispute in Preston in 1921 from the NUFW, a craft union, which wanted all women coremakers in the district to be dismissed before a single male coremaker became redundant.[30] During a dispute in 1925 at J. Stone and Co. one official said he had been instructed by his district committee to oppose the introduction of female labour into London: 'it was the definite resolve of his union in London to oppose the employment of women in Engineering. In particular at this time when so many craftsmen were out of employment he protested against a craftsman's work being given without change of method to semi-skilled and unskilled labour.'[31] (There had been no change in method but the firm had employed men and boys on work – mainly assembly – on which other electrical firms had employed women.) This attitude could be expressed as hostility to women, but was motivated by fear of unemployment and a desire to protect the position of unemployed members. An earlier dispute at Fairbairns, for instance, saw the AEU representative insisting that 'the firm should take into consideration the industrial depression at the present time and try to employ as many of the male population as possible as they can. There is always other work which can be found for girls without bringing them into the engineering industry.' The union was, however, 'prepared to encourage re-organisation in the industry' as long as it was not 'to be to the detriment of their unemployed members'.[32]

In all these disputes unions aimed at least to secure guarantees that female labour would not be extended further than had already occurred. Often they failed as employers were reluctant to tie themselves to definitions of women's work in their firm, usually promising that it would only be extended, if necessary, to 'suitable' jobs. During the 1930s, on the other hand, they met with more success as employers, and particularly their representative, the EEF, became

30. EEF, Preston Question, Women Employed on Coremaking, NUFW. Local Conference Notes, 7 Mar. 1921, Workmen's Arguments. MRC MSS.237/3/1/89, F(6)39.

31. EEF, London Question, Transference of Work Previously Done by Skilled Workmen to Another Class of Workpeople, Messrs J. Stone and Co. Ltd, AEU. Works Conference Proceedings, 21 Aug. 1925, p. 2 [Cruse, AEU Official]. MRC MSS.237/3/1/89, F(6)41.

32. EEF, Fairbairn, Lawson, Combe, Barber Ltd, Local Conference Notes, 5 Jul. 1926, Workmen's Arguments. MRC MSS.237/3/1/89, F(6)43.

increasingly cautious on the issue of women's work. An example of this new caution is found in the textile firm Platts in 1933. At the time of the dispute over their introduction of girls to needle sorting, the firm was planning to turn the whole manufacturing operation into a female one, displacing male semi-skilled workers on light operations 'of a very simple character' – milling, drilling and simple assembly. A detailed report was made to an EEF official who was also shown round the works but Platts agreed that 'if the advice of the Federation is opposed to such a change, we certainly would not press to put it into operation'.[33] Only three years after the national lock-out, during the dispute at J. Stone and Co., the EEF had advised the London Association that:

> while the specialisation and progress in the direction desired by the firm is desirable and should not be interfered with, it is essential that in giving effect to such specialisation each case as it arises should be dealt with discreetly so as to avoid as far as possible friction with the unions. This is particularly desirable in the case of the London area having regard to the antagonistic attitude of the Unions in connection with the employment of female labour on productive engineering work. Under the circumstances the Board were of the opinion that the firm should at all stages keep close in touch and act in conjunction with your association.[34]

The ability of craft unions to resist female employment was helped by cautious attitudes such as these and a tightening labour market after 1934. Demand for skilled engineering labour began to revive as the market for engineering products recovered from the worst effects of the slump in world trade that had occurred between 1929 and 1932. The Leicester Engineering Employers' Association reported in 1934 that 'practically no skilled men of any category could be obtained in the Leicester Area'. The association had appointed a subcommittee to investigate the question but blamed failure to train a sufficient number of juveniles. In Derby 'firms were scouring the country for certain classes of skilled labour'.[35] With the onset of rearmament from 1935 increasingly serious shortages of skills emerged as activity now revived in the older heavier sectors as well as in skill-intensive new trades like aircraft.[36] A cautious

33. EEF, Copy of Letter from Mr W.R. Hall to Mr H. Pearce, 28 Aug. 1933. MRC MSS.237/237/3/1/89, F(6)53.

34. EEF, Letter to London and District Association, 21 Oct. 1925. MRC MSS.237/3/1/89, F(6)41.

35. East Midlands Joint Standing Committee of Engineering Employers Minutes, 25. Jul. 1934. MRC MSS.288/EMJ/1/4.

36. Zeitlin, *Sinews of Flexibility*, ch. 4, p. 7.

attitude to demarcation disputes became more common, especially
as the EEF actively discouraged any confrontation over 'dilution'
after 1936. In almost all disputes coming to central conference
from 1933 onwards the EEF dissuaded firms from their proposed
employment of women. In 1937, the EEF told Henry Hope Ltd that
'for the last few years the policy of the Federation has been that if
the question of dilution has to be faced it will have to be faced as a
broad national issue'.[37] They had therefore discouraged Ingranic
Electric earlier in the year from introducing women to work previously done by boys after protests from the AEU's executive. As early
as 1933, the EEF had responded to a firm in the West of England
proposing to introduce twenty women into a separator works with a
detailed questionnaire about the changes involved. The firm was
then discouraged from going ahead. Three years later, it was again
stopped from employing women, this time on viewing work. Its local
association was told: 'The amount of engineering work involved in
the Government's Defence Programme has led the Trade Unions
to anticipate emergency measures to deal with the situation and
they have been particularly alert to take exception to any measure
which savours of dilution.'[38]

More evidence that union resistance to women's employment
was tightening and union strength in the workplace beginning to
revive is found in another dispute at marine engineers Vickers in
1937. There had been a history of disputes over the introduction
of women at its Barrow works in 1930, 1931, 1933 and 1937. Only
in the last example did the employers offer to revert to original
practice. All parties were aware of the national context and implica-
tions of this dispute and a bargain was struck. The AEU asserted its
determination to 'do everything in our power to stop any further
inroad of females being employed at Barrow. There is no war on
but they are trying to create a war atmosphere and I hope the
Federation will at least bring not only Vickers of Barrow into line
but any of the firms which are members of the Federation.'[39] For
their part, the EEF made an offer on future dilution: 'if the employers are reasonably met on jobs of this sort, unions will be able

37. EEF, Proposed Introduction of Female Labour in Relation to the Dilution
Issue. Henry Hope and Sons Ltd, Birmingham Association. Extract from Minutes of
Special Meeting of the Management Board held on 22 Jul. 1937, p. 2. MRC MSS.237/
3/1/89, F(6)71.
38. EEF, Letter to West of England Association re. Listers Ltd, 13 Jul. 1936. MRC
MSS.237/3/1/89, F(6)54.
39. EEF, Central Conference Proceedings with AEU, 11 Jun. 1937, p. 3. MRC
MSS.237/3/1/89, F(6)66.

to control the development of the employment of women in ways which do matter'.[40]

The AEU feared the effects of mass production and specialisation with which female labour was associated. J.T. Brownlie, president of the union, believed that 'the development of the machine tool . . . will ultimately mean that you have got a large number of machine operators and a very small number, comparatively speaking, of the old handicraftsmen or the highly skilled fitter or mechanic'.[41] This was the 'machine question' which the union tried to answer by pressing for fixed minimum wage rates for each machine, 'pricing out' the threat of female, boy and unskilled labour. Its attitude to female labour should be seen in this context. It could not oppose what it saw as the fragmentation of skilled jobs but it could try to claim the new jobs that emerged as belonging to skilled men – if not to men at the peak of their ability, then to apprentices and older men. The skill shortages and ability of the unions to resist the extension of women, especially after 1933, and the caution advised by the EEF in dealing with this issue all suggest that, in practice, union fears about the future impact of female employment were misplaced.

The 1922 lock-out was the most important event in engineering's industrial relations between the wars but the greater power of managerial prerogative it apparently gave to employers did not, on its own, influence female employment. The circumstances in which women were introduced varied. There had to be a number of factors in place for women to seem a profitable choice of labour. Perceived suitability was not all. The EEF response to firms who did seek to employ women was a mixed one, tending to become more cautious in the 1930s. Meanwhile, skilled unions were increasingly able to resist the extension of women's employment not least because the need for skilled labour had not been eroded.

The 'woman's rate'

Engineering's extensive collective bargaining system not only dealt with issues of disputed work; it was also responsible for national wage rates and other conditions of employment for all its workers. Using evidence from negotiating conferences this section examines

40. Ibid., p. 7.
41. EEF, Special Conference Proceedings with AEU, 27 Oct. 1920, pp. 494–510, pp. 518–26. MRC MSS.237/1/12/5.

the criteria that shaped women's pay and earnings. There is no mistaking the narrow view taken by the EEF of women's employment in the industry. It assumed that there were natural limits to the use of female labour. Not only must marriage 'have a pronounced bearing on any question of detailed training and instructional schemes in the industry for women', the progression of women within the industry to higher grades of skill and responsibility, 'is remote and is not to be seriously contemplated', for, as a general principle 'the male is the more appropriate of the two sexes for gaining the necessary experience and giving continuity of service in the Production Shops of the Engineering and its Allied Industries, and therefore it should be recognised, so far as employment of labour is concerned, that the male is the mainstay of the industry'.[42] As we shall·see, the EEF's view of women as peripheral workers meant that they were not formally included in important procedural and national agreements and this was to have significant consequences for their pay and working conditions.

It is not surprising then to find the federation admitting in 1932 that for male and female wages 'the arrangements made have been in certain respects on an entirely different basis'.[43] Generally speaking, negotiations about wages and working conditions were held separately for men and women, even where the agreements reached were similar and where the unions concerned represented both men and women. The tendency of the EEF to treat women 'on an entirely different basis' is also shown by their non-inclusion in some important agreements governing wage conditions. More than once the EEF questioned whether agreements made with general unions apparently on behalf of their whole membership automatically applied to their female members. Nor were women formally included in the basic procedural agreements which governed the industry's collective bargaining.

In the early 1920s, engineering employers were quick to reduce wages inflated by the exceptional circumstances of wartime to a more 'appropriate' level. They did this as part of their return to normality, regaining control of their industry from government, but also as a response to post-war slump and price deflation. Part of the industry's return to normality was a clear return to the idea of the 'rate for the grade' in wage payment. In the history of women's wages, the war was seen as an exceptional time when women, instead

42. Ibid., pp. 9–10, paras. 39–41.
43. EEF, Extension of the 1922 Agreement to Women, Patternmakers' Committee Report (1932), p. 2. MRC MSS.237/3/1/89, F(6)52.

of getting a 'woman's rate' as they did before and afterwards, received the rate for the job. In practice, as Chapter 3 showed, even in wartime the wage rate was still defined by *whose* job it had been so that, for example, 'split' work had to be paid at the fully skilled man's rate rather than on the basis of an assessment of the job content. War had not significantly undermined the idea of grades of labour with corresponding rates of pay and at a time of financial retrenchment it was easily resumed. In May 1921 the EEF imposed a new scale of wages for women, based solely on sex and age, beginning with 16s. a week at 14 rising to 28s. at 21. In areas like Birmingham and the Midlands where women had been employed in engineering before the war employers were still concerned about being tied to rates they considered too high. Alexander Ramsay, then full-time chairman of the Birmingham Association, put forward a new set of reduced rates but his proposal was held back until a reduction in men's wages had gone through. Even though women's wages were already far lower than men's, the EEF was still anxious to maintain a kind of parity in the reductions being made. It was felt that the women's war bonuses could not remain untouched while men's were lowered. It was not, strictly speaking, a question of maintaining a differential as there was no suggestion that women's wages should be linked to upward movements in men's rates. Later in the same year another lower schedule was put forward by Mr Dumas of the electrical firm BTH in Rugby. The management board agreed that any new schedule adopted would need to be flexible, operating as a minimum to allow for higher rates where female labour was difficult to obtain. The 'war' or 'cost of living bonus' component of the schedule was to fluctuate until the total amount of the bonus was eliminated. Dumas and Ramsay were together asked to draw up a new set of rates. In conference with the NUGW, a schedule was arrived at giving girls of 14 10s. a week rising to 24s. at 21. In December 1922, the EEF enforced the new scale although the union had rejected it by ballot. It was known as the Women's National Schedule.

Uniform rates all over the country were not expected to result from the imposition of this new pay scale. The Engineering Employers thought that while some would abide by the original scale, now called Schedule A, other firms would adopt the new scale, Schedule B, and adjust it according to the prosperity of the trade, supply and demand for labour, the nature of the particular work done and the ability shown by the woman or girl concerned. The relation between wages paid to females and wages paid to boys

and youths might also be a factor. The management board of the
EEF therefore thought it impossible to give a lead but advised
employers to take account of all these circumstances and 'provide
a fair and reasonable wage for the female labour employed on the
various operations'.[44]

The existence of two schedules and the fact that the lower one
had been made a minimum scale meant that actual wage rates paid
to women did vary. Apart from the reasons anticipated by the EEF
itself, variations arose where unions were able to negotiate higher
rates with individual firms. In 1927 and 1935 almost a third of
women in federated establishments were on the lower scale, Schedule B, while the rest were paid at higher rates.

What ideas informed the drawing up of female wage scales in
engineering? What was the 'fair and reasonable wage' which the
EEF advised local employers to pay when adjusting these scales to
suit their own circumstances? Employers treated women as a gen-
eric class of labour with a 'corresponding economic rate', as it did
juvenile and other male labour. An 'economic rate' took into account the kinds of circumstances outlined above – the prosperity of
the trade, supply and demand for female labour, the nature of the
job, the ability of the individual worker – but it was also fenced
around by social and cultural notions of what was fair for women.
A lower wage was fair because women were only expected to con-
tribute to a family income, not to be its sole provider. It was fair
because, unlike that of men, the destiny of women was marriage
and motherhood not a lifetime in paid employment. To a limited
extent fairness included recognition of specific skills and expertise
on particular operations. But this was on an individual basis within
the broader category of female labour.

The different basis on which men and women were treated was
reflected in the exclusion of women from agreements on working
conditions and even from the basic procedural agreements which
governed the industry's collective bargaining. While general wage
rates for men could not be altered without prior negotiation, for
example, employers were free to impose either one of the national
scales on their female employees. Not until the Atherton dispute in
1932 were women conceded the same right as men to negotiation
before general changes in wages took place. That dispute arose when
three firms in the bolt and nut trade joined the Bolton Association

44. EEF, Minutes of the Management Board, 7 Dec. 1922. MRC MSS.237/1/6/2,
p. 52.

of Engineering Employers and were required to conform to conditions agreed between the EEF and the unions. They had never differentiated between women and girls in wage payment before and had no recognised time rates, everyone being employed on piecework. Female workers at the firms went on strike when given notice that the EEF's Schedule B was to be adopted. It meant lower pay for many of them. When at the request of the NUGW the EEF refused to recognise women's right to prior negotiation, men at the firms also came out on strike. The dispute was resolved in July 1932 when the EEF agreed to apply the 1922 agreement to women. This dispute raised the whole question of whether women members of trade unions were automatically subject to the industry's procedural agreements in the same way that male members were. In this case it was claimed by the employers that wages and working conditions affecting women had always been the subject of separate negotiations made on a different basis to those of men. They did however eventually concede the principle that female members of unions shared in the general agreements made by their unions.

The same question had been raised ten years earlier when the NUGW was forced to ask for the overtime agreement of 1920 to be explicitly extended to women so that men and women might receive overtime pay at the same rates. The agreement had been made when the NUGW was still a male union and before it took over the NFWW, but many employers assumed, along with the union, that the agreement applied to union members whether they were male or female. The EEF, though, objected: 'if you were to take into your organisation males, which would be the usual form, we have nothing to say against your contention, but when you come to bring a different sex in, that is a fundamental difference'.[45] The agreement was, however, formally extended to women in 1922 on equal terms. The point of these examples is that in both cases it was necessary for the unions to establish that their female members were automatically party to wage agreements made by them on behalf of engineering workers generally.

Effect on earnings

Women's earnings reflected the iniquities of the 'woman's rate' and were probably never more than half those of men. Most women

---

45. EEF, Thos. Golver and Co. Ltd, Gothic Works, Edmonton, Central Conference Proceedings with NUGW, 14 Jul. 1922, p. 10. MRC MSS.237/3/1/198, O(13)46.

earned more than the schedule rates described above because they were employed, not on ordinary time work with its flat rate, but on a system of payment by results. By 1935 four times as many women were paid in this way as on a flat rate and their earnings were therefore higher. In that year, for example, the average earnings of those of 18 and over on time work for a forty-seven-hour week were 28s., while for those on payment by results it was 34s. 6d.[46] Evidence collected in 1924, 1928 and 1931 showed male earnings to be almost twice those of women in most sections of engineering.[47]

Disparities between men's and women's earnings may have been even larger. The EEF's figures exclude, for example, overtime payments and special increments and may not be a good reflection of average earnings over the course of a year, as the general unions pointed out in conference with the EEF in 1935. We know that there was a tendency for trades employing large numbers of women, like wireless manufacture, domestic appliances, lamps and gramophones, to be seasonal. They worked part of the year at high pressure, taking on more workers and if necessary working overtime, and for the rest of the year with fewer workers and/or short-time working. It was also claimed that younger, cheaper women, taken on in the busy period, were retained at the expense of older women once business slackened, thus continually producing a cheaper workforce, although evidence from the EEF shows that in practice most of the female workforce was adult. About 80 per cent of women in federated firms were aged 18 or over in 1927 and 1935. In motors and motor cycles in 1933 64 per cent of the female workforce was aged over 21. Similarly in telephone manufacture two-thirds were adult. In other light engineering firms and lamps the workforce was divided half and half.

A further source of inequality was the failure of the EEF to include women in important agreements governing wages and working conditions in the industry. Time rates for women were, as we saw above, largely determined by age and gender. Most men and women worked under some form of piecework or payment by results, but once again, not on the same terms. Sometimes different percentages over base rates were paid to men and women. The adjustment of piecework prices under the forty-seven-hour week introduced in 1919 was made in the case of men on a 33.3 per cent basis and in the case of women on the basis of 25 per cent. In other

46. EEF, Meeting of the Special Committee re. Women's Wages, 19 Jul. 1935. MRC MSS.237/1/6/12, p. 10, p. 13.
47. M.L. Yates, *Wages and Labour in British Engineering* (1937), p. 120.

words, it was accepted that piecework should yield a lesser percentage of extra earnings for women than for men.[48] In 1922, however, when the lower scale of wages was introduced, this inequality was corrected.[49] Employers generally complied, as an EEF questionnaire in 1928 showed. In Birmingham, however, the payment of equal piecework rates was 'general but not universal practice'.[50] Other employers adapted practice to conditions in their factory. A London firm employing 1,000 women stated that 'In the case of female workers most of the personnel are unskilled when engaged and as the nature of the work varies a great deal it is often necessary to give an enhanced piecework price at the commencement of the job and finally adjust it when the operators become proficient.'[51] Another firm from East Anglia makes a similar point, though it is not clear that piecework prices were enhanced in order to compensate as in the example above:

> The conditions applicable to female employment are rather different to those applicable to skilled male employment. In the nature of things, female employment is unskilled or at best semi-skilled, and there are frequently considerable learning periods during which female labour cannot be expected to earn full bonuses on piecework. These conditions may vary considerably in different factories, but the conditions in this factory where changes are frequent, are obviously very different from those in one where mass production in large quantities is the practice.[52]

Women were also not included in the national agreements between unions and the EEF on payment by results and so the terms on which their piecework price could be changed were different. The 1920 agreement between the NUGW and the EEF which applied to men only guaranteed that where employers altered the piecework price because of a change in the 'material, means, or method of production', earnings would not be reduced. A dispute arose at the Manchester electrical firm Ferranti's in 1928 when a change in the method of production led the firm to lower the

48. EEF, Extension of the 1922 Agreement to Women, 1932. MRC MSS.237/3/1/89, F(6)52.

49. EEF, Minutes of Meeting of the Management Board, 26 Jan. 1928, Proposed National Agreement in Respect of Female Labour, p. 1. MRC MSS.237/3/1/231, P(14)40.

50. EEF, Systems of Payment by Results, Appendix A, 'Copy of correspondence received from certain federated associations relative to this question', Mar. 1928, p. 11. MRC MSS.237/3/1/231, P(14)40.

51. Ibid., 'Summary of replies received from federated associations', Mar. 1928, p. 7. MRC MSS.237/3/1/231, P(14)40.

52. Ibid., p. 6.

piecework price for certain jobs on which women were employed. The effect of the new price was to reduce their earnings by 5s. a week. It was then that the NUGW tried, unsuccessfully, to have the agreement of 1920 extended to women.[53] That agreement had also guaranteed male workers a time rate in case their earnings under piecework were to fail. Women did not have this safety net of a guaranteed time rate wage.

Women were not always paid overtime at the same rate as men, either – even though the NUGW's Overtime Agreement with the EEF was extended to women in 1922. In 1928 some firms and districts were paying women at time and a quarter instead of at time and a half. Particular firms had their own quirks for which no explanation is offered. It was the practice of a firm in Liverpool, for instance, 'to pay overtime rates only after a full week has been worked. This is contrary to the conditions applicable to male workers where each day stands by itself.'[54]

This exclusion of women from important agreements relating to working conditions such as overtime and piecework prices, together with variations in the actual practice of given firms, made women vulnerable to low wages in a way that men were not. The use of bonus payment schemes by some employers has been seen as another factor resulting in a unique disadvantage to women in the industry. Glucksmann argues that as assembly line workers they were the first of the engineering workforce to experience a new kind of payment by results – the group bonus. From her examples, which included the Phillips radio factory at Mitcham, she describes how assembly line workers were paid differently to female machine operators on piecework. Under the new system there was a pre-fixed rate of production per hour paid to a group of workers as a single production unit and a bonus on top. Bonus points might be docked as a penalty or form of quality control. Meanwhile the speed of the line was controlled mechanically by the employer. She concludes therefore that women were subjected to unprecedented degrees of capitalist exploitation and subordination in a way that the men who worked to service the line or as rate fixers, bonus clerks and supervisors were not.[55]

53. EEF, Payment by Results for Female Workers, Central Conference Proceedings with National Union of General and Municipal Workers (NUGMW), 13 Jan. 1928. MRC MSS.237/3/1/231, P(14)40.

54. EEF, Systems of Payment by Results, Appendix A, 'Summary of replies received from federated associations', Mar. 1928, p. 7. MRC MSS.237/3/1/231, P(14)40.

55. Miriam Glucksmann, *Women Assemble. Women Workers and the New Industries in Inter-war Britain* (1990), pp. 182–9.

It is not clear how widespread group bonus was even in motor manufacture and electrical trades. It may have been the practice of the most advanced employers. As we saw in Chapter 4, many women, while employed on payment by results of some form – not usually specified – did not work on assembly lines but on other kinds of hand and machine operations. Thus, among the women employed by federated firms group bonus is unlikely to have been a common experience. It is also the case that men, especially in the motor trade, experienced group payment and speed-up as well as women. In 1936 an AEU organiser from Luton claimed that at Vauxhall Motors 'instead of a worker drawing bonus individually, it is pooled'. Another member, from Southall, described a components firm where a complicated scheme of group output payment was established: 'they work in groups. Times are fixed by a rate fixer. In addition there is an accumulated bonus – 92 per cent of efficiency. All points above 92 go up at the rate of $^{1}/_{4}$d for 2 points.'[56] Gang working among men had always been the norm in aircraft. At Boulton and Paul Aircraft Ltd in the mid-1930s there were several gangs of twenty men, each headed by a section leader whose own bonus depended on that of the gang; 'the result is that they are being speeded up', reported the AEU. These workers were divided among themselves and disciplined each other in the same way as women on the line: 'the old hands can earn time and a third, but the new ones (. . . the majority . . .) cannot earn bonus . . . and there is bad feeling between new ones and locals because the old ones think they will be tied down to the 25 per cent bonus'.[57] Group bonus schemes were not, then, confined to women and it is not clear how widespread their use was even in the trades where most women worked. More significant for the relationship between men's and women's experience of work and pay in the engineering industry was the determination of the EEF to treat women as peripheral workers. The attitude adopted by the EEF resulted in lower, gender-based rates of pay. It also meant women were excluded from important procedural agreements. They were then disadvantaged in terms of working conditions and pay in a way not experienced by male workers.

* * *

56. AEU, Report of a Conference on Motor Manufacture and a Survey of Organisation, Wages and Conditions, 6 and 7 Feb. 1936, p. 15. MRC MSS.259/Special Reports presented to the National Committee.

57. AEU, Report of a Conference on the Aircraft Industry, 24 Oct. 1935, p. 11. MRC MSS.259/Special Reports presented to the National Committee.

This chapter has shown that the apparently improved bargaining position of employers after the lock-out of 1922 was not important in affecting the direction taken by women's employment. Evidence from the EEF suggested that employers' use or non-use of female labour was conditional on a number of circumstances or factors of which adherence to an ideology of appropriate gender roles was only one. Similarly, for craft trade unions, a 'gendered' ideology was part of their opposition to women's employment and how it was articulated but not its central motive. Their opposition is more usefully seen as an attempt to keep control of a shifting division of labour in the interests of their members. In the 1930s their ability to resist the extension of female employment was strengthened by a tightening labour market and skill shortages. The EEF and some employers became much more cautious in their approach to female labour disputes.

The EEF as an institution did, however, have a significant impact on how women were employed and paid. For instance, it actively began to discourage employers from extending their employment of women from 1933. It clearly saw women, by virtue of their gender, as marginal to the engineering industry. It not only imposed a gender-based system of low pay (with the support of employers), but also always attempted to separate female from male workers when interpreting procedural and other agreements.

The emphasis in this chapter on opposition by unions to women workers will be shifted to their support for and recruitment of women as members in Chapter 6. It will address the role of the general workers' unions in women's recruitment and pay as well as the attitudes of women themselves to trade unions, bargaining and strikes.

CHAPTER SIX

'A Specialised Line': Women and Trade Unions, 1919–1939

General trade unions are often described as no different to skilled unions and employers in their approach to women workers. While craft unions did not admit women members, the activities of general unions are said to be motivated only by a concern to prevent them undercutting male wages. A common view is that the attitude of most trade unions towards women workers appeared to differ little from that of employers. Both craft and general unions shared with employers a belief in a gender-based hierarchy of labour, in which women's skills were never acknowledged. They were 'directly responsible' for restricting women's opportunities.[1]

This chapter looks at the response of general unions to women as potential members and their negotiations on women's pay. It argues that they did have an outlook different from that of both skilled unions and employers. As we shall see, their recruitment of women was not motivated solely by a concern for the livelihoods of existing male members. The 'defensive incorporation' of the First World War now competed with a more positive approach to the organisation of women. At the same time, the TGWU and NUGW increasingly challenged the EEF's gender-based system of pay, basing their claims for higher wages on other criteria. In spite of these moves, women's unionism failed to grow significantly. The last section of the chapter demonstrates, however, that it would be wrong to conclude, as some unionists did, that women were not interested in the defence of pay and working conditions. The circumstances

---

1. Harriet Bradley, *Men's Work, Women's Work. A Sociological History of the Sexual Division of Labour in Employment* (1989), p. 115; Miriam Glucksmann, *Women Assemble. Women Workers and the New Industries in Inter-war Britain* (1990), p. 194; S. Lewehak, *Women and Trade Unions. An Outline History of Women in the British Trade Union Movement* (1977).

in which they worked and their experience of collective bargaining were more likely to encourage spontaneous and unofficial industrial action than trade union membership.

Organising women

The largest engineering unions were organisations of skilled men. The most significant of these was the AEU. In 1922 it had considered a revision of its rules to make all wage earners in the engineering and shipbuilding trades eligible for membership but the proposed revision was defeated. Even after 1926, when it opened two semi-skilled sections for men, its outlook remained defensive, conservative and hierarchical. Two other craft unions which recruited from the electrical engineering and motor trades – the ETU and the NUVB – also excluded women on principle for most of this period. The only unions likely to recruit women engineering workers therefore were those whose membership was open to all – the TGWU and the NUGW. The TGWU had been formed in 1921 from an amalgamation of a number of unions including the WU, which, as we saw, had a history of recruiting women in the metal trades of the Midlands. The TGWU succeeded in recruiting a small number of women in the motor industry out of strikes which the union then intervened to settle. However, the union was not actively seeking new members. Not until the mid-1930s did Ernest Bevin, its general secretary, sanction large-scale recruitment in engineering.[2]

The NUGW, later NUGMW, was more active in engineering and in other areas of female employment too, including laundries, hospitals and local government, and what follows is therefore mainly concerned with this union. Unfortunately, it is not possible to calculate how many of its women members were engineering workers. In 1927 it had just 204 female engineering members in the Midlands (one of the main centres of women's employment in engineering and metal working), 1,505 in the whole of its Northern District, 804 in Sheffield and 319 on the East Coast, less than 3,000 in total.[3] In that year there were 42,000 women and girls employed in federated engineering firms alone. These figures suggest ambivalence, if not reluctance, to promote women's organisation on the part of the union. During the First World War it had rejected resolutions

2. S. Tolliday, 'Militancy and organisation: women workers and trade unions in the motor trades in the 1930s', *Oral History*, 11. 2 (Autumn 1983), p. 42 and p. 45.
3. NUGMW, Executive Council Minutes, 2 Jun. 1927.

for the appointment of a woman official and a woman organiser for each district.[4] In 1921 it took over the NFWW, one of the main sources of female union membership during the war, which then became its women's department. However, the union refused to accommodate the new department within its own financial and administrative working. It would not pay for additional women organisers beyond the three agreed to at the time of the merger. Instead the department paid for them out of its own women's provident fund. In effect, the size of the department was frozen for more than a decade. It was not until 1932, three years after her appointment to the Labour cabinet, that the union agreed to appoint a deputy for its women's officer, Margaret Bondfield. Even then, Dorothy Elliott was styled as the new temporary national woman organiser, rather than full-time deputy. In 1925, the executive council had placed women organisers under the direct control of district secretaries rather than the women's department. It had also said that these women officers would not attend the women's national committee. There was thus no direct means of communication between those recruiting women and the women's department. Bondfield offered her resignation 'in the absence of effective co-operation and with no acceptance by the District authorities of her position as consultative officer on women's representation from a national point of view', but it was not accepted.[5]

Part of the problem was the union's inability to make up its mind whether women were a special group requiring special provisions and tactics, or a kind of unskilled labour equally well recruited (along with male labour of this type) in the usual way through workshops and factories. While the women's department was denied any active involvement with recruitment locally, the broad-based national campaigns they proposed were also rejected. In December 1931, for example, Bondfield presented the National Executive Committee with a set of proposals for recruiting more women which included special training groups for organisers, intensive concentration in certain areas of women's employment, more research work and a press and radio advertising campaign. None of these were acted upon because workplace recruitment was felt to be more effective. It was also cheaper. 1931 was a year of depression when the engineering unions had been obliged to accept reduced working conditions for their members.

4. Marion Kozak, 'Women Munitions Workers During the First World War' (Ph.D. thesis, Hull University, 1976), p. 316.
5. NUGMW, NEC Minutes, 12 Mar. 1925, p. 6. MRC MSS.192.

There were, however, more positive moves towards women's organisation by the union. In August 1928, a conference was called to consider how women might be more effectively organised and, together with head office officials, conference delegates formed a committee. In the same year that Bondfield's proposals for a national campaign were turned down, some role for the women's department in local recruitment was finally conceded. It was agreed that it should advise districts of potential membership, though 'all efforts shall be subject to District approval and co-operation'.[6] There were other positive signs. By the 1930s the union was using demands for higher wages as a means of recruiting women and the EEF was correct about their propagandist purpose. In 1935 the union executive approved a wages claim 'if for no other reason than to enable the Districts to obtain the fullest propagandist effects from such a course and with the object of strengthening organisation amongst those workers'.[7] Accordingly, districts were to be told of the number of women employed locally and where they worked so that they could take full advantage of the outcome of the negotiations. A leaflet was prepared to promote women's organisation in engineering and printed locally so as to allow the inclusion of relevant local material. The union had been disturbed by (unfounded) reports in May the previous year that the AEU was to begin recruitment of women 'despite the fact that our union had for long been recognised by the AEU and generally as the main factor for the organisation of women in this trade'. In response the union produced a statement in the form of a history of their organisation of women to be circulated to districts as propaganda for recruitment.[8] In May 1937 a report was drawn up with proposals designed to lead to effective organisation among women in engineering.[9]

In spite of these efforts from the centre to step up the recruitment of women, there were tensions within the union about their worth. The general secretary in 1935 thought that 'if the machinery of the union was to be used in support of the economic interests of women in the Engineering Industry we ought to be able to command a far greater degree of loyalty among such workers than was revealed by the membership returns'.[10] The value of making applications for higher wages on behalf of women who did not usually

6. NUGMW, NEC Minutes, 6 Aug. 1931, p. 9. MRC MSS.192.
7. NUGMW, NEC Minutes, 7 Feb. 1935, p. 6. MRC MSS.192.
8. NUGMW, NEC Minutes, 31 May 1934. MRC MSS.192.
9. Report was not found.
10. NUGMW, NEC Minutes, 7 Feb. 1935, p. 6. MRC MSS.192.

respond to recruitment drives was still in question at the end of the decade.

There were tensions, too, in the union's motives for organising women. Speeches urging that the union establish itself as '*the* organisation for the organisation of women' in 1936 were enthusiastically received, but one delegate to the union's biennial congress voiced the familiar view that the main reason for organising women was that unorganised they were a menace to the livelihoods of men. In the mid- to late 1930s the union at the national level was moving away from this idea and towards a conception of the rights of the woman worker. In 1935 it was agreed that if any improvement in wages and working conditions was achieved by the union for men, an application should be made for similar improvements on behalf of women. Three years later, the policy of the union was to ask for a wage advance for adult workers, the same for men and women. But these commitments were still tempered by a feeling that organising women did not pay.

Some leading unionists believed that organising women was not worthwhile because they were a shifting, unstable workforce whose loyalty to trade union principles could not be assumed. The general secretary made this clear in 1938 in his opposition to equal pay for male and female union organisers, saying: 'I don't believe you can make the organisation of women as remunerative [as of men] . . . I start with the conviction that they will be in and out, and that they will never be a stable element within the organisation.'[11] One cause was their shorter industrial life. 'I am bound to admit', said one male branch secretary:

> that the organisation of women is perhaps harder than the organisation of men because of the fact that girls (for after all is said and done it is mainly girls and not women whom we organise) are not looking forward to an industrial career; in the main they are looking forward to getting married and leaving industry, and consequently they won't look at the question of organisation in exactly the same manner as the ordinary man who is working in the factory.[12]

'We have to recognise', said another, 'that a change takes place in the personnel of a factory amongst the women workers every 5 or 6 years.'[13] In other words, unionists believed the turnover of women in industry made it difficult to build up a stable membership and encouraged a different outlook to that of the male worker.

11. NUGMW, Report of the Biennial Congress, 20 May 1938, p. 221. MRC MSS.192.
12. Ibid., p. 222.   13. Ibid.

Youth was commonly perceived to be the newest obstacle to trade union growth even though, as we saw in Chapter 2, evidence from the EEF shows that most female engineering workers were adult not adolescent. Anne Godwin, then a member of the Central Committee for Women's Organisation on the London Trades Council, nevertheless described how in 1932 'we stood at the corner of the street in an outer suburb, where the factories have gone out to meet the fields, and watched the workers streaming by; groups of men, a few middle-aged women and girls – lines of girls, battalions of girls, 14 year olds, 16 year olds, 20 year olds, in a never ending stream'. It was, said her companion, '*the* sign of the times'.[14] Like women, youths were seen as lacking traditional loyalties. They had not the same stake in the workplace as men. A delegate to the biennial congress of 1938 thought that 'there is definitely a psychological problem associated with the organisation of adolescent youth, whether it be boys or girls'.[15] Another, two years earlier, felt it 'more difficult to get girls of 15 to 18 to stick together in harmony than the men'.[16] Young, short-term, with an eye to marriage and not a career, women in this view made unreliable trade unionists. If employers provided the right conditions, it was thought, women would not see the need for trade unions. Dorothy Elliott, the union's national woman organiser, described in 1936 'the great modern factories run under the best conditions' as an obstacle to the recruitment of women:

I would like to say to the women in those industries – forget for the moment that your piecework earnings are comparatively high; that you have a dining room in which you have pretty table-cloths and flowers in vases, and remember the strain on your nervous system and the effect on your health, of the concentrated speeding-up and high production in the best days of your life.[17]

Mostly, though, there was little attention given to the effect on union recruitment of the circumstances in which women worked. Some sections of the union turned to supposed female psychological attributes in explaining their failure to recruit more women members. They looked less to the material constraints of women's – frequently seasonal – work in engineering and more to notions of quiescence and domesticity. These and other ideas expressed by

14. *General and Municipal Workers' Journal*, May 1932, p. 165. MRC MSS.192.
15. NUGMW, Report of the Biennial Congress, 20 May 1938, p. 219. MRC MSS.192.
16. NUGMW, Report of the Biennial Congress, 15 Jun. 1936, p. 115. MRC MSS.192.
17. Ibid., p. 111.

delegates at biennial congresses suggested that women were at best difficult and at worst impossible to organise and could never match men as a source of union members. The main motive for recruiting them therefore lay in controlling the threat they might pose to the livelihoods of men.

However, as the campaigns to recruit women in engineering and pressure from the women's department described above suggest, this was not the only view. Instead there was a competition of views within the union on the necessity for and merits of women's organisation. Not all unionists, for example, drew the same conclusions from women's shorter industrial life. If youngsters were not discerning enough about the merits of trade unionism, grown women could be too discerning about what the union had to offer them. Far from being apathetic, they were seen as more astute 'buyers' of trade union services than men. Such women could not be expected to join merely out of custom, tradition or work group pressure. One member felt that 'when they come into the union, unless we keep moving, I am afraid we are going to lose them because they are not satisfied'.[18] The union's national executive expressed a similar view, which suggests that the shorter industrial life of women was seen to sharpen and focus their expectations of unions, rather than to lower them. As its report on the biennial congress in 1938 put it:

> in their organising efforts our representatives should be able to approach women in the Engineering Industry with a more attractive and positive programme regarding skilled, semi-skilled and unskilled work, rather than to offer only the provisions of the agreement for the avoidance of disputes, particularly as that agreement had, on more than one occasion, nullified satisfactory progress in relation to wages claims for male workers in the industry.[19]

Here it is assumed that women, who were not expected to have a career in industry, still had an interest in work and the conditions in which it was carried out that was at least equal to men's and that this was a factor to be used in recruitment.

Alternative views existed on the issue of pay too. This was clearly shown, again in 1938, when the Tottenham women's branch proposed equal pay for the union's men and women organisers. The general secretary, as we have seen, spoke against the motion. Sounding much like the EEF in its wage negotiations with the union, the

18. NUGMW, Report of the Biennial Congress, 15 Jun. 1936, p. 115. MRC MSS.192.
19. NUGMW, Report of the Biennial Congress, 20 Jun. 1938. MRC MSS.192.

executive said that wages paid to the four women organisers should remain at a more or less constant ratio to the men's and not be equalised up to the same level. The reasons given were that the organisation of women was less remunerative, that men and women did not share equal responsibilities in the 'rough and tumble' of organisation, that they were 'a specialised line'. If equal pay for equal work were granted 'the women employed might be far less in numbers'. The women that they recruited would be a shifting population who paid lower contributions. They were less valuable to the union not only in terms of revenue but as members. They were changeable and not loyal.[20] Several men spoke for the motion, though not the national woman organiser. One man's comments to delegates indicate perhaps that she, like he, had been warned off. He told them:

> I was assured by one member of the Executive that if I happened to speak in favour of this resolution I should find myself in a hot shop! I don't mind a hot shop . . . and I should be ashamed of myself if I let the opportunity go by without saying that, in my view, the question of sex should not enter into this matter, but the job and the value of the job should be the criterion.

Another male delegate, from the Midlands, pointed out that he often dealt with 'engineering employers who are substituting women for men on various jobs on machines and I am fighting my way every week asking for equal pay for equal work and yet inside our own organisation, while this principle is enunciated in our rule book, we ourselves are not carrying it out'. A woman delegate from the Northern District foresaw the difficulties the union's mixed attitude to women's work and pay might cause in the run up to dilution in preparation for war:

> I am quite sure that the seriousness of it is not overlooked by our General Secretary, because he is aware, I am sure, that in the near future we shall probably be faced with the question of the dilution of labour and whether you will be able then in the interest of your men members to demand the rate for the job. What are you going to look like if your own house is not in order?[21]

The vote on equal pay for union organisers was lost but the discussion surrounding it illustrates the variety of viewpoints on women's pay. It confirms that there were positive and negative

20. NUGMW, Report of the Biennial Congress, 20 Jun. 1938, p. 134. MRC MSS.192.
21. Ibid., p. 218.

ideas about the purpose of equal pay and women's organisation, both at the centre and locally. There was no clear cut acceptance by the union of wage rates related to sex and not to the job, especially during the 1930s. But the leadership could be ambiguous in its motives for organising women and tepid in its approach to the problem, not just on ideological grounds but on grounds of cost too. Women brought in half contributions, 3d. a week instead of 6d. The work of organisation had constantly to be renewed as women left industry for marriage. Meanwhile, the numbers yielded seemed very small compared to the male membership of the union. These considerations were always competing with the idea that women workers as a group were a permanent feature of industry and needed to be organised, some said to protect men's livelihoods but others as a matter of equity and justice, to remove division and to improve the position of all workers.

Negotiating women's wages

Soon after the First World War, the NUGW were supporting equal pay for women in terms of which the all male AEU would have approved. In 1921 at a dispute in a motor cycle works in Sheffield a local official claimed: 'We in the NUGW strongly advocate that where women are employed they shall receive the same wages as men. I venture to submit that if this were done men should be employed right throughout the country instead of women . . . my opinion is that women's duty is at home to look after the children, when they are married.'[22] Undoubtedly prejudice of this kind existed throughout the union, including, as we saw, at its highest levels. As late as 1938, the union's general secretary was still voicing this kind of sentiment behind official support for equal pay. However, equal pay for equal work was the union's declared policy for women in industry and it was not always interpreted in this negative way by its male and female organisers and delegates, as their contributions to biennial conferences showed. At the same time, wage claims became the focus for the union's organising efforts among women engineering workers and negotiations were generally led by the union's national woman organiser. In these negotiations the union began to move towards new criteria for women's pay, based not on sex and age but on the value of their work.

22. EEF, Phelon and Moore Ltd, Central Conference Proceedings with ETU, 11 Mar. 1921, p. 9. MRC MSS.237/3/1/89, F(6)36.

In wages claims during 1927 and 1935, the union argued that current rates were too low for single women, especially those with dependants, a factor not taken into account by the EEF. But, married or single, female rates caused hardship, being lower than those paid by the trade boards in other industries. They referred to one district where they said 'women were waiting for an opportunity to transfer their services to other industries as soon as trade in those industries became more brisk'.[23] The view of female labour being presented here is one in which women did not have skills or abilities specific to engineering. They could be transferred to other industries and their pay in the engineering industry was decided not by their specific abilities and experience but by the action of supply and demand in the local labour market and the price paid for female labour in other trades. While useful experience and expertise could be acquired (and rewarded in merit bonuses) by particular women, it was not rewarded in women as 'a class' or category of labour. Individual women might show special abilities and give several years of continuous service, as they did at GEC, but women as a class did not.

This view begins to shift. While they usually based their claims on comparisons with women's wages in other industries, especially those controlled by a trade board, the NUGMW and TGWU did begin to argue for industry-specific skills for women as a class, though with little result. In 1927 the NUGMW claimed, for instance, that 'women employed in the engineering industry are not paid rates of wages to which they are entitled having regard to the nature of their work'.[24] No rise was conceded. In 1935 the unions argued their claim more forcefully in terms of women's contribution to the prosperity of the engineering industry and the value of their work. As they now put it, 'in the added prosperity of the trade and the increased production which you have in the trade the women have played as great and in those particular sections a greater part towards getting that production and in doing the work of the trade than the men'.[25]

Employers were also asked to see women and girls as either independent 'economic units' or as much needed contributors to family income in a period of depression. The union opposed the

23. EEF, Special Committee re. the Wages of Female Labour. 6 and 7 Dec. 1927. MRC MSS.237/1/6/7, p. 125.

24. Ibid.

25. EEF, Special Conference Proceedings with NUGMW and TGWU, 19 Jul. 1935, p. 9 [Dorothy Elliot, Women's Officer for the NUGMW]. MRC, MSS.237/1/13/39.

idea of the 'family wage' paid to men (regardless of their circumstances) on the grounds that it held down the standards of wages for women and, because women were still poorly organised, it therefore undermined wage standards generally.[26] This claim resulted in a 1s. a week increase from 1936. A further claim at the end of that year was eventually granted – a shilling on the cost of living bonus.[27]

General unions have been criticised for adhering to the age- and gender-based wages structure for women.[28] But a climate of financial retrenchment and the inability of the unions whether they negotiated for men or women to resist national wage reductions left them with little choice but to whittle away at the system of wage payment laid down by the EEF. While the leadership of the NUGMW shared with employers and others a cultural perception of what was fair for women workers, within the union alternative views competed for attention and held support. These negotiations also show that the union increasingly challenged wages for women that did not take into account their worth to the industry's most successful sectors or their economic independence as workers.

At the same time, experience of disputes brought the union to recognise that women as well as men had ideas of tolerable levels of effort, pay and working conditions. Thus the early 1930s saw the NUGMW arguing that women should be included in the procedure on the same grounds as men and supporting women workers in defending customary standards of work and pay. Both developments are examined in more detail later.

For these reasons, the view that there was no difference between the outlook of general unions and that of employers is hard to sustain. The AEU and the engineering employers may have shared a presumption that skill was a form of property possessed by certain men but the NUGMW, who were probably recruiting more of the semi-skilled and unskilled workers in engineering than any other union, did not. Their attitude to women was less negative than has been suggested.

Women's attitudes to trade unionism

As we saw above, some sections of general unions failed to put women's attitudes to union membership in the context of their work.

26. NUGMW, Report of the Biennial Congress, 15 Jun. 1936, p. 109. MRC MSS.192.
27. EEF, Female Labour Sub-committee Minutes, 10 Nov. 1936. MSS.237/1/6/12.
28. Penny Summerfield, *Women Workers in the Second World War. Production and Patriarchy in Conflict* (1984), p. 170.

Instead women were simply seen as, by nature or social role, uninterested in and unresponsive to trade union issues. Other unionists did recognise, however, that they had little to offer women, especially in terms of higher pay. This section suggests that women were interested in and motivated about the issues which trade unions existed to defend: pay and working conditions. But it also argues that the circumstances of their work and their experience of collective bargaining tended to discourage union membership or lead them to spontaneous and unofficial industrial action.

Seasonal work, overtime and short-time working affected most of the radio and motor components firms employing women, even those whose conditions of work would have been among the best. The sector dominated by firms such as GEC also included many small producers on the margins of profitability at which conditions of employment for women were far worse. At Grosvenor Electric Batteries seasonal demand, the relocation through labour exchanges of young women from depressed areas and managerial hostility combined to produce a factory at which it was impossible for any union to make inroads. In 1933 it had no washing facilities and those who worked there did so for fifty-five hours a week at piece-work prices yielding little more than 26s., barely equivalent to time rate earnings under the EEF schedules. Deductions for transport were also made from the wages of those recruited from depressed areas. During the months from September to December, a pool of girls and young women was added to the permanent workforce according to the amount of work to be done and paid only on piecework. At that time, an observer from Watford Trades Council wrote:

> the factory is working to its fullest capacity and to cope with the work extra staff is employed . . . from what we learned at the factory gates it was evident that the staff was recruited from the North of England and South Wales . . . Staff seeking trade union recognition are liable to instant dismissal. Efforts [at recruitment] during October and November were unsuccessful because of the company's attitude, another factor against us is the fluctuating staff . . . ten members, young women brought in from Newcastle on Tyne, lapsed because at Christmas they were returning home.[29]

In spite of constraints like these and contrary to the presumptions of some unionists, women did have notions of acceptable pay

29. TUC, Correspondence between Watford Trades Council, the Labour Party and the Organisation Department, Jan. 1933. MRC MSS.292/615.61/4.

and conditions which they were prepared to defend through industrial action, though not necessarily through the channels of the union and the industry's collective bargaining procedure.

EEF disputes files provide examples of women acting in defence of customary standards of pay. In 1932, for example, women employed on machines facing nuts and bolts at Marsden and Son in Oldham, went on strike because they could not earn their usual piecework rate. Their complaint was about the organisation of work in the factory: frequent change-overs to new runs, waiting too long for materials and prices too low to compensate for these delays. In addition, 'although the girls are getting short runs, they feel that even if they had a good run of work they would not be able to make satisfactory balances'.[30] Their complaint had a national context. Piecework earnings were reduced for both men and women with the imposition of new working conditions on the unions in July 1931. Except for the fact that these women went on strike before going through the bargaining procedure, this dispute is similar to those brought forward by men after 1931 on the same issue. Certainly the employers' response was the same. They blamed the depression and a lack of continuity in orders for failure to earn the piecework rate and would not revise the base rate or the piecework price.

There are other records which show that women were prepared to use trade unions and to invoke collective bargaining procedure in defence of wages. When firms in Chelmsford transferred from the higher A scale to the lower B scale of wage rates in 1926, women at one firm agreed to the reduction on the condition that it was 'phased in', while others, through the WU, contested the right of the employers to transfer from one scale to another without going through the procedure. In June 1930 the NUGMW, acting on behalf of women employed by a Manchester firm, questioned whether after having established a rate of 28s. per week for women of 21 and over the firm was entitled to take on 'fresh starts' at the lower rate of 24s. – scale B. The women concerned objected to the breaking of a rate that had been customary at the firm even though the firm was officially entitled to transfer from scales A to B without discussion. The union objected, as they would have done where male wages were concerned, that such a change could not be made without first going through the procedure.[31]

30. EEF, Marsden and Son. Notes of Local Conference, 10 Jun. 1932, p. 2, Workmen's Arguments. MRC MSS.237/3/1/89, F(6)51.
31. EEF, Extension of 1922 Agreement to Women, Patternmakers' Committee Report (1932). MRC MSS.237/3/1/89, F(6)52.

The Atherton dispute, referred to in the last chapter, again shows women taking action in defence of their earnings and customary methods of pay. Its conclusion also saw the NUGMW finally succeeding in getting their female members included in the industry's main procedural agreement. The 'wage for age' rate imposed by the EEF in 1921 was not customary in the nut and bolt trade, and would have meant lower wages for some of the women concerned. The women went on strike in April 1932 and although their protest failed it did give rise to the concession that women be included in the Managerial Functions Agreement along with male workers.

All these examples suggest that women, as well as men, had a firm notion of their work and of the conditions in which it should best be carried out and a customary expectation of pay and earnings which led them to oppose change. They also show women using the industry's collective bargaining system. But women's defence of their earnings could be turned against unions as well as employers.

In 1922 a dispute at a firm in Edmonton ended with the women who began the strike leaving the union. It arose over the payment to women in its enamel shop of an overtime rate which was less than that which had been agreed nationally between employers and unions. Women in the brass finishing shop, however, had remained at work until pressure was put on them by the union to stop work. At this, the women in the shop where the dispute began 'tore up their cards and remained at work'.[32] They apparently objected to the union spreading the dispute and causing a loss of earnings to workers not directly affected by the change.

'Speed-up'[33] and 'Bedaux', notorious catch-words in the trade union movement, triggered further spontaneous, unofficial action among women workers. Spontaneous strike action by women workers followed the introduction of Bedaux at Lucas in 1932 and changes to a group bonus system known as the 'Kodak' at GEC in 1935. Attempts to replace the 'Kodak' were viewed as a form of speed-up, involving the re-timing of jobs and therefore threatening earnings levels. Both these changes were pioneered on women workers and both met with spontaneous refusal. For four days women workers gathered on the firm's Magnet Sports Ground. The motive behind a sudden strike was presumably to get a quicker and more immediate response than the drawn out process of conferences which took

32. EEF, Thos. Glover Co. Ltd, Central Conference Notes, 'Further Correspondence' to Local Association, 27 Jun. 1922. MSS.237/3/1/198, O(13)46.
33. 'Speed-up' referred to the greater pace and intensity of work associated with time and motion study, stopwatch timing and mechanised conveyors.

place between trade union officials and employers while the cause of the dispute remained in place. A quick response was important where pay was at issue and their actions suggest that women may have felt frustrated with, or estranged from, collective bargaining procedure.

Estrangement from the aims and procedures of trade unions may explain why women's industrial action tended to begin suddenly and unofficially with strikes and sit-ins and then fail to develop into unionism. Steven Tolliday has used the example of the Bedaux strike at Rover in 1930 to demonstrate very clearly how women and their workplace struggles were marginal to the overall aims of unions like the TGWU and the NUVB and too few in number to influence them nationally. As part of its plan to introduce volume car production, breaking with the quality market in order to promote a mass produced small car, Rover turned to the Bedaux system of work measurement and pay. The scheme was to be piloted on female trimmers. The TGWU engineering group secretary was persuaded by the firm to bring the trimmers round to the new scheme but failed. In mid-August when the scheme was introduced, female workers took spontaneous action. Eight women were sacked for refusing to work under the new conditions and the rest walked out. Pickets prevented replacements from the labour exchange from getting through. Some women were enticed back and a few more taken on. But when skilled trimmers belonging to the NUVB were asked to do cushioning work normally done by women the unofficial strike spread to include men. Eventually a settlement was arrived at over the heads of the women who began the strike and who now returned reluctantly to work. Its terms were never put into practice, however, as Rover was forced to abandon its mass production policy.

Militant action such as that taken at Rover by the female trimmers could not be sustained or capitalised on without institutional support and unions like the TGWU were unable or unwilling to provide it. The TGWU's intervention in the Rover strike was not motivated simply by a wish to recruit more women. By gaining new members at the factory they could secure, says Tolliday, 'a toehold inside a domain of a craft union as a possible springboard for wider *male* recruitment'.[34] Similarly, the NUVB decided to admit women in December 1931 following the end of the dispute in order to regain control of ground which it felt had been conceded to the TGWU. In conference the union noted that 'the development of

34. Tolliday, 'Militancy and organisation', p. 48.

female labour in the production of the motor car has gone beyond our power to erase. . . . It is not anticipated that this will develop beyond the motor car centres but it will give us a control that now belongs to others.'[35] These trade unions had a wider range of aims and interests than just building on shopfloor struggles. The NUVB wanted to preserve itself as an institution in competition with the TGWU. It also wanted to avoid being brought into conflict with the EEF by the unofficial action of women in the trade. Its chief aim was containment, not expansion. Tolliday's examples from the motor trade suggest not that women were unreliable trade unionists but that trade unions had little to offer them.

* * *

This chapter has shown that there were differences in outlook between general unions, other unions and employers. Organisations such as the NUGMW had no choice but to operate through the schema of wages based on sex and age set up by the EEF but, as the internal records of the union show, their position on women's pay did differ from that of employers. This can also be seen at negotiating conferences with the EEF where they increasingly put forward wage claims based on criteria that engineering employers did not accept. Two significant differences between employers and general unions were the suggestion that women be treated as independent economic units and the recognition that they had, as a whole class of labour, acquired skills that contributed to the prosperity of their section of the industry and that these should be rewarded. Evidence from the NUGMW also shows that its recruitment of women was not motivated solely by a concern for existing male members whose livelihoods it wished to protect. But these positive differences did not result in a larger female membership. The last part of the chapter has argued that the circumstances in which women worked, their experience of collective bargaining as well as the ambivalence of union leadership, meant that women's interest in pay and working conditions was more likely to translate into spontaneous and unofficial action than increased unionism.

The emphasis on the differences between general and craft unions is continued in the next chapter. A study of dilution will show how the outlook of the general unions described here informed a distinctive and positive approach to women's pay during the Second World War. The outlook of the AEU, on the other hand, although apparently more radical, was much more shaped by a negative concern to protect the interests of its existing members.

35. Ibid.

CHAPTER SEVEN

The Second World War: Dilution, 'An Arrangement for Men'?

Once popularly seen as a force for unprecedented social and economic change in the lives of women, the role of the Second World War has undergone a revision in the last twenty years. For Arthur Marwick, writing in 1974, its impact on women 'brings one to the heart of the whole question of whether the war brought about significant social and economic change'.[1] His view was that the war emancipated women, giving them new social and economic freedoms and bringing about lasting changes to their lives. Later studies disagree. Penny Summerfield and Harold Smith in particular show how wartime changes to women's lives were only part of a temporary adjustment to an emergency and that after 1945 pre-war patterns were restored.[2] The question is no longer whether the war brought about radical or lasting changes for women but why did it not?

For Summerfield the answer lies in patriarchy. Dilution – the process by which women were introduced into new jobs in wartime – was plainly 'an arrangement for men'. The AEU and other unions negotiated the dilution agreement in order to protect men against undercutting and permanent displacement by women. Both tried to promote the interests of men at the expense of women. Divisions

1. Quoted in Harold L. Smith, 'The effect of the war on the status of women', in H.L. Smith (ed.), *War and Social Change. British Society in the Second World War* (1986), p. 208.
2. Penny Summerfield, *Women Workers in the Second World War. Production and Patriarchy in Conflict* (1984); Smith, 'The effect of the war'; S. Lewenhak, *Women and Trade Unions. An Outline History of Women in the British Trade Union Movement* (1977); Sarah Boston, *Women Workers and the Trade Union Movement* (1980).

in the workplace therefore not only existed between the skilled and unskilled but 'were profoundly rooted in gender differences'.[3] Summerfield suggests that all trade unions were 'so enmeshed with patriarchy' that they would always sacrifice the interests of women to those of men.[4]

It is true that in negotiating the dilution agreements, unions wanted to protect the jobs and pay of those who had left the industry and, in doing so, they were defending an established gender division of labour. But their aim was also, more simply, to protect themselves against a rival workforce. This chapter will argue that the AEU's concern with women's work and pay under dilution was part of its broader interest in the growing body of semi-skilled workers – male and female – over whom the union had no control. General unions like the NUGMW and TGWU also wanted to restore the status quo at the end of the war and remove competitors, but in their case they negotiated dilution on behalf of female as well as male members and wanted to ensure fair treatment of the former as well as to protect the latter against undercutting. In these ways, as this chapter will show, the relationship between trade unions and women dilutees was not the unambiguous gender divide other historians often describe.

What of the 'gendered' motives of engineering employers who proved reluctant to move women into work recognised as men's? Women dilutees lacked the ability of fully skilled men and could not be reasonably expected to replace them. Beyond the practical constraints of dilution, however, the custom of employing women on unskilled and semi-skilled work combined with doubts about their abilities and restricted training schemes to produce limited expectations. But the main influence restricting women's employment under dilution was a determination to limit the impact of wartime changes on women's 'normal' peacetime pay. Engineering firms clearly wanted to maintain the customary gender-based system of wages. The fear of employers faced with dilution was that equal pay for women on men's work would bring about a general rise in wages for all women. As we shall see, the tradition of the 'woman's rate' gave employers a cost advantage they did not want to lose and led them to continue to employ women on women's work and, where possible, to redefine disputed work as female.

3. Summerfield, *Women Workers*, p. 161.   4. Ibid., p. 170.

Organising for war

From 1936, engineering firms were told that the EEF's labour policy during the expansion of armaments production was to encourage the training and upgrading of semi-skilled male labour. Female dilution, on the other hand, would have to be faced as a national issue. As well as upgrading male engineering labour, the EEF in January 1939 was discussing with the Ministry of Labour the availability of suitable unemployed men. The Temporary Relaxation of Existing Customs Agreement reached with the AEU just before war broke out permitted the employment of an 'alternative class of worker', but only where unemployed skilled men were not available.

These measures proved inadequate once war began. Throughout 1940, therefore, the minister of labour and engineering employers were pressing the EEF for an agreement with the trade unions which would enable more women to be employed. In May 1940 the Extended Employment of Women Agreement (signed separately by the AEU and the general unions) provided for the temporary extension of female employment into jobs previously done by men in order to meet wartime emergencies and increase output. For the first two years of war the government relied on voluntary solutions like these for new manpower requirements. Under fierce criticism from government departments of the inadequacy of this laissez-faire policy, Ernest Bevin, the new minister of labour, began to introduce compulsory measures aimed at concentrating and extending the employment of women on essential war work. By 1943 only those women under 40 with heavy family responsibilities or charged with the care of a war worker could avoid mobilisation.[5]

The women who entered engineering in the First World War had been volunteers; the Second World War brought conscription and as a result many more women than ever before worked in engineering factories. Between 1939 and 1943 an extra 1.5 million women entered the 'essential industries'. In engineering their numbers rose from 97,000 to 602,000 or from 10 to 34 per cent of the workforce.[6] The industry had never seen such a huge and compulsory influx of women workers. The following sections consider how employers and unions responded to the challenge posed by dilution on such a scale, examining their attitudes and motives in drafting

5. Angus Calder, *The People's War. Britain 1939–45* (1971), p. 383.
6. Summerfield, *Women Workers*, p. 29.

the agreements which permitted the employment of more women than ever before.

Employers

The main objective of the EEF in negotiating dilution on behalf of engineering employers was to control the cost of women's wages. They feared that the predominance of men in the industry would enable unions to claim that work previously done by men but elsewhere in the industry recognised as suitable for women was 'men's work' and so raise the rate for a given job. In drafting and implementing the dilution agreement employers were determined to limit the impact of wartime changes on the present and future cost of female labour.

During the negotiation of the Extended Employment of Women Agreement in 1939 and 1940, the EEF was therefore reluctant to concede to the demands of the general unions for equal pay for women employed on men's work. Instead, it wanted a rate fixed by individual employers according to 'the nature of the work and the ability required'. What the EEF seems to have had in mind is the existing Women's National Schedule supplemented by a special 'ability bonus' such as those already paid to women on an individual basis in government filling factories and throughout the industry. The employers' body was under pressure from member firms to concede nothing more. They had already made it clear to the EEF that they were afraid of the effect conceding equal pay to women dilutees would have on women's rates generally. Firms in Liverpool objected to the EEF's management board that equal pay for women on men's jobs could result in 'what may now be regarded as skilled female labour' leaving women's work 'for the purpose of obtaining a higher rate of wages under the Agreement'. Alternatively, employers might be compelled to pay a higher rate simply 'in order to retain the women already trained in the industry'. Likewise, Manchester firms employing large numbers of women feared dislocation and chaos in ordinary female employment as women sought out the better paid jobs. English Electric in Bradford also pointed out the difficulty of 'reverting to anything approaching the present scale' after the war if equal pay were conceded now.[7]

7. This and preceding quotations from EEF, Replies of Local Associations of Engineering Employers to Circular of 11 Dec. 1939 on the Extended Employment of Female Labour. MRC MSS.237/3/1/301, W(4)34.

During negotiations, therefore, the EEF made clear its refusal to agree to 'new conditions out of all reasonable proportion to conditions which have become well-established in the industry by industrial negotiation and custom'.[8] Alexander Ramsay, director of the EEF and former chairman of the Birmingham Association, where many of the industry's women workers were employed, insisted on the different nature of female labour. Men's and women's wages were decided on a different basis, even where the work done was the same, he argued. In his words: 'the men's wages have been regulated and are regulated around the central factor that they are in industry for life . . . they have to marry and rear families, and there can be no question that, in the broad arrangement of our social habits, industrial wages have been based on an acknowledgement of the responsibility which men have to bear'.[9] Equal pay, on this basis, was inconceivable. He proposed that the employer be left free to decide wage rates for women on men's work.

The question of the wage to be paid to women replacing men remained a problem, then, with employers wanting freedom to decide their own rates while unions refused to give way on equal pay. Ernest Bevin, former leader of the TGWU, and minister of labour since May 1940, upheld the union view. The EEF's women's committee, therefore, put forward a compromise involving probationary periods and phased-in payment of an equal rate, with a clear implication that their purpose was to make equal pay more palatable – it would not have to be paid straight away – rather than to reflect the lower value of female labour until it was fully trained and competent. Two years later the EEF told the Huddersfield Association in reply to its query about applying the dilution agreement to part-time workers that 'the probationary periods . . . are not a strict measure of the time required to become proficient on a particular job. [Their] real object is to provide a reasonable period within which the base rate and bonus can be increased from the women's schedule to a figure related to that of the man replaced.'[10] In other words, probationary periods were not so much intended to reward the growing competency of the worker as to lessen the burden of higher wage costs on the employer. The proposal for

8. EEF, Conference Proceedings with NUGMW and TGWU, 1 May 1940, p. 4. MRC MSS.237/3/1/301, W(4)34.
9. Ibid., p. 45. See also his evidence to the Royal Commission on Equal Pay, *Minutes of Evidence* (1945–6), paras 2858–9, p. 204.
10. EEF to Huddersfield Association, 16 Jul. 1942. From EEF, Broadway House, file titled 'Part-time workers' (n.d.).

probationary periods was accepted and became part of the Extended Employment of Women Agreement signed on 22 May 1940. This agreement together with the earlier Relaxation of Existing Customs Agreement signed with the AEU was to shape the work and pay of women dilutees in the industry. Each side referred to both together as the dilution agreement or, more usually, the relaxation agreement.

Women dilutees were now formally guaranteed equal pay but, as the drafting of this agreement shows, there was no acceptance of equal pay for equal work as a matter of equity for women workers. Instead employers were concerned to limit the impact on their members of higher wages for women both during and potentially after the war. Equal pay meant that cost-conscious employers had an interest in seeing that women's work in wartime did not differ very much from women's work in peacetime.

When it came to implementing dilution, therefore, employers tended to reinforce the pre-war division of labour. Their concern that equal pay would bring about a general rise for all women meant that they were reluctant to move them into work recognised as men's and were keen to show that men's work in a given factory or district was recognised as suitable work for women elsewhere. Instead of the pre-war practice of the industry being overturned by dilution, it probably spread further, to new districts and firms. A typical attitude was that of the Bolton Association, who wrote to the EEF in December 1939 insisting that:

> there should be no deviation from the National Schedule of Rates for Women Workers by the payment of the men's rate. It is essential that firms should continue to be in the position of employing women on every type of work on which female labour has been established in the engineering industry prior to there being any question of placing women on men's work at men's rates.[11]

As this example suggests, employers avoided placing women on work considered to be 'men's work'. Where possible they also re-defined a man's job as female according to the custom of the trade (rather than the factory). AEU officials in Coventry, for instance, complained about the view taken by local employers that 'if women have been employed on specific work by other employers in the district, firms who have previously only employed males on the same work are entitled to employ women without registering them

11. EEF, Replies of Local Associations of Engineering Employers to EEF Circular of 11 Dec. 1939 on the Extended Employment of Female Labour, p. 4. MRC MSS.237/ 3/1/301, W(4)34.

and at the women's schedule of wages'.[12] By extending women's work in these ways employers were able to avoid the costs of equal pay under the dilution agreement. It was claimed that they also downgraded jobs for the same purpose, requiring women to accept assistance when they did not need it, for example, or making minor organisational changes such as dividing jobs between two women.

The electrical firm Metropolitan-Vickers, a large employer of women before the war, provides evidence of how employers avoided equal pay for women dilutees. In line with EEF policy women replaced apprentices and 'handy youths' while the latter were transferred to men's work. By March 1941 this process of male upgrading was complete. Women were now needed to replace men and the question of their pay had to be faced. The works manager advised the factory's superintendents that 'if the work you are putting women on is of a simple nature and not of extreme accuracy and if they are operating under a setter up, then you should pay them the women's rate'.[13] In other words, work commanded a woman's rate if it was 'simple' and carried out with skilled assistance, whoever generally did it. Women's pay was being decided without much reference to whether the work they did was a man's work, or considered suitable for women in other firms and districts. Women who worked in an engine details department, for instance, were doing the same work as men in a blading department. Neither set up their own machines but they were each paid at different rates. The details department feared that the discrepancy would be noticed and lead to a claim for equal pay.[14] Women may also have been compelled to accept skilled assistance when it was not required, in order to deny them the full rate of the man they had replaced. In reply to his fears, the works manager told the details superintendent that 'women are not entitled to men's rate unless and until they work on level terms with a man. This, to my view, includes setting up and responsibility for sizing of parts. Therefore with the provision of setters permanently, the women will be on women's class and women's rate.'[15] In other words, regardless of the competency or experience of the women workers they would always be required to accept the

12. EEF, Management Board Report, 1 Jan. 1941, p. 1. MRC MSS.237/3/1/243, R(6)12.

13. Associated Electrical Industries (AEI) file, 'Women on men's work 1918–', Memorandum from Works Manager to Superintendent Detail, 19 Jan. 1942. GEC-Alsthom, Trafford Park, Manchester, formerly Metropolitan-Vickers.

14. Ibid., Superintendent Detail and West Works Extension to Works Manager, 17 Jan. 1942.

15. Ibid., Memorandum from Works Manager to the Above, 2 Feb. 1942.

aid of a setter-up. Practices like these gave rise to a feeling within the factory that women were being prevented from earning equal pay because certain jobs and tasks were kept from them. The women's works committee asked that 'opportunity be given to girls to prove that they were worth advancing beyond the limit of seventy-five per cent for men'.[16] It alleged that setters-up prevented or discouraged women from doing more complex operations because they were afraid they would be blamed for resulting bad work. At the same time women were reluctant to be trained for more skilled work because their short-term earnings could not be guaranteed.[17] Here, fear of trade union disruption and an evident desire to control the cost of female labour combined with women's own reluctance to take up training to limit their replacement of men and entitlement to equal pay.

These examples from Metropolitan-Vickers show how difficult it was in practice for women to receive the same pay as the men they had replaced. First of all, they had replaced mainly boys and youths. Then, when they replaced semi-skilled men, it was on work which could be said to be suitable for them and it seems any work which was simple and limited in range was 'women's class and women's rate'. Finally, for a combination of reasons, they rarely replaced a skilled man fully.

Employers feared that dilution would disturb the customary lower pay of women, perhaps irrevocably. There was alarm that they could lose control of women's wages and the basis on which they were decided. This account of the drafting and implementation of the dilution agreement by employers has shown that fear of losing a customary cost advantage led them to continue to employ women on women's work and where possible to redefine disputed work as female. At the same time, as we shall see below, they attempted to regain control of women's pay by negotiating a new set of 'women's rates'.

Trade unions

The chief fear of trade unions facing dilution was undercutting: a job formerly done by a man would be downgraded by employers

16. Ibid., Memorandum from Superintendent, Mechanical Dept., to Chief Supervisor of Women, Miss A.G. Shaw, 4 Sept. 1943, in response to a request from Miss Mitton, Chairman of the Women's Works Committee.
17. AEI file, 'Women on men's work 1918–', see N. Power, Mechanical Department to Superintendent, 5 Nov. 1943 and agreement reached 25 May 1944.

who were able to show that in other firms or districts such work was normally done by women. The rate would be lowered and the scope for male employment after the war narrowed. The objective of trade unions in negotiating dilution was therefore to prevent the cheapening and downgrading of men's jobs. But this was not simply an attempt to protect and promote the interests of a gender and, in line with the evidence of the last chapter, there were genuine differences of attitude between general and craft unions that cut across the boundaries of gender.

Chapter 6 showed how the general unions' attitude to women workers was shaped by a growing sense of fairness and equity as well as by a desire to protect male jobs and pay. Unlike the AEU, the general unions were negotiating dilution on behalf of female as well as male members and wanted to ensure fair treatment of the former as well as to protect the latter against undercutting. In all the discussions which took place between November 1939 and May 1940, for example, the NUGMW and TGWU repeated their basic claim that:

> where it is a case of a woman substituting a man, and who can do the work and give the same output and meet the requirements of the employer, there should be no penalty because of her sex and provided she gave an equal return to the male whom she superseded, she should have the same rate of pay.[18]

They also attempted to protect the position of women already employed in the industry by asking for preference to be given to them over inexperienced newcomers when dilution was put into practice. In 1942 the TGWU reminded the EEF president of its request that 'women who were in the Engineering Industry prior to the outbreak of war should have the first opportunity of being transferred onto work under the Relaxation Agreement'. The union argued that where employers failed to do so it was because they could not afford to release experienced women from their normal jobs. The complaint became the basis for a new wage claim: 'if it is so important they want to keep them in this class of work [i.e., women's work] and cannot for that reason transfer them under the Relaxation scheme where they would get a much higher wage, there ought to be some compensation.'[19] This example confirms

18. EEF, Conference Proceedings with NUGMW and TGWU, 1 May 1940, p. 7. MRC MSS.237/3/1/301, W(4)34.

19. This and preceding quotes from EEF, Central Conference Proceedings with NUGMW and TGWU, 11 Sept. 1942, p. 226. MRC MSS.237/1/13/64.

that general unions saw their role as to protect and promote the status and pay of all the engineering workers they represented, not simply men. It shows them continuing to work for practical improvements in women's pay. It is further evidence too that employers avoided disrupting normal practice on women's work and pay wherever possible (by tending to move newcomers on to diluted work and retaining experienced women at their usual jobs and rates of pay).

In negotiating dilution general unions were also of course considering the interests of their male members liable to be replaced by women. This does not mean, however, that they wanted simply to promote the interests of men over women. Just as it had done with women workers, the union was once again trying to obtain a guarantee that workers who had a history in engineering 'should have a greater moral claim on the Industry than men who might be brought out of agriculture or a retail shop'.[20]

The position of the AEU during discussions on dilution was admittedly more straightforward than that of the general unions who represented female members in the industry and employed national women officers on their behalf. It is not surprising that some scholars have interpreted the AEU's view of the dilution agreement as 'an arrangement for men'.[21] Until 1943 the union still excluded women from membership and its general secretary declared in February 1940 that 'the AEU was and always had been opposed to the introduction of women into the industry . . . Not with the consent of the union would women be brought in, in normal times.'[22] But in negotiating dilution the union was not only defending the interest of a gender but protecting itself against competition from rival workforces. Mounting skill shortages in the 1930s had strengthened the position of craft unions like the AEU and their ability to resist such competition. Their first relaxation agreement, signed in 1939, therefore allowed other groups of men to be employed on 'skilled men's work' but only where existing supplies of craft labour were inadequate. Furthermore, any such changes required the AEU's approval and pre-existing practices were to be restored at the end of the war. Several times the union asked the Ministry of Labour to identify as dilutees men put forward for engineering work through labour exchanges so that they

20. Quoted in Gary Howard, 'Trade Unions and Dilution: The Coventry Engineering Industry During World War II' (MA thesis, University of Warwick, 1994), p. 49.

21. Summerfield, *Women Workers*, p. 154.   22. Quoted in ibid.

would not be taken on at the expense of skilled men.[23] During negotiations on the extended employment of women, its main concern was with the method of recording changes in female employment so that, once again, the pre-war division of labour between itself and rival groups could be restored at the end of the war.

It should be clear by now that the dilution agreement was not intended either by unions or by employers to work in favour of women dilutes. On the other hand, it was not simply an arrangement for men, rooted in a desire to maintain gender difference. For employers, as we saw, the issue was cost. For unions the main objective was to prevent employers from cheapening and downgrading the work of their members through the use of a rival workforce – male and female dilutes. General unions like the NUGMW, however, were also more positively motivated. They negotiated the dilution agreement in order to ensure fair treatment for their female members and other women in the industry.

Women's pay under dilution

Most women, for reasons given above, continued to do work classified as female and to receive female rates of pay. For most of the war women received half the rate of pay of skilled men and only two-thirds of the rate of pay of unskilled labourers.

Trade unions objected to low female wages and the failure of the dilution agreement to achieve equal pay, but were their complaints motivated by anything other than a desire to protect standards of pay for men and to keep women out of those jobs in the long run? What follows describes negotiations about women's pay, examining trade union motives and attitudes. It argues that general unions like the NUGMW attempted to improve women's pay, bringing it closer to the lowest rate for male workers and insisting that it reflect more adequately the value of the work done. In doing so their main concern was to deliver improvements in pay to the majority of women who worked in the industry. The AEU, on the other hand, while apparently more radical in its proposals for women's pay, was motivated by concern for its primarily male members.[24] Its involvement in the issue of female pay and grading was

23. Dilutees: Letter from TUC in Respect of the AEU re. the Classification of Persons Entering the Engineering Industry as Dilutees (1944–6). PRO LAB 10/287.
24. The admission of women to membership of the AEU in 1943 is discussed in Chapter 8.

part of a broader strategy to control rewards in the growing category of semi-skilled engineering work.

Negotiations during 1941 show the general unions continuing to pursue new criteria for women's pay, criteria which conflicted with that of employers. They aimed for pay based on the nature of the work rather than the age of the worker, parity with male pay and a national minimum wage. As the subsequent history of the union's grading proposals reveals, these aims were positively motivated, not to protect male pay but to deliver better wages to women who worked in the industry.

Before the war general unions had great difficulty in arguing for a new basis for women's wages given the determination of the EEF to uphold the custom of 'the woman's rate' enshrined in the Women's National Schedule. The disruption to work and pay caused by the war, however, now gave a new impetus to the unions' efforts, persuading employers of the need to revise the basis on which women were paid. There was a confusing variety of wage rates to which women were entitled according to age, place of work (government controlled or private) and the practice of particular firms. Payment under the dilution agreement created yet another 'anomaly' in women's wages. On the employers' side, these disparities provoked fears that control of women's wages was being lost and that they needed to be tied to a new, unified rate much as they had been before the war. For the general unions, on the other hand, the concerns of the engineering employers at last offered an opportunity for them to redefine and update the basis for women's pay.

In July 1942 they requested a comprehensive revision to the Extended Employment of Women Agreement. The claim was based on the inadequacy of the existing women's wage scale and the trouble and confusion caused by the relaxation agreement in the absence of a 'uniform basis for deciding what is women's work and what is men's work'. As we saw, the EEF wanted to regain control of women's pay and the basis on which it was decided. Its women's wages committee therefore recommended that 'the time has come when we should seriously reconsider the position of women's wages in relation to the anomalies and difficulties arising from the operation of the Women's Relaxation Agreement, chiefly resulting in discrimination in rates and earnings.'[25]

At an informal meeting with unions in October 1942 detailed grading proposals offered to base women's wages on the nature of

25. EEF, Management Board Minutes, 24 Sept. 1942. MRC MSS.237/1/1/40.

their work. In deciding the appropriate grade 'the primary factor to be taken into account is the merit of the job or process as performed at the time, due regard being paid to subdivision and the means provided to assist the worker'.[26] A month later rates were proposed for each grade, rising finally, with probationary periods, to 'the appropriate skilled man's district rate and national bonus'. When the general unions counter-proposed higher rates and contested the work of each grade, the claim was referred to the Ministry of Labour.[27] It was sent back unresolved and on 3 December a provisional agreement was signed between the EEF and the general unions which, subject to the consent of the AEU, increased the minimum time-work pay of women over 21 to 50s. a week. It also set up a series of four grades with the fourth equivalent to the men's skilled rate.[28]

These negotiations between general unions and employers appeared to establish for women the principle of 'the rate for the job', instead of expressing a woman's rate as a percentage of a man's as the dilution agreement had done. But the basis of payment was still generally the Women's National Schedule, with increases. Payment under the skilled grade, grade four, of 'skilled jobs, involving a skilled man's range of work, performed by the same means and methods as hitherto, taken over in toto from men without additional supervision or assistance', would presumably have been as much of a dead letter as in the original agreement and for the same reasons. The grading agreement did not challenge pre-war arrangements on women's pay as reports in the press seemed to suggest. As the EEF later noted, it 'did not in point of fact grade women in the true sense of the term. Grades 2, 3 and 4 were merely an alternative to the Relaxation Agreement and the practice in the establishment or normal developments in engineering practice were still to be taken as criteria in determining the appropriate payment.'[29] In recognising the categories of men's and women's work the agreement did not remove the danger of employers using the concept of work 'commonly performed by women' to redefine jobs as female and to downgrade them. Even so, in differentiating between the work of women, instead of paying a 'woman's rate' to

26. EEF, Management Board Minutes, 29 Oct. 1942. MRC MSS.237/1/1/40.

27. EEF, Management Board Minutes, 26 Nov. 1942. MRC MSS.237/1/1/40.

28. EEF, Special Central Conference Proceedings, 3 Dec. 1942. MRC MSS.237/1/13/65.

29. EEF, Minutes of a Meeting of the Employers' Side of the Joint Negotiating Sub-committee on Grading, 9 May 1944, p. 3. MRC MSS.237/3/1/114, G(2)3.

all those on 'women's work', it represented an upgrading for many women in engineering and better pay. In this sense the agreement negotiated by the general unions was a positively motivated move to improve the position of women workers in a way that equal pay, in intention and in practice, was not.

Together the grading agreement and other claims for higher wages show the general unions doggedly pursuing improvements in women's pay. These were not intended, first and foremost, to protect standards of male pay, as the equal pay clause of the dilution agreement had been. Moreover, they were aimed at the majority of women in the industry, who had not replaced a skilled man and who failed to qualify for equal pay. These efforts by general unions were intended to deliver practical wage increases to most of the industry's female workers and, for the first time, to bring their pay more in line with the nature and value of their work.

The AEU remained aloof from the wage claims and grading negotiations described above. It viewed the question of women's grading as part of a broader strategy to harness the changing nature of engineering work and new divisions of labour for the benefit of its (largely male) membership. The AEU would not separate male from female grading, therefore, and linked claims on women's grading to an overhaul of the whole wages structure. Its proposals were therefore more radical – an abolition of the woman's rate – but only for those in the important category of semi-skilled work currently performed by both male and female labour. For those employed on recognised women's work there were no radical changes or improvements. The AEU did not take the same interest as the general unions did in improving the status and remuneration of most of the industry's women workers. This is perhaps not surprising as women's grading and the overhaul of the wages structure of which it was part actually grew out of a longstanding attempt on the part of the AEU to grade male labour which the EEF had resisted since the early 1920s. Similarly, its pursuit of equal pay under the dilution agreement was aimed at preserving the position of its members, during and after the war, rather than improving the pay of women.

The AEU refused to consent to the new grading agreement for women arrived at by employers and general unions in December 1942 and declared its intention to make a joint approach with the general unions on women's wages and conditions. For the rest of the war the AEU pursued joint grading of male and female work through conferences and through a joint sub-committee with employers. On the face of it what the union wanted was grading in the true sense of the term, irrespective of the sex of the worker. If they could not have comprehensive grading they wanted the 'rate for the job' guaranteed by the dilution agreement. Their approach was exemplified by the dispute at Rolls-Royce in Hillington, near Glasgow, during 1942 and 1943. A long and complex dispute, it showed how, when faced with new work and a high proportion of semi-skilled labour in a new factory, the aim of the AEU was to achieve either equal pay under the dilution agreement or comprehensive grading. The union's involvement in women's pay and grading in this dispute and more generally was part of its plan to devise a clearer and more up-to-date set of wages which would establish negotiated rates for a growing body of semi-skilled workers, male and female.[30]

In doing so the union seemed to be seeking a fundamental change in the wages structure of the engineering industry. It would abolish the idea of a 'woman's rate', as the general unions' earlier agreement had failed to do. Yet, in practice, the effect of the AEU's involvement in grading negotiations was to reorientate them towards male workers. In seeking a grading scheme related to work only, irrespective of whether the operator was a man or a woman, the AEU was, said Tanner, 'visualising the position which might arise after the war when the existing Relaxation Agreements were terminated' and employers might be tempted to keep women on.[31] These new proposals were not, then, about challenging the pre-war arrangements on women's pay but rather about protecting the pay of AEU members after the war. In March 1944 Tanner admitted that comprehensive grading of work was not what the union had in mind:

we are prepared to admit that there is in the Industry work which is recognised as women's work – . . . but we feel that even in that work there is a need for grading and there would also be a need for a schedule of rates of pay. We are prepared to agree that such a schedule should be on the present basis, that is to say a basis of rate for age.[32]

30. For more detailed accounts of the Hillington dispute see Richard Croucher, *Engineers at War* (1982), pp. 285–91; Harold L. Smith, 'The problem of equal pay for equal work in Great Britain during World War II', *Journal of Modern History*, 53 (Dec. 1981), pp. 664–5.
31. EEF, Minutes of a Meeting of the Joint Sub-committee, 23 Mar. 1944, p. 1. MRC MSS.237/3/1//114, G(2)3.
32. Ibid., p. 2.

All that the union really seemed to be asking for was a new schedule of rates for women. The rates were still to be related to age, not work, a requirement to which the general unions were opposed. Pay would continue to be tied only or mainly to the sex of the worker.

The real interest of the AEU was in the grading of 'work which is somewhat undefined and comes in the categories of skilled and semi-skilled done at present by men, women and boys and in some cases apprentices – and we have had cases . . . in this class of work where women were actually teaching men'.[33] It was only in the field of work not *recognised* as women's but in which women were now employed as well as men and boys that 'an appropriate rate should be fixed for each class of job regardless of whether it is done by males or females'.[34]

When the AEU was unable to persuade the employers to accept a grading scheme of this kind, it concentrated its energy instead on ensuring that the equal pay clause of the dilution agreement was applied. The joint sub-committee on grading continued to meet, but the issue of women's pay and grading was not actively pursued by the AEU. It was the general unions who, in May 1944, suggested to the AEU that the sub-committee meet to discuss the 'urgent position regarding women's rates', the need for 'an immediate substantial advance' and their policy on grading.[35] A wage increase was made three months later but in answer to a claim put forward by the general unions in May the previous year, not as a result of pressure from the joint sub-committee.

What does all this reveal about attitudes and motives? Were both sides supporting equal pay and negotiating women's grading only in order to preserve the position of men, protecting male standards of pay and thereby keeping women out of 'male' jobs in the long run? The AEU clearly wanted to preserve its position and that of its members in the future. In putting forward its own grading proposals it was concerned to protect the livelihoods of union members after the war. Its grading scheme, while apparently radical, was not intended to effect fundamental changes in women's pay, such as abolishing the woman's rate. Instead, it was intended to meet the challenge of another competing workforce – that of semi-skilled workers, men and women, whose rates of pay it had no power to negotiate. As these proposals failed, it returned to devoting its

33. Ibid.   34. Ibid.
35. AEU, Executive Council Minutes, 23 May 1944, p. 174. MRC MSS.259/1/2/95.

energies to the payment of equal pay under the dilution agreement. But in supporting equal pay under that agreement it was influenced by its view of women dilutees as custodians of its members' jobs and wages.

To the general unions, the AEU's pursuit of equal pay was impractical and not likely to improve women's wages significantly, as the operation of the dilution agreement had shown. They were more interested in delivering wage increases to women through the grading scheme they had already negotiated.[36] The NUGMW felt that the AEU had deliberately frustrated its efforts to get improvements for its women members in engineering while 'pinching our members' on a recruitment programme of comprehensive grading and equal pay. It was the general unions who, throughout the war, pressed for rates and conditions that would bring women's pay into line with the kind of work done and benefit most of the women in the industry.[37] This they did on the grounds of 'equity' and 'fairness'. The grading agreement they reached with the employers in December 1942 was not a radical alteration of pre-war arrangements but it represented an upgrading for many women and better wages. These efforts by general unions did not aim to protect male standards of pay, as the dilution agreement had done, but were positive attempts to deliver wages increases to most of the industry's female workers, and to bring their pay more in line with the nature and value of their work.

Women's work under dilution

As we saw above, the objectives of both employers and unions in drafting and implementing dilution agreements was to restrict the employment of women on men's work, limiting the cost of female labour and preserving jobs for those who had left the industry. Not surprisingly, therefore, most women continued to do work classified as 'women's' and to be paid accordingly.

This reality is in stark contrast with the views of certain contemporaries. Caroline Haslett, president of the Women's Engineering Society, predicted in 1942 that from then on it would be the job that mattered and not the sex of the worker.[38] Observers like Haslett

36. Croucher, *Engineers at War*, p. 285.
37. NUGMW, Proceedings of Biennial Congress, 10–13 Jun. 1945, p. 88. MRC MSS.192.
38. From Margaret Goldsmith, *Women at War* (1943), p. 199.

assumed that dilution would promote integration in a formerly segregated industry, achieving equal pay and acceptance for women as skilled workers. Evidence about the kind of work done by women in wartime suggests the opposite.

Many women munitions workers were employed to do work similar to that which they had done before the war. The 1943 Wartime Social Survey of women industrial workers found 71 per cent had been in paid work before the war. Of the 45 per cent of these now employed as 'machine and tool operatives' and 'assembly and repetition workers', nearly half had been 'machine and assembly workers' before the war.[39] The official history of wartime labour confirms that many women dilutees were employed as semi-skilled workers and only a very small proportion in the highly skilled grades.[40] Three-quarters of the women employed in engineering during the war were paid under the Women's National Schedule and classified as doing 'women's' work.[41]

Trade unions clearly wanted to protect the jobs and pay of those who left the industry while employers wanted to postpone the payment of men's rates to women on men's work by employing other men instead (youths and semi-skilled men) and by ensuring that women's employment was extended first and as far as possible on recognised 'women's work'. Thus, in keeping with the relaxation agreement and the EEF's policy in the face of the rearmament drive, many firms employed men in preference to women dilutees. As the MP Elaine Burton noted in 1941, 'most firms seem to be taking on in every case men of over forty before giving women a chance. It is only when it is impossible to find a man suitable that a woman is called in.'[42]

Employers were also criticised for being short-sighted in their deployment of women, who were seen as no more than a wartime expedient. *The Engineer* complained, for instance, that employers were not using women dilutees as freely as it claimed they had in the First World War. They were blamed for being 'resistant and unenterprising', especially in the machine tool industry and in shipyards.[43] Dilution was shaped by the assumption that those who came in would leave as soon as the war ended and dilution agreements were made in order to ease that process. Dilution of skilled work,

---

39. Geoffrey Thomas, *Women at Work. Wartime Social Survey. An Enquiry Made for the Office of the Ministry of Reconstruction* (1944), p. 9.
40. P. Inman, *Labour in the Munitions Industries* (1957), p. 80.
41. Harold Smith, 'The effect of the war', p. 217.
42. Quoted in Summerfield, *Women Workers*, p. 58.   43. Ibid.

even for the duration, was not seriously contemplated. Not only would it be too disruptive in its effects on women's pay, but engineering employers did not think women dilutees capable of replacing fully skilled men. A typical view was that of the Preston Association, who in 1939 told the EEF that 'although some women may be able to do a few of the jobs carried out by men they could not be classed as equal to a skilled tradesman'.[44] Dilution of skilled work was not anticipated by the EEF either. In conference with the AEU in May 1940, Alexander Ramsay predicted that 'the great bulk of the dilution will unquestionably be in relation to semi-skilled labour'.[45]

According to Mass-Observation,[46] this assumption created a frame of mind which limited the training and use of womanpower.[47] It offered the aircraft industry as an example where custom and prejudice prevented the best use being made of female labour. Believing women to be unsurpassed on repetitive, unskilled mass-produced work, employers failed to train them up to the semi-skilled levels more suited to the building of heavy aircraft. An aircraft worker wrote to *The Times* in January 1942 that 'the factory I work in is now passing an average of 40 women a month through its training school. Not one of them is being equipped with the necessary groundwork of knowledge to take the place of the men who are being drawn off to the services and to other factories.'[48]

Government training was relatively modest in scope. At first confined to unemployed men, during 1940 admission to government training centres was broadened. By the beginning of 1941, women and girls over 16 were eligible for entry. In the same year the number of such centres was increased by four, making thirty-eight in all. The sixteen-week courses of instruction they provided were felt by employers to be too long, too generalised and too theoretical. From 1942, therefore, the length of the training period and the concentration on producing skills like instrument making,

44. EEF, Replies of Local Associations of Engineering Employers to EEF Circular of 11 Dec. 1939 on the Extended Employment of Female Labour, p. 4. MRC MSS.237/3/1/301, W4(34).

45. EEF, Central Conference Proceedings with AEU, 22 May 1940, p. 5. MRC MSS.237/3/1/301, W4(34).

46. Set up in 1937 by the journalist Charles Madge and the anthropologist Tom Harrison, Mass-Observation conducted detailed studies of everyday life, work and leisure in Britain, drawn from the evidence of trained investigators and thousands of volunteer 'observers'.

47. Mass-Observation, *People in Production. An Enquiry into British War Production, Part I. A Report prepared by Mass Observation for the Advertising Service Guild* (1942), p. 117; pp. 121–2.

48. Ibid., p. 114.

draughtsmanship and machine operating were reduced. From then on, the bulk of trainees were to be given a preliminary grounding, lasting four to eight weeks, in simple repetitive work. Most of these trainees were women. The Emergency Training Scheme begun in June 1940 already provided classes at technical schools and colleges in simple repetitive processes and by 1941 two-thirds of its 40,000 trainees were women. The Auxiliary Training Scheme introduced in December 1940 was, by comparison, a failure. Employers did not take to a scheme which saw them training workers over and above their own requirements for transfer to other employers who lacked training facilities of their own.[49]

As well as doubts from employers about their ability for more skilled work and limited training programmes, women faced hostility from men. Again, Mass-Observation gives an example of the managing director of an aircraft firm who told them that men and women had worked together in gangs but that the best was not brought out of the women 'as the men, perhaps quite naturally, were inclined to use them as assistants or labourers'.[50] Penny Summerfield attributes the highly segregated employment of women war workers to the opposition of skilled men. In 1941, for instance, women made up only 10 per cent of the workers in railway engineering and 5 per cent in marine while 'in shipbuilding and repairing, with their own particularly craft-minded unions, women dilutees never formed more than six per cent and four per cent of the workforces at any point during the war'.[51]

It is true that skill shortages left employers vulnerable to pressure from craft unions. There were a number of disputes over the employment of women led by the AEU in the first two years of war. In Rolls-Royce at Crewe, 600 men went on strike against the employment of women on capstans previously operated by boys who had in turn been upgraded. What concerned the union's executive was the introduction of women into a factory in a district where women had not been employed in engineering before. Up until May 1940, the AEU was enforcing its own relaxation agreement by preventing women from being employed before unemployed craftsmen. In March 1940 Burnley Aircraft Products Ltd were prevented by the local AEU from employing girls on soldering of ammunition boxes. In anticipation of this kind of opposition, and in line with

49. H.M.D. Parker, *Manpower. A Study of War-time Policy and Administration* (1957), pp. 375–82; see also Note on Training, Jun. 1940, LAB 26/59.
    50. Mass-Observation, *People in Production*, p. 123.
    51. Summerfield, *Women Workers*, p. 155.

EEF policy, employers tended to upgrade boys and youths first and then move women on to the jobs they had vacated.[52]

Mass-Observation showed how custom and the experience of employing growing numbers of women on semi-skilled work between the wars played a significant part in shaping employers' expectations. But there were also practical limits to the degree to which a woman dilutee could quickly replace an experienced and fully skilled man. The skill-intensive nature of production (not simply exclusion by craft unions) limited the scope for dilution. In shipbuilding, where there was little repetition work and therefore less scope for deskilling than in light engineering, female employment failed to grow significantly. New machinery introduced during the war, like hydraulic riveting machines, 'reduced the *quantity* of labour required rather than altered its *type*'.[53] Craftsmen were therefore still in demand, a demand made more acute by the shortage of such labour in the mid- to late 1930s. In shipbuilding, the take-up of female dilutees could only go so far without a balancing quota of skilled men being needed.[54] Similarly, in the new purpose-built factories, shortages of skilled labour limited the scope for upgrading which in turn limited the demand for semi-skilled and unskilled workers. Employers could also be reluctant to make their skilled male workers available for transfer. While such men were likely to be needed in the future, dilutees were seen as a wartime necessity without a permanent place in peacetime production. For this reason, managements were anxious to preserve the maximum number of skilled men so that they might be in a better position than their competitors both during and after the war. 'Some managements', recorded Mass-Observation, 'are retaining skilled workers when there is not enough work for them to do, in hope of further contracts or in the fear of further contractions of the labour force.'[55]

The greatest increases in women's employment came in those trades which had employed the largest proportion of women before the war, such as electrical engineering. This is not surprising given employers' concern to control costs by expanding the number of women on 'women's work' and the proven ability of women in that trade. Dilution agreements, meanwhile, were fashioned to restrict women's work and pay so as not to threaten the normal, peacetime practice of engineering employers.

52. See, for example, Correspondence of EEF to General Secretary, AEU, 8 Jan. 1941. MRC MSS.237/3/1/243, R(6)13.
53. Inman, *Labour in Munitions*, p. 126, my italics.   54. Ibid., p. 137.
55. Mass-Observation, *People in Production*, p. 107.

* * *

The war failed to produce any radical revision in the pre-war arrangements for women's work. Practical constraints, conservatism and the idea of women workers as a temporary, emergency measure were important reasons. But the main cause, as we saw in the last section, was the determination of employers to limit the costs of female labour both during and after the war. This meant that the employment of women was expanded on work already recognised as female, and that new and sectionalised work tended to be redefined as female with female rates of pay.

The basis for women's pay was not fundamentally altered either, in spite of the adoption of the principle of equal pay in the dilution agreements. Craft and general unions wanted to protect the future position of their members against the encroachments of a rival workforce. The AEU's involvement with women's pay and grading was part of a broader, defensive strategy to control rewards in the growing category of semi-skilled work. But its pursuit of grading, like its pursuit of equal pay, was therefore motivated more towards safeguarding the position of its members than improving women's pay. General unions were, however, more positively motivated to improve women's pay through the dilution agreement (which was negotiated on behalf of their female members too) as well as through wage claims and the grading scheme. It is true that, in their new grading proposals, both craft and general unions continued to acquiesce in the idea of 'women's work' and a 'woman's rate', but that is not surprising given the determination of the EEF over more than twenty years to maintain both. It is important to remember that unions were restricted not simply by their own motives but by what the engineering employers were prepared to concede. When in 1944, for example, the EEF decided to continue to negotiate grading it was with the proviso that the unions 'were under no delusions as to the Federation's views on the equality of rates between males and females'.[56]

Yet the war did bring some changes to how unions viewed women as wage earners. Four years after the dilution agreement was first negotiated, all sides can be found bringing forward claims for the payment of the labourer's rate as a minimum to women on the grounds that women were 'not less skilled or able than a labourer, but less organised', that they 'too had financial responsibilities'

56. EEF, Minutes of a Meeting of the Management Board, 24 Feb. 1944, p. 1. MSS.237/3/1/114, G(2)3.

and, possibly for the first time, that women 'deserved wages which would permit a full life'.[57]

This chapter has examined the war from the perspective of employers and trade unions. It has shown how their actions, in pursuit of different objectives, combined to shape employment opportunities for women and their rates of pay. But it has questioned the view that dilution arrangements were intended, first and foremost, to uphold gender differences. The next chapter will look at women's own experience of work in wartime engineering.

57. EEF, Gramophone Co., London, Central Conference Proceedings with AEU, TGWU, NUGMW, 10–11 Aug. 1944. MRC MSS.237/3/1/114, G(2)3.

CHAPTER EIGHT

Would Women Stay?
The Effects of War Work

The previous chapter described how trade unions and employers shaped the opportunities open to women working in wartime engineering. It argued that in negotiating dilution unions wanted to protect the jobs and pay of their members, especially those who had temporarily left the industry. They were afraid that dilution would be used to enlarge the category of 'women's work' and that jobs formerly done by men would be cheapened and downgraded. These were the grounds on which they defended equal pay for women replacing men. Employers feared that equal pay for women on men's work would bring about a general rise for all women and they were therefore reluctant to move women into work recognised as 'men's'. When they did, it was into work which could be redefined as 'female' according to the custom of the industry.

As a result, the last chapter concluded, the war did not bring about radical or lasting changes to the type of work most women did. The distribution of women within the industry continued to reflect the pre-war pattern. Women never formed more than 16 per cent of the workers in marine engineering, for instance, while in 1944 they formed 60 per cent of all electrical engineering workers.[1] Many women dilutees were employed as semi-skilled workers and only a very small proportion in the highly skilled grades.[2] Three-quarters of the women employed in engineering during the war were paid under the Women's National Schedule and were therefore classified as doing 'women's work'.[3]

1. Penny Summerfield, *Women Workers in the Second World War. Production and Patriarchy in Conflict* (1984), p. 151.
2. P. Inman, *Labour in Munitions Industries* (1957), p. 80.
3. Harold L. Smith, 'The effect of the war on the status of women', in H.L. Smith (ed.), *War and Social Change. British Society in the Second World War* (1986), p. 217.

This chapter will look at how women experienced their war work and its effect on whether they would want to stay in the industry. It argues that, while women had their disenchantments, as Mass Observation discovered, the disinterest and passivity it described concealed more complex attitudes related to the kind of work women did and the alternatives available to them. This suggests that wartime munitions production left many women engineering workers ambivalent about remaining in the industry. What follows will examine the sources of that ambivalence, looking first at their experience of work, then at trade unionism and lastly at their attitude to demobilisation.

Doing your bit?

Not only was war work not new or radically different work for many women but, as Harold Smith points out, most of those who came into engineering at this time did not welcome the opportunity, nor did they go into it voluntarily. Rather, they were obliged through a series of compulsory measures from 1941 to enter war work and from 1942 they were conscripted. This must, as he suggests, have affected attitudes both to the work itself and to continuing in the industry after the war.[4]

War work, as the last chapter showed, often meant not skilled or varied tasks but monotonous, repetitive and simple hand or machine operations. Mass-Observation claimed that the main objection to the monotony of war work came from those conscripts who had worked in non-industrial jobs or in jobs involving initiative. On the other hand, women who had gone into industry before the war, of their own accord, 'were in the main satisfied or even enthusiastic ... though they may be dissatisfied over details'.[5] But even some of those who had worked in the industry before the war complained about the monotony of wartime production. In 1941, during a 'war work' exhibition, a woman who had worked in radio manufacture complained that:

> we used to make about seven wirelesses a week, so we were doing different things following on all the time. Not like this, going on the same. It's monotonous. I wonder how many she has to turn out a

4. Smith (ed.), *War and Social Change, passim.*
5. Mass Observation, *People in Production. An Enquiry into British War Production. Part 1. A Report prepared by Mass Observation for the Advertising Service Guild* (1942), p. 156.

day? And standing all the while too – of course you sit down at that job (pointing to a girl checking sizes of holes in capstans) and there's no noise, but wouldn't it be awful? I'd go potty doing that all day. And you haven't done anything when you've finished. You haven't made anything. These jobs are only fit for young girls – 14 year olds could do that.[6]

War Factory, a Mass Observation account of life and work at a radar systems factory in Gloucestershire, described attitudes among the mostly young female conscripts to their work. The machine shop called for simple, repetitive tasks, paced by the worker and 'involving neither mental nor physical effort of any kind'.[7] The main preoccupation of the women who worked there was 'how to make the time between breaks pass as quickly as possible, and to wait for the evening to come'.[8] There was no interest in work, production, efficiency or the finished product and the atmosphere of the shop is described as 'slapdash and carefree'.[9]

The monotonous nature of the work described here resulted in torpor and passivity. Other contemporary commentators described a link between seemingly dull, senseless work and the motivation and attitudes of women war workers. Editor of the *Left Review*, Amabel Williams-Ellis, writing in 1943, thought subdivided wartime production meant that 'many war workers hardly know what they are doing, and sometimes doubt if they are on a war job at all'.[10] Many would like to know more. 'I wish we could tell better what we're doing and how they finish it off', a young woman in an engineering factory told her. Another woman from a filling factory wanted to 'go round all the different departments and see the whole thing and have it explained'.[11] A 35-year-old is recorded as saying, 'If I was going in for factory work I'd like to do it properly – learn to do a more complicated job. You don't feel you're doing nothing like this.'[12] A showing of the finished product did arouse real interest in their own work among the young women in *War Factory*. But the type of work on which women were engaged had a more significant effect. In contrast to the simple monotony of the machine shop for example, the more complex work of assembly was reflected in better pace, motivation and concentration. Most assembly jobs took twenty minutes or half an hour each, and required 'a

6. Quoted in Summerfield, *Women Workers*, pp. 54–5.
7. Mass-Observation, *War Factory* (1943; Cresset Library edn, 1987), p. 26.
8. Ibid., p. 43.   9. Ibid., p. 56.
10. Amabel Williams-Ellis, *Women in Wartime Factories* (1943), p. 23.
11. Ibid., p. 27.   12. Ibid., p. 48.

fair degree of at least manual skill and also attention'.[13] Unlike the machine shop, assembly also had an output target for women to aim for.

Long hours accentuated the monotony of war work and the feeling that real life was being sapped away. At this factory, a twelve-hour day was worked, six days a week. Travelling to and from work ate further into the little time available for leisure, shopping and chores. But, according to *War Factory*, shorter hours, a demonstration of how one's work fitted in with the finished product and even the provision of more complex and demanding work could only have a limited effect on motivation. The reason for this was the debilitating effect of war work itself and the reluctance of the women to see it as anything other than an interruption of normal life. Many of the women observed were not simply dissatisfied with their jobs but resented the disruption the war had brought to their 'real' lives. According to their observer, Celia Fremlin, the women's 'attitude of passive waiting for the day to be over does not imply merely lack of interest in the actual jobs to be done. It implies also a profound and very significant reluctance to accept the 12 hours spent in the factory as part of real life at all'.[14] 'Real life' had been postponed for the duration or squeezed into the few hours remaining between work and bed. Again, in the words of their observer,

> they regard their new lives not as an exciting adventure, full of personal and social possibilities, but as something to be put up with until at last the peace life can be taken up again. The ambition that keeps girls going is not the hope of achieving something in the new life, but the hope that the peace will return soon ... the all-absorbing hope is that present conditions and all appertaining to them will, as soon as possible, have vanished, never to be thought of again.[15]

But shaping this profound resentment of war factory work as depriving them of leisure, pleasure and 'normal' life was an awareness of their temporary status in the eyes of employers and others. Women were not encouraged to develop a personal or permanent interest in their war work. Chapter 7 showed how dilution was openly premised on the *temporary* extension of women's employment and was concerned to ensure the return of fighting men to their jobs at the end of the war. Mass-Observation studies demonstrated how cautious employers with an eye on peacetime production limited the training and work opportunities available to women,

13. Mass-Observation, *War Factory*, p. 56.
14. Ibid., p. 43.   15. Ibid., pp. 121–2.

assuming that they would leave as soon as normal peacetime production resumed. On both sides of industry, Mass-Observation noted
the idea 'that the new trainees are interlopers with something in-
efficient or unpleasant about them'.[16] Chapter 7 also indicated how
the Ministry of Labour decided against a wide-scale training programme for women because they were mainly temporary dilutees
or employed on the simple repetitive tasks deemed to be 'women's
work'. As we shall see below, the AEU admitted women to a special
category of membership which underlined their segregated and
temporary status. Similarly, government propaganda aimed at recruiting women presented war work as a labour of love, helping out
the men who had gone to fight in an emergency which demanded
self-sacrifice. Wartime propaganda films like *Jane Brown Changes Her
Job* emphasised the woman dilutee's pride in completing a task for
someone else and her satisfaction in knowing she has helped 'to
put another plane in the shed for the boys'.[17] The message given to
women through arrangements for dilution, government propaganda
and their recruitment to craft unions like the AEU was that this was
not work undertaken for the personal possibilities it might provide
but work undertaken for others. The future demobilisation implied
in all aspects of dilution must have discouraged women from devel-
oping a permanent interest in war work and the attitudes described
in *War Factory* are therefore not surprising.

Trade unionism

Women's passivity and disinterest as war workers was seen to extend to their attitude to trade unionism. Mass-Observation reported
that women were 'abysmally ignorant of politics and trade unionism'
and a report on the engineering firm English Electric at Bradford
found women to be 'absolutely disinterested in any form of organisation or unionism'.[18] A more rounded depiction of their wartime
experience suggests, however, that women could and did seek union
membership and take industrial action but, as we shall see, they did
so only in specific contexts and over issues that mattered to them,
such as pay. Otherwise trade unions were perceived to be not genuine in their support of women workers or as irrelevant to women's

16. Mass-Observation, *People in Production*, p. 122.
17. S.L. Carruthers, 'Manning the factories: propaganda and policy on the employment of women 1939–1947', *History*, 75. 244 (Jun. 1990), p. 240.
18. Quoted by Summerfield, *Women Workers*, p. 182.

FIGURE 8.1   *Female trade-union membership, 1939–49 (in thousands)*

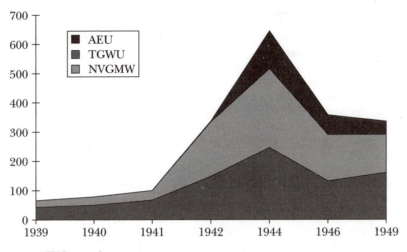

Source: TUC annual reports

needs, either by emphasising their temporary status as war workers or not actively taking up issues that animated them, like hours of work and pay.

As Figure 8.1 shows, there was a great expansion of trade-union membership generally among women during the war. The number of women members doubled between 1938 and 1943 from about 900,000 to 1,810,000. In the case of TUC affiliated trade unions, the figures trebled. 1942 to 1943 was a peak year when women's trade-union membership grew by just over 10 per cent compared with 1 per cent growth for men. The AEU (which began the war as a male only union) had 143,000 women members by August 1944.[19] However, the figures given here both for industry generally and for engineering in particular were a small proportion of the possible membership. In October 1944 the TUC calculated that three-quarters of the women in industry were unorganised.[20] Clearly, there was still a vast number of women workers who were not interested in trade unionism and trade-union leaders continued to complain that women needed to develop a trade-union 'consciousness' and that they lacked loyalty, discipline and a sense of responsibility.[21]

19. Vera Douie, *Daughters of Britain. An Account of the Work of British Women During the Second World War* (1950), p. 114.
20. Margaret Goldsmith, *Women and the Future* (1946), p. 60.
21. Summerfield, *Women Workers*, p. 159.

Given the temporary view women were encouraged to take of their war work, joining a trade union may simply have seemed irrelevant to many of them. An example of this is given by Margaret Goldsmith, who quotes one munitions worker, a keen unionist, talking about the different attitude of her neighbour at work:

> take the woman who works next to me in the shop. Her husband's in Libya. Every shell that goes through her hands, she hopes will be one up for him against the Germans. She told me this one day. So you see, she's working for her husband as well as for England . . . and what she gets paid or what she belongs to doesn't make much odds to her.[22]

For this woman, as for many others, war work was work undertaken for others, helping out the men who had gone to fight. A real life Jane Brown, she had no permanent or personal interest in her employment.

Contemporary studies also claimed that traditional union issues had little or no appeal to wartime workers. Thus, while much trade-union effort was directed at achieving better pay, Mass-Observation thought women were less interested in wage increases than male workers. The young single women portrayed in *War Factory* were not, according to their observer, as susceptible to financial incentives as men were – increased leisure time meant more to them – and joining a trade union to secure better pay presumably had little appeal, although unfortunately there is no discussion about it in the observer's report.[23] Reduced opportunities for spending and a lack of consumer goods probably weakened financial incentives generally for the young and single.

Hours and working conditions were said to animate women more than pay and trade-union involvement. The same report which claimed women were apathetic about trade unions said that they took part in works committees much more eagerly, obtaining, in one instance, a reduction in overtime hours. When asked by Mass Observation in 1942 about improvements they would like to see in their own job women regarded hours as a more important element in working conditions than men. It is important to remember how much working hours had risen during wartime. Before the war, employment of women for not more than forty-eight hours a week, excluding overtime, was normal. In engineering, the usual hours

22. Margaret Goldsmith, *Women at War* (1943), p. 206.
23. Mass-Observation, *War Factory*, pp. 119–20.

were forty-seven with a maximum of fifty-four and a half including overtime. Many women worked more than fifty-five hours a week between 1941 and 1942, both in royal ordnance factories and in private firms. At the end of that year, the hours allowed for women in about 6,500 factories were between fifty-five and sixty. Hours at a minority of royal ordnance factories were even higher. Despite women's interest, trade unions did not tackle the issue of working hours as vigorously as they did that of dilution and pay for women on men's jobs. This suggests that women's ambivalence towards unionism was, at least in part, caused by the failure of trade unions to take up issues important to female workers.

Unions like the AEU, which first began to recruit women members during the war, did not do so in order to represent issues of importance to women. When the AEU decided to admit women members for the first time in its history in January 1943 it was immediately suspected, with reason, of not genuinely reflecting women's interests. The union's decision was openly portrayed as a temporary war measure designed to protect the position of the rest of the industry's workers. Members were asked when casting their votes to note that 'the opening of the ranks of our Union to women will safeguard the wages and conditions of all engaged in the engineering industry'.[24] A low poll showed a majority of voters in favour of admitting women. By the end of 1943 the union had gained about 140,000 new members, a figure roughly equivalent to three-quarters of the TGWU's entire membership in the industry. A year later the numbers of women members had grown to 900,000. However, those who joined did so on a temporary, segregated basis and their recruitment was openly spoken about as a means of influencing their demobilisation. It was, recorded the union's *Monthly Journal,* 'the stress of circumstances, arising from the war situation' that 'compelled the union to deal with the question of admitting women'.[25] Women were issued with special membership cards marked Section V (Temporary Relaxation Agreement) and their role in the union was circumscribed. No women officers were appointed to represent these new members nationally. An annual women's conference elected six delegates to the union's national committee but they were only allowed to advise on women's questions and had no voting rights. The impression is that for the AEU women remained the temporary leaseholders of male jobs and that its main motive in

24. AEU, Report of Executive Council to the 24th National Committee, Jun. 1942, p. 322. MRC MSS.259/4/15/42.
25. AEU, *Journal,* Sept. 1942, p. 229. MRC MSS.259/4/14/56.

recruiting them and pressing for equal pay was to remove the threat of cheap labour from its male members.[26]

The way in which some women were recruited to the AEU further suggests little respect for the wishes of the women themselves and shows the union taking advantage of their ignorance of procedures. One tactic was to recruit the female collector or steward of the general union and have her bring all that union's female membership with her, handing out application forms without informing them they had a choice. This happened at the Lancashire Dynamo and Crypto Company in 1943. Only two TGWU members remained. At another firm where this had happened, a member wrote to the union's district officer, saying:

> I did not know until last Saturday when I wanted to pay my contribution to the Secretary that she had sent in the registration . . . several of us are not going to transfer and would like to know what our position is, how and to whom we should pay our contributions or, if the majority transfer, if we are left without a union?[27]

Uncertainty about these questions may have deterred many other women from resisting a transfer of membership.

Pressure was applied by male co-workers in an effort to get women to join the AEU. Women who transferred were supposed to resign from their former union. Forty-eight women did so at Sebro Ltd, all using the same wording for their letters. The TGWU official pointed out that 'those who went over were in a shop greatly outnumbered by male AEU members'.[28] At an engineering firm in Bristol women were determined to transfer, feeling 'that as all the men employed by the firm belong to the AEU it will be in their interest to belong to the same Union'. At Pye Radio in Cambridge the man who set up the machines operated by women TGWU members persuaded twenty-two of them to leave: 'what do you want to belong to the T&GWU for? We are the proper union for all workers in the Engineering Industry to be attached to . . .'[29]. Only two remained.

The aim of this poaching by the AEU during 1943 was to drive out or 'crowd out' the general unions. They attempted to recruit

26. Women members of another formerly all-male union, the ETU, were similarly restricted. Those belonging to its special women's section were only allowed to be stewards for members of their own section and to vote at their branch only on matters concerning women.
27. TGWU, quoted in Letter from Park Royal District Officer to Area 1 Secretary, 16 Jan. 1943. MRC MSS.126/T&G/3/SACK 51/308/E (460.c/10.sf16).
28. TGWU, Letter from District Officer to General Secretary, 12 May 1943. MRC MSS.126/TG/3/SACK 51/308/E (460.c/10.sf16).
29. Ibid.

male as well as female members, though most of the complaints concerned women. The 'poached' unions were sceptical about the AEU's motives. 'It is quite obvious', wrote one official:

> that they intend to enrol all women whether already organised or not, and so get a majority, and then make conditions for the women to suit themselves and so crowd our members out of it until eventually the women will be glad to join the AEU for the sake of a hearing or having any matter dealt with.[30]

The union's main motive in recruiting women, as in pressing for equal pay, was to remove the threat of cheap labour from its male members. As one woman saw it:

> if they hadn't let us in and didn't make a fuss to raise our wages, we'd be as skilled as the men by the end of the war and yet working for smaller wages. See? And the boss would want to keep us on after the war instead of taking the men back. If we get into the Union, and get men's pay, the boss will prefer to take the men on after the war. There wouldn't be a proper reason to keep us on now would there?[31]

In spite of barely concealed negative motives like these, women did see a positive appeal in the AEU. It did not always have to use pressure or coercion to recruit women from other trade unions. A forthright adoption of equal pay drew women's support. A woman organiser for the TGWU who resigned taking thirty-two other women with her gave the AEU stand on equal pay as her reason:

> I've always had the same complaint regarding Crane Drivers and Painters who I insisted were doing a man's job and should have been paid accordingly. Well, I got little response only that we were getting our scheduled rate of pay and in our case more than what other firms are paying their girls, but I still think something should have been done to get that Schedule altered. It's alright patting themselves on the back and thinking we're well paid, that's not enough. They want their rights when a woman definitely replaces a man, that's why we join a union, to prevent cheap labour, but what I want to point out is that thanks to the AEU Shop Stewards only, Crane Drivers have at last got what they're entitled to, a man's wage.[32]

30. TGWU, Secretary of Stretford Branch, Salford to Area Secretary, 8 Feb. 1943. MRC MSS.126/TG/3/SACK 51/308/E (460.c/10.sf16).

31. Quoted by Goldsmith, *Women at War*, p. 105.

32. Copy of Letter from Mrs I. Davidson, Steward at Henry Simon's Ltd, Stockport, sent by Salford Area Secretary to Acting General Secretary, 17 Jun. 1943. MRC MSS.126/TG/3/SACK 51/308/E (460.c/10.sf16).

The AEU was aware of this appeal. At a Bristol aircraft firm in February 1943, the AEU shop steward approached the female workers about their rates of pay and told most of them that they should be receiving 75 per cent of the full district rate. 'Whilst so far none of them have attempted to transfer to the AEU', wrote the TGWU's area secretary to the union's national office, 'there is a growing feeling that if they do so they will, within a very short period, receive this seventy-five per cent of the District rate.'[33]

While Mass-Observation showed that women were generally less dissatisfied with their pay than men, the examples given above suggest that pay was nevertheless an important issue for women. Ministry of Labour figures showed women's earnings in war industries to be about half those of men but only about a fifth of women surveyed by Mass-Observation thought their wages were too low.[34] The implication was that pay was unlikely to draw women – of any age – into trade unionism. In contrast to the evidence of Mass-Observation, however, these examples of poaching suggest that pay did draw women into the AEU because what it claimed to offer – the rate for the job or a high percentage of it – unlike the existing system, was clear, straightforward and fair. The last chapter showed how the equal pay clause of the dilution agreement was evaded or avoided by employers. Where it was put into practice obvious differences arose between the earnings of women on 'women's work' and those on 'men's' which were felt to be unfair. In addition, the nature of the job, merit allowances and special 'leads' all gave rise to differing wage packets. A Mass-Observation report of women working at BSA revealed confusion and resentment over discrepancies in their pay.[35] In this context, the clarity of the AEU's insistence on the rate for the job had an obvious appeal.

However, in line with the evidence of Chapter 6, pay was an issue which could be turned against trade unions, drawing women into unofficial industrial action. Weekly reports of the industrial commissioners to the Ministry of Labour Industrial Relations Department suggested that women 'were goaded into action by the numerous mysterious inequalities they experienced in things like merit allowances, output satisfaction with pay bonuses and holiday pay as well as basic wages'.[36] Contemporaries saw this as simply another example

33. TGWU, Bristol Area Secretary to General Secretary, 22 Feb. 1943. MRC MSS.126/TG/3/SACK 51/308/E (460.c/10.sf16).
34. Mass-Observation, *People in Production*, pp. 119–20.
35. Richard Croucher, *Engineers at War* (1982), pp. 281–3.
36. Summerfield, *Women Workers*, p. 172.

of women's industrial immaturity and lack of trade-union discipline. Summerfield quotes a Ministry of Labour official saying that 'disputes relating exclusively to the wages of women and girls are proportionately more prone to result in strike action than where men are concerned' because 'women had less experience of trade unionism and factory discipline' than men. But such action was also a sign of their dissatisfaction with, and estrangement from, existing trade-union procedure.

An unofficial strike of about 600 women at Fairey Aviation Co. in Lancashire during 1943 confirms women's impatience with the inequalities in their pay but questions whether it was simply lack of trade-union discipline or inexperience which fuelled unofficial action. A successful claim for equal pay for women working on heavy milling machines and routing machines created dissatisfaction among those on 'women's work', and other women workers began to send resolutions through their branch asking for further wage increases. Machine shop women struck for a week until they were promised that a claim for an increase in the basic rate would be made. The firm made enquiries of rates at other local aircraft manufacturers and decided that no further increase in the basic rate could be given. The decision provoked a strike by the machine shop workers which the TGWU organiser was unable to prevent. The next day women on assembly and electrical work joined the strike. The union clearly saw this as a problem for them as much as for management and blamed equal pay. 'We might have had no trouble at all', noted the TGWU official, 'if we had not been partially successful in the claim put forward some months ago.'[37] The disputes procedure was followed, however, and work was resumed pending a works conference. There, on the women's behalf, the union accepted an offer to raise certain piecework prices if necessary and to set out clearer criteria for merit advances. Not satisfied with this outcome, the machine shop, composed of about forty women, remained on strike. Their demand was much more radical than either management or union would concede. They wanted men's rates of pay for the 'woman's class' of job. These forty strikers elected a strike committee of six female TGWU members and two female AEU members to represent them in place of the official TGWU organiser. The illegal strike was in its fourth week when the Ministry of Labour industrial relations officer advised them to

37. TGWU, Letter from National Secretary, A. Dalgleish, to Organiser, Fairey Aviation Co., 10 Sept. 1943. MRC MSS.126/TG/3/SACK 51/308/E (460.c/10.sf16).

return to work. The strikers voted unanimously to continue but resumed work when threatened with prosecution by the ministry. This remarkable dispute ended in failure, but not just for the strikers. The TGWU lost members as the machine shop women resigned in order to join the AEU. As the TGWU organiser wrote, they left because 'we had been unable to obtain seventy five per cent of the men's rate for them whilst they were on dispute and . . . they had resumed work under the same conditions as they ceased work'.[38]

Far from being satisfied over pay, this dispute shows the lengths to which some women were prepared to go in order to improve it. It certainly shows women flouting trade union procedure but also demonstrates how that procedure failed to serve their interests. In fact, they were barely part of it. Negotiations were conducted and a settlement reached on their behalf. Not until they elected their unofficial strike committee were women themselves directly involved.

Elsewhere, too, women transferred to the AEU as a protest at trade union procedure which was seen as not treating women's interests seriously or urgently enough. These transfers also question women's passivity or immaturity regarding trade unionism. When the AEU began to poach women TGWU members at a firm in Salford in 1943, the women used it as an opportunity to mark their dissatisfaction with the TGWU. When the organiser met the women concerned in the canteen, discussion was 'heated':

> many members were very dissatisfied at the length of time it took to get anything settled when we had to deal with anything outside. This seemed to be a very sore point and they expressed the fact that in future they were going to get things done and done quickly, and not to have to wait weeks and then the case to gradually peter out to be forgotten. . . . We had a rather uncomfortable time for about ten minutes.[39]

The examples given above reveal more than the passivity and lack of interest described by Mass-Observation. They indicate that women could take trade unionism seriously enough to leave and seek membership of another union that they believed would be more effective. They also indicate that the issue on which they did so was pay and that they felt frustrated by the drawn-out collective bargaining procedure that existed between the unions and the EEF.

38. Ibid., Letter from TGWU Organiser at Fairey Aviation Co. to Dalgleish, 28 Sept. 1943.
39. TGWU, Secretary of Stretford Branch, Salford to Area Secretary, 8 Feb. 1943. MRC MSS.126/TG/3/SACK 51/308/E (460.c/10.sf16).

Most women, in common with most men, remained outside trade unions. At its peak, the number of women organised was never more than a third of the possible total. In *War Factory*, assembly workers, who were distinguished by an involved and 'responsible' attitude to their more complex work, were also more vocal in their grievances. Unlike the machine shop workers, they had a critical attitude to their environment which was constructive and thought-out. 'They have something of the more sophisticated worker versus boss attitude', said their observer, Celia Fremlin, 'and are critical of the whole management in a way one never meets in the machine shop.'[40] But this 'against management' attitude was never, it seems, translated into trade unionism. The same was true for many women who worked in engineering. Even those who did belong could sign away their membership of one trade union for another without too much thought. A 'form' went round the shop and most people signed it. Their woman organiser changed her union and so did they. It may have reflected apathy or inexperience but this chapter has also argued that women's attitudes were shaped by a perception that trade unions were irrelevant to them as war workers or not genuinely and effectively serving their interests. In some contexts, especially where pay was at issue, women did seek union membership or take industrial action. They also took action against unions themselves either by pursuing unofficial action or by transferring their membership elsewhere. It is further evidence, in line with that of Chapter 6, that women could be interested in and motivated about issues which trade unions existed to defend, like pay and working conditions.

Attitudes to demobilisation

The day the war is over I'll be the first one out of here. I'll be down that path before they've finished announcing it.[41]

I'm not going to work the day out! When peace starts, I'm going, I don't care whether its morning, afternoon or evening![42]

Most historians agree that women war workers generally did not want to continue to work after the war. By 1944 the government was no longer concerned about the 'problem' of displaced women workers. Their draft employment policy presented in May of that

40. Mass-Observation, *War Factory*, p. 61.   41. Ibid., p. 51.   42. Ibid., p. 52.

year accepted the forecasts of economists that the war would be followed not by slump but by shortages. It was assumed therefore that there would be jobs for those women who wanted them. The government was also informed by a survey made in late 1943 that a high proportion of women who had entered industry as a result of the war would want to return home when it ended.[43]

This survey found that married women under 34 years old mostly did not want to continue to work, a preference which was influenced by the type of work women did. Less than half the 'labourers and packers' surveyed wanted to go on working after the war compared with three-quarters of professional and administrative workers. Yet women in general thought that married men with dependants should have first right to a job after the war.[44] Mass Observation reports confirmed that most women working in factories did not want to remain there. Marriage or a return to home life was an almost universal post-war target, especially among those aged over 25.[45] In answer to the question whether women doing men's jobs should be allowed to go on doing them, 43 per cent of the women asked said 'no', almost the same percentage as for men. But a larger proportion of women than men, nearly a third, answered that it 'depended on post-war conditions'.[46]

The influences shaping women's preference for a return to domestic life were numerous. As the reports above suggest, women often shared with men the social expectations of what their respective roles should be. Many of them were conscripts. Women who had been compelled to take up war work, directed to factories far from home and accommodated in hostels and billets were likely to be glad to finish their war duty and return to their own lives. Given the monotony and fatigue described among the machine shop workers in *War Factory*, it is not surprising that the women there were keen to see their war work over and done with. Furthermore, patriotism and propaganda which had suggested that their war work was to be a temporary 'sacrifice' encouraged women to make way for returning men. There were also practical obstacles to continued employment. Nursery provision began to be withdrawn in 1944, making it hard for married women with young children to

43. Geoffrey Thomas, *Women at Work. Wartime Social Survey. An Enquiry Made for the Office of the Ministry of Reconstruction* (Jun. 1944).
44. From Sarah Boston, *Women Workers and Trade Unions* (1987), pp. 204–5.
45. Mass-Observation, *The Journey Home. A Report Prepared by Mass Observation for the Advertising Service Guild* (1944), p. 56.
46. Quoted in Goldsmith, *Women and the Future*, p. 71.

work even if they wanted to. The government grant to day nurseries was halved and many were closed down or became prohibitively expensive.[47] It is significant that Mass-Observation found 'a good many women' who 'expressed the desire to continue in part-time work'.[48]

Some women did want to stay at work, and not only the widowed or single. A small AEU survey was conducted in 1945. The survey was sent to a selection of AEU branches comprising in all 26,000 women members. Only 2,000 or 7 per cent replied.[49] Their responses showed that 79 per cent of married women who had no paid employment before the war wanted to stay in industry, provided they were not depriving a man of his job. Half of those who wanted to stay on were dilutees, while two-thirds of all those who replied wanted to keep their jobs.[50] Penny Summerfield gives examples of several protests over the closure of factories where large numbers of women worked, such as Vickers Armstrong in Blackpool and Manchester and Shorts aircraft factory in Rochester. In May 1945 women working at the Ferranti factory in the North West protested against a return to textiles where wages and conditions were felt to be inferior.[51] Former cotton workers at the royal ordnance factory in Chorley were unwilling to re-enter 'some of the old mills from which they had come'.[52]

The chances of women dilutees keeping their jobs, even if they wanted to, were slight. As we saw in Chapter 7, part of the purpose of the dilution agreements was to ease the removal of dilutees at the end of the war. In August 1944 the AEU agreed with employers that, where necessary, the names of dilutees should be submitted first for removal from firms at the end of the war. The female engineering workforce was accordingly halved between 1944 and 1945.

* * *

The attitude of women war workers is portrayed through Mass Observation as largely passive and disinterested. This chapter has argued that women's experience of war work was shaped by dilution arrangements and other factors which underlined their temporary, segregated status and often confined them to meaningless and monotonous work. As a result they were unlikely to develop a

47. Boston, *Women Workers and Trade Unions*, pp. 221–2.

48. *The Journey Home*, p. 59.   49. *Engineering*, 18 Jan. 1946, p. 54.

50. Quoted by Carruthers, 'Manning the factories', p. 247 and Gary Howard, 'Trade Unions and Dilution: The Coventry Engineering Industry during World War II' (MA thesis, University of Warwick, 1994), p. 47.

51. Summerfield, *Women Workers*, pp. 160–1.

52. Inman, *Labour in Munitions*, p. 201.

permanent or engaging interest in engineering production. Similarly, examples of inter-union poaching and women's strikes betray more complex attitudes among women than the apathy towards trade unionism that is usually attributed to them. Their experience both of war work and of trade unions contributed to women's ambivalence about remaining in the engineering industry and their willingness to leave wartime employment.

CHAPTER NINE

Post-war Divisions of Labour

Social historians of war see the period following the end of the Second World War as one of return to pre-war conditions, with intense segregation of work along sex lines and a renewed emphasis on home and family in the lives of women. In the case of engineering, this is broadly true. Female employment was still highly segregated in particular trades such as electrical engineering and motor vehicles. Wartime gains like the provision of nurseries were lost as government funding was withdrawn. Unions failed to dislodge the Women's National Schedule as the basis for female pay or to achieve parity with male pay. But pressures during these years created by labour shortage and the export and rearmament drive did start to undermine the categories of 'women's' work and pay. While the EEF held out on women's wages, individual employers faced pressure to improve wage rates and difficulties in respecting the boundaries between male and female, adult and youth work. More confident of full employment for its male members, the AEU took a less negative and defensive stance towards women as workers and union members, describing a positive role for them in the future of the industry.

An unexpectedly early end to the war robbed the new Labour government of a period of gradual readjustment. The cancellation of the Lend Lease Agreement by America which shortly followed brought about a currency crisis as Britain was forced to pay for American goods imported during the war. Dramatic increases in exports over wartime levels of between 120 and 150 per cent were required both to reduce 'the largest external debt in history' and pay for imports of food and raw materials.[1]

1. Alec Cairncross, *Years of Recovery. British Economic Policy 1945–51* (1985), p. 7.

Among the problems faced by the engineering industry in the rapid reconversion to peace was acute labour shortage, compounded by little effective planning on the part of government to meet peacetime labour needs.[2] In 1946 it was estimated that the number employed on civilian work in the engineering industry was still less than two-thirds of the 1939 figure.[3] *Engineering*, the industry's trade journal, complained that government war contracts had continued for longer than expected and consequently fewer workers than planned were being released from munitions work to civilian production.[4] Relatively short-term problems of distribution like these were made worse by actual shortage. The return of former soldiers to civilian jobs failed to bridge the gap between the supply of and demand for engineering labour. During 1946 the Essential Work Order was gradually withdrawn from industry and women no longer needed permission to leave their jobs. Large numbers of them took the opportunity to go. Between 1943 and January 1947 the female engineering workforce was more than halved.[5] Other potential labour was also drawn away by the raising of the school leaving age to 15 and the conscription, for a further eighteen months, of men.

Government was therefore obliged to restore employment controls in the winter of 1946–7 to direct labour once more into essential work and to launch a (largely unsuccessful) remobilisation campaign in 1947 aimed at persuading older women back into industry. In engineering, shift working and longer hours were also introduced in order to maintain production.

The remobilisation campaign failed to have a significant impact on the supply of female labour to industry. Only a third of the target number of women was recruited. Susan Carruthers blames the campaign's narrow concentration on conventionally female occupations like textiles, nursing, teaching and domestic service, restrictive government policy on nurseries and its tepid support for equal pay. It seems likely, however, as Jim Tomlinson has recently shown, that the provision of nurseries had limited effect on the supply of female labour. More important were hours of work, time for shopping and the kinds of job available. The limited nature and subsequent failure of the government's campaign probably had more to do with its justified pessimism about women's enthusiasm for a

---

2. S.L. Carruthers, 'Manning the factories: propaganda and policy on the employment of women 1939–1947', *History*, 75. 244 (Jun. 1990), p. 248.
3. *Engineering*, 18 Jan. 1946, p. 53.   4. *Engineering*, 11 Jan. 1946, p. 27.
5. Harold L. Smith, 'The womanpower problem in Britain during the Second World War', *Historical Journal*, 27. 4 (1984), p. 939.

return to work than to sexist views about women's role. After all, as Tomlinson observes, 'Given the conditions of the period, a lack of enthusiasm to respond to government blandishments would have been rational, especially . . . for those women who had already worked long hours over a number of years during the war.'[6] As we shall see below, engineering firms were aware of this problem and consequently forced to offer new incentives, including improved conditions and more part-time work, in order to induce women to return. Male labour was in demand too and the labour market in general remained tight as the Labour government achieved its goal of full employment. By the end of the decade engineering employers were still complaining that they were hampered by a lack of available labour, especially skilled male labour. Semi-skilled and unskilled adult men were at a premium in many districts and there was little surplus female labour.[7]

What follows will look at the effect of the post-war labour situation on the attitudes and approaches of engineering trade unions and employers to women's work and pay. It argues that labour shortages and the modernising reconstruction plans of the trade unions gave rise to more positive and radical attitudes towards women engineering workers. But failure of these plans and the intransigence of the EEF on women's pay also led them back to the pragmatism and defensiveness shown during the war. On the employers' side, individual firms were forced into change by acute shortages of female and other labour. They were obliged to offer incentives like higher pay and part-time working to women and forced into expedients such as using the dilution agreements in peacetime and moving men on to women's work. In other words, a tight post-war labour market began to undermine the concepts of 'women's' work and pay.

Trade unions

Chapter 7 showed how the AEU, in its handling of dilution, was motivated more by a wish to protect the livelihoods of its members and to control status and rewards in the growing category of

---

6. Jim Tomlinson, *Democratic Socialism and Economic Policy. The Attlee Years 1945–1951* (1997), p. 192.

7. EEF, Amendment of Relaxation Agreement, 1951–5, File 7, Letter from London Association, 7 Sept. 1951. MRC MSS.237/3/1/251, R(6)256.

semi-skilled engineering work than to represent the interests of women *per se*. Its equal pay and grading proposals were therefore also less radical than they at first appeared. Equally, its recruitment of women as union members was intended as a way of controlling or influencing their dismissal at the end of the war.

In contrast, the post-war situation was more complicated. Public commitment to full employment and the experience of labour shortage helped to temper the anxiety of the AEU and its male members about female employment after the war. In March 1946 the editor of the union's *Monthly Journal* was confidently informing its readers that 'the post-war demand for engineering products of every kind is such that a high and stable level of employment is assured for the engineering trades'.[8] It was in this context of continuing demand for all kinds of labour that the union's national committee affirmed the right of wartime women to take part in the post-war development of the engineering industry, acknowledging 'the experience gained and skill attained'.[9] As before, the union continued to oppose cheap labour, but its opposition was expressed less negatively and in the new language of reconstruction. Thus, 'women's work' and the Women's Schedule (of wages) were still portrayed as a threat but now it was the health and stability of the industry as a whole, including its women workers, that was being defended, rather than male jobs and pay. Accordingly, the union sought not simply equal pay for women on men's jobs but, more broadly, 'a stable wages structure on improved standards' of which parity between women and unskilled men was part. But women's pay and grading remained unresolved. Failure to make progress with the new wages structure meant that the union could be seen as promoting the employment of women and valuing their experience and skill (as the quotation above suggests) while also trying to ensure that they were dismissed before skilled and semi-skilled men in the reconversion to peace.[10] It also meant that the union simultaneously opposed the existence of female work and pay because it deterred the women who were needed as part of the post-war development of the industry and because it threatened the livelihoods of men and narrowed the scope for their employment.[11]

8. AEU, *Monthly Journal*, Mar. 1946, p. 66. MRC MSS.259/4/14/60.
9. AEU, National Committee, Aug. 1946, Resolution 30, in AEU *Monthly Journal*, Aug. 1946. MSS.259/4/14/60. See also Royal Commission on Equal Pay, *Appendix VII* (1945–6), para. 20, p. 79 and *Minutes of Evidence* given on 3 Aug. 1945.
10. See, for example, *Monthly Journal*, Feb. 1946, p. 48. MRC MSS.259/4/14/60.
11. AEU, *Monthly Journal*, Feb. 1946, p. 44. MSS.259/4/14/60.

As we saw in Chapter 7, the AEU had been attempting to negotiate a new wages structure with comprehensive grading during the war. In peacetime the grading campaign was re-invigorated as part of the union's broader modernising programme for the engineering industry. In 1945 the National Engineering Joint Trades Movement, an organisation joining the AEU with the Confederation of Shipbuilding and Engineering Trade Unions, produced a series of proposals to promote productive efficiency and full employment in an industry it claimed had become 'cautious and restrictive in its outlook'.[12] Like engineering's technique and equipment, 'the wages structure is a reflection of past methods and a dead era'. The Women's National Schedule too was out of date. At a wages conference in 1949 the unions repeated their belief that 'with the present development in the Industry the work carried out by males and by females was coming closer together and, as a consequence, women today were employed on work calling for a higher degree of skill and responsibility'.[13] However, improvements in women's pay related to grading of their work continued to run aground on the insistence of the AEU and other unions that men's and women's pay be considered together, as part of a unified structure of wages based more clearly on work content. The EEF meanwhile refused to link men's and women's work or pay and would not concede changes for women that might be seen to preface a new national grading scheme. The unions were accordingly forced to divide their claim into separate proposals for men and women, both of which were then refused. A joint committee of employers' and unions' representatives had been set up to explore grading in 1944 but while the union side now wanted a scheme for all workers, employers remained opposed to the grading of men. A subcommittee was formed in 1947 to examine more closely women's grading and to put on paper a scheme for discussion. The employers involved included Lucas, GEC, Osram Lamps and Pye Radio. Privately they found grading of women to be possible but had no intention of introducing it in case it was seen as opening the door to male grading. Alexander Low, secretary of the EEF and chairman of the employers' side of the subcommittee, felt that the result of their discussion with the unions was already foregone and that 'we will ultimately

12. National Engineering Joint Trades Movement, Memoranda on Post-war Reconstruction in the Engineering Industry (1945), para 9. PRO SUPP 14/137.
13. EEF, Equal Pay, Conference Between the Committee in Regard to the Employment of Women and Representatives of the Unions, 15 Jul. 1949. MRC MSS.237/3/1/91, F(6)95.

come to the point of saying that grading so far as women are concerned is as impossible as it is in the case of men, but I do believe it is necessary to indulge in further exploration and consultation with the unions before that conclusion is reached'.[14] The subcommittee was eventually dissolved unilaterally by the EEF as serving no useful purpose.

The general unions, especially the NUGMW, had made less radical proposals for women's pay during the war which, while still recognising the category of 'women's work', would have brought their pay closer to the lowest rate for male workers and reflected more adequately the value of the work done. After the war, though, they were more explicitly committed to equality of wage rates between men and women and equality of opportunity in access to training for skilled jobs. Unlike the AEU, they were unambiguous in their support for the retention of women workers. The TGWU, for example, passed a resolution in July 1947 that 'those women who acquired special skill or experience during the war in a particular job or trade should have full opportunity to continue to use their experience and skill to the benefit of the country'.[15] The national delegates' conference of women in the same year resolved that:

> The attitude of mind that a woman was something half-way towards a man insofar as her standing and efficiency in industry was concerned should be broken down once and for all and, accordingly, in all future negotiations the drive should be to establish the principle of equal pay for equal work without regard to sex, with a discontinuance of the policy of seeking to secure so-called women's schedules.[16]

In practice, though, the general unions and the AEU continued to seek improvements in women's wage rates under the schedule as the only realistic way of delivering increases in pay. These claims were made jointly. The general unions continued to regard the AEU's separate claims for equal pay for women as 'unreal' and 'purely for propaganda purposes and in order to increase their membership'.[17]

Both general unions and the AEU were in stalemate with employers in their attempts to change the basis of women's pay by relating it to job content and to levels of pay for unskilled men. Instead of a comprehensive reworking of the basis for pay in engineering, grading

14. Ibid., Letter from A. Low to A.B. Waring at Lucas, 11 Jun. 1947.

15. TGWU, Biennial Delegates' Conference Proceedings, 18 Jul. 1947, p. 42. MRC MSS.126/T&G/1/4/12.

16. TGWU, National Delegates' Conference of Women Members, Resolution 1 (iv), 25 Apr. 1947. MRC MSS.126/T&G/1/4/12.

17. NUGMW, Report of Congress 19–22 Jun. 1950, p. 130. MRC MSS.192.

negotiations dragged on unresolved. Dilution agreements remained in place, in spite of the end of the war, allowing for the employment of a different class of labour on recognised men's work but leaving the notions of 'men's' and 'women's' work intact.

Employers

As we saw above, the EEF refused to abandon the Women's National Schedule and only went through the motions of considering a new grading scheme, but for individual employers the labour shortage after the war did create pressures to improve on the schedule rates and provide other incentives for women to work. It also led to the retention of wartime dilution agreements and, in some cases, expedients which tended to undermine the boundaries between male and female work.

The electrical firm Metropolitan-Vickers came under pressure after the war to increase female pay and improve working conditions in order to attract women workers back into its Trafford Park factory. During 1946, labour difficulties threatened to stop production in four of its main manufacturing departments. Up to half the women working there were expected to leave immediately with the lifting of the Essential Work Order. The works manager complained to the site's director in March 1946 that many women had already left for domestic reasons and of those who remained 'absenteeism, particularly on Saturday a.m.s is very serious . . . if we take any disciplinary action it provokes an immediate application for release, and nearly all applications for release are successful'. Further losses were expected 'because of more attractive and higher paid work [outside]'. A particular difficulty was posed by the loss of twenty-two women without notice from the coil-winding and insulation departments. At least sixty women were now needed to maintain output to other departments within the factory using coils and the female labour shortage was causing a serious production bottleneck. Meanwhile the works manager predicted: 'We cannot expect that our wastage will be made good by new recruitment because of the transport difficulties, the unattractiveness of the work, and the fact that we can only pay Women's National Schedule and a small merit award.'[18]

18. This and preceding quote from AEI file, 'Women workers – general 1918–', Works Manager to Director E.W. Steele, 7 Mar. 1946, GEC-Alsthom, Trafford Park, formerly Metropolitan-Vickers.

The preferred solution was to transfer proficient women from within the factory on to the work, so that production would not be lost, but no compulsion could be used for fear of women leaving the factory altogether. Instead the small 5s. merit award was offered, and improved amenities: hot and cold water, aprons and gloves. The motion study section was asked to consider a rearrangement of the work which would allow workers to sit down. Winding and insulating large coils was especially difficult, slow and dirty work and the management acknowledged that 'The girls will not stay long on this work, whilst there are more attractive operations in the factory, or worse still, more highly paid and attractive operations outside.'[19] As feared, no one volunteered for transfer. Management responded to complaints from women workers that they could earn more in textiles by contacting a local firm, Vantona Textiles, to compare rates. One superintendent at the factory concluded that 'something should be done to increase the earnings of adult women in the Main Works. Whilst no one can guarantee what the results are likely to be, the financial return will be one of the main factors with which to retain and attract women.'[20] He proposed to increase the women's piecework bonus and, as with male employees, to provide a higher bonus figure than stated in national agreements. He also put forward merit awards for arduous and intricate jobs like the one described above and general merit awards for other women on time work, for example, inspectors or storekeepers.

The experience of acute labour shortage informed the firm's response to the EEF's enquiry on the suitability of the unions' grading proposals. These were thought too vague and likely to prevent firms from using labour with flexibility. The coil-winding work in question, for example, was simple in content but very important to the production of the factory. If it were put in a low grade category it would be even harder to persuade proficient women workers to transfer to it, as production required. But the firm went on to make a general point that with the raising of the school leaving age and the maintenance of conscription a shortage of male and female labour would occur and that 'Competition will therefore arise and if the Engineering Industry is to obtain an adequate share of female labour the wage rates will have to be

19. Ibid., circular 4 Mar. 1946 includes 'Statement – steps being taken to increase output of Plant Dept.'.
20. Ibid., Superintendent of Mechanical Department to Works Manager, 27 Mar. 1946.

made attractive.' The same applied to male labour but in its case competition from other employment was less strong as 'there is a natural bias in perhaps the majority of boys to seek employment in the Engineering Industry'.[21]

This does not mean that women were regarded as a labour force without special skills or experience and interchangeable between industries. The firm clearly wanted women experienced in engineering because they would meet output targets best; but it shows their recognition that in retaining women, persuading others to return and recruiting new workers they needed to offer more than the low wages of the Women's National Schedule.

A serious shortage of female labour faced Lucas as it tried to meet customer requirements, especially of items not manufactured since before the war. As civilian car production gathered pace after 1946, the components manufacturer found itself 900 workers down on its pre-war strength and forced to turn to male labour and to recruitment of women from the North of England, Scotland, Wales and Ireland to help make up the shortfall. A female personnel supervisor visited labour exchanges in Cardiff and Durham where women and girls were obliged to be interviewed by her before they received their unemployment benefit. Recruits, of whom there were few, were billeted by the firm's welfare officers and put through its now expanded training schools. For Irish recruits, 'we had something like the catholic equivalent of the Salvation Army to meet them in Liverpool and to send [them] down to us and our welfare officers looked after them'.[22] A year later the personnel manager confirmed that 'women have only been obtained in the Birmingham factories by continual recruitment in Southern Ireland' backed up by the extensive use of part-time and some evening shift working.[23] By 1952, 6,000 women and girls were employed of whom half were part-time workers. This avoided the need for nurseries, and childcare arrangements remained informal. According to the same personnel supervisor:

we couldn't have a nursery. . . . We hadn't got anywhere we could properly house a nursery . . . somebody who had been on afternoon shift would look after the children in the evening and they left them

21. This and preceding quotation, ibid., Director and General Manager of Works to Bailey, Chairman of EEF, 21 Mar. 1946.

22. Interview with MW 24 Feb. 1993.

23. Lucas Industries Plc, General Survey of Works and Products Including Capital Programmes and Maintenance and Reconstruction for the Financial Year 1948/9.

with their older children too. . . . It was very convenient for neigh-
bours to come if the women were going to work so that they could
share their responsibilities.[24]

As at Metropolitan-Vickers, female labour shortages forced the firm
to improve working conditions, experimenting with better lighting
and ventilation, new colour schemes, and a reduction of 'arduous
and unpleasant operations'. The personnel department also put in
a plea for better earnings to attract and retain women employees of
the standard they needed. But the female labour situation did not
start to ease for Lucas until after the mid-1950s.

The post-war labour shortage also led to the retention of wartime dilution agreements in many engineering firms. In striking
contrast to the First World War, none of the relaxation agreements
were abolished in 1945. As the EEF wrote to the director of the
London Association in 1951: 'the impingement of the export drive
and the re-armament programme . . . has made it very necessary for
the Agreements to remain in operation.'[25] In practice this seems to
have affected men more than women. While the Extended Employment of Women Agreement was little used, the EEF noted how 'so
far as the AEU (skilled men) Agreement is concerned, each year
since the end of the War we have received many hundreds of regis-
tration Forms affecting thousands of dilutees'.[26] Even so, individual
firms were forced to use male and female labour in ways which
began to undermine the boundaries between their work.

During the war, Liverpool employers had encountered difficulties in establishing the category of women's work in an area with
little previous female engineering employment. Post-war shortages
now threatened to reverse those demarcations they had managed
to establish. In February 1946 the Liverpool Association of Engineering Employers told the EEF that the labour exchange could not
provide women for jobs such as spot welding, spray painting and
simple assemblies and had offered unskilled and semi-skilled men
instead. Members were 'a little nervous about putting men on to
the work', the association told the EEF, 'in case they are unable to
revert to their practice, if and when, female labour should become
available'. In their response the EEF sought the advice of other
districts, among them Birmingham where BSA was employing men
on women's work in order to maintain continuous production of

24. Interview with MW 24 Feb. 1993.
25. EEF, Amendment of Relaxation Agreement, 1951–5, File 7, Letter from the
Director of the London Association, 11 Sept. 1951. MSS.237/3/1/251, R(6)256.
26. Ibid.

cycles and motor cycles. They were paid at the firm's minimum rate for production workers while the piecework price formerly paid to women was increased by 50 per cent. Lucas, as a well-established employer of women, was more cautious about employing men in this way because of the consequences for 'normal' production. Precautions included placing men doing women's work on the night shift, which women were debarred from working. Otherwise, they worked on the firm's lowest male operator's rate and in jobs where some women were already employed. Record cards were stamped 'employed on women's work due to temporary shortage of women', before being signed by the worker and initialled by foreman or superintendent. The Liverpool Association were advised to ensure that work groups stayed mixed, with at least some women employed so that work would be harder to establish as 'male'.[27] These examples show the strains and contradictions labour shortage brought about for employers attempting to keep control of the definitions of male and female work.

Part-time working was a less controversial means of overcoming the shortage of female labour and one which many engineering firms developed from their wartime experience. In the middle of 1944, *Engineering* noted, there had been 900,000 part-time workers in the industry, and although problems of training and supervision were likely to continue to present difficulties, 'a continuation of some form of part-time work may be an important factor in increasing production so long as the present manpower shortage persists'.[28] It was an explicit attempt to recruit the workforce which had been encouraged through government policy to give up work at the end of the war – women with domestic responsibilities.

Arrangements for part-time working were already established in the radio industry and branches of light engineering like lamps. Here part-time work was probably intended mainly to allow for the seasonality or instability of demand, rather than to accommodate women's home responsibilities. For instance, it had been common among radio and lamp firms for 'part-timers' to come in from 8 a.m. to 5 p.m. every other day. Sometimes women worked on a rota system which gave them two full days and three half days off a week.[29] From 1944, when records were first kept by the EEF, to

27. EEF, Female Labour Shortage, Liverpool Association. MRC MSS.237/3/1/ 72–5, E(3)70.
28. *Engineering*, 18 Jan. 1946, p. 54.
29. EEF, file marked 'Part-time workers' (n.d.) [1942–50]. EEF Head Office, Broadway House, London.

1950 the number of part-time workers remained high or increased in female trades like lamps, telephones and plastic moulding, where they now formed a fifth of the workforce. In electrical engineering and motor vehicles the figure remained constant at around 15 per cent. In 1951 Villiers Engineering Co. Ltd in Wolverhampton introduced a 'pairing' scheme between sixty women living in the same area, so that 'while one is working a shift at the factory, the other attends to the domestic duties of both. The women then change places . . .'.[30] Approximately half the firm's workforce was female and the women concerned were employed in machine shops and on inspection duties.[31] Pye's television factory in Cambridge relied largely on the employment of women to produce 2,000 sets a week. In 1947, it had recruited a number of married women on the not very catchy slogan of 'Make your own hours to suit your domestic responsibilities'. By 1950 much of its workforce was employed part-time.[32]

No employer seems to have gone as far as lamp manufacturer Ismay's in its attempts to attract women workers. In 1946 the female residents of Ilford were startled by the appearance of fifty posters issued by the firm offering free medical, dental and 'sun ray' treatments, free stockings and shoe repairs, 'good hot meals', no Saturday work, paid summer and autumn foreign holidays in return for 'clean, light, interesting work of varying nature'. 'Girls! What other job offers you all this?' Not many.[33] The firm also set up at this time a 'Key Operators' scheme with higher earnings promised to women of 'special ability and efficiency'.

Sometimes the focus of recruitment for part-time work was not simply women with domestic responsibilities but married women who had left engineering with valuable experience. In June 1948 the East Anglia Association of Engineering Employers, for example, told the EEF that 'some of the part-time workers are married women who had considerable experience with the firm before marriage and are of more use than the later full-time recruits'.[34]

* * *

30. *Engineering*, 22 Jun. 1951, p. 754.
31. *Wolverhampton Express and Star*, 13 Jun. 1951.
32. *Engineering*, 14 Jul. 1950, and Wages and Working Conditions of Part-timers, East Anglian Association to EEF, Jun. 1948. MRC EEF MSS.237/3/1/311, W(4)98.
33. Essex County Archives: Ismay of Ilford 1946/7 D/F 14/25. The foreign holidays were visits to families abroad who also worked at lamp factories.
34. EEF, file marked 'Part-time workers' (n.d.) [1942–50]. EEF Head Office, Broadway House, London.

Neither engineering employers nor trade unions wanted to see an indiscriminate return to home and family life for women workers in their industry. Post-war pressures meant they wanted to retain and attract women who had worked in wartime (and before). The AEU had conflicting responses to the challenge of the reconstruction era. It promoted women's employment (as semi-skilled workers) in the engineering industry together with a new unified wages structure as part of its modernising programme. Unresolved negotiations over grading and failure to achieve its wages plans produced defensiveness too – proposals to make women redundant before men or support for equality of rates that was mainly intended to prevent women from displacing men, for example. The general unions emerged in this period as, apparently, radicalised. They had abandoned separate grading of men and women in favour of joint grading and were publicly committed to equality of rates between men and women. But they were also still pragmatic and sceptical in approach. Meanwhile engineering firms were handicapped by the low rates of the Women's National Schedule and forced to offer additions to nationally agreed pay rates as well as other incentives, like part-time working, in order to retain workers or to draw experienced women back into the industry. They were also forced into expedients which aimed to keep the concepts of women's and men's work intact – Lucas registering men on women's work, for instance – but which began to blur them and reveal disadvantages. For the first time employers were forced to change their practices in ways that began to question the value of the tradition of the 'woman's rate' and 'women's work'.

Conclusion

This book has demonstrated the complexity of women's employment, challenging the particular importance given to male dominance – whether through gender ideology or through exclusion and job segregation – which pervades most historical explanations of women's work. The role of ideology in directing women into low paid and low status work is not, of course, denied. Within engineering, for example, the EEF clearly discouraged comprehensive training for women workers, whose main goal, in its view, was marriage and not an industrial career. The promotion of women within the industry to higher grades of skill and responsibility 'was not to be seriously considered'. Their wages were 'made on an entirely different basis' related to their social position as women and not to their skills as workers. It was men who were to be encouraged as the 'mainstay' of the industry.[1] Trade unions who recruited women were, in the eyes of the EEF, 'introducing a fundamental difference' and it was reluctant to extend agreements, apparently made on behalf of all engineering workers, to women. The question is whether male dominance of this kind is the key to understanding women's work. The present study has instead deliberately highlighted other factors which have influenced employers' use of labour.

Those who stress the agency of ideology neglect what is a more complicated picture. For these writers, employers, driven by gender ideology, defined women's work as consisting of unskilled, fragmented, repetitive tasks and modern production techniques. But, as we saw, this view leads to an account of women's employment

1. EEF, *Report to the Administration Committee by the Sub-Committee of the Administration Committee in Regard to Female Labour* (Jun. 1934), pp. 9–10, paras 39–40. MRC MSS.237/3/1/89, F(6)56.

based solely on the theme of male dominance in a deskilled, tightly controlled labour process. It gives no role to the other factors which influenced firms beyond preconceived notions of women's suitability for certain kinds of work. It also neglects the complexity of women's employment which was not, even among leading employers, associated with the newest and most advanced forms of production.

To broaden the range of influences acknowledged as affecting female employment was the aim of chapters 3 and 4. These showed how, during and after the First World War, the continued importance of skill and flexibility within engineering production were important in shaping employers' use of female labour. There were genuine economic concerns about the peacetime viability of the wartime methods of production with which female labour had been so closely associated. In consequence, inter-war employers, even in mass production trades, were unable to pare down their reliance on skilled male labour and on male production workers as much as they might have wished. This in turn questioned whether women were employed only within the setting of deskilled and rigorously controlled work. Chapter 4 demonstrated that, in an industry composed of different sectors exposed to different variations in profitability, competition and market stability, as engineering was, it is difficult to talk of tightening managerial control. With the market for the goods of new industries centred on novelty in design and variable demand, British engineering firms could not afford to imitate wholesale their American counterparts. Instead of being inevitably compelled towards ever greater control, they achieved only an uneven degree of deskilling which, as Chapter 3 showed, influenced both how women were employed and their degree of control over the work process. As we saw, it involved a reliance by employers like Lucas and GEC on women's experience, competencies and flexibility in order to meet a variable demand for their products, and vulnerability to pressure from organised labour from the mid-1930s onwards. In Chapter 3, then, unstable markets and a continuing need for a relatively experienced and versatile manual workforce (female and male) were added to the factors which influenced women's employment.

The weight given to ideology and other influences in employers' choice of labour was examined in Chapter 5. A study of female labour disputes between the wars revealed that employers resisted defining 'women's work' (beyond its semi-skilled or unskilled nature) so that they might remain free to decide how work was allocated.

Significantly, in the absence of union power following the lock-out, they did not automatically opt for female labour. Instead there had to be a range of factors in place for women to seem a profitable alternative to male workers. Engineering employers responded to a number of influences like cheapness, volume of work, competition, labour supply, and opposition from unions. A socially defined notion of suitability was only one factor in employers' choice of labour.

As well as broadening the explanation of women's employment beyond male dominance in order to take account of other influences and causes, the present study has re-evaluated the role and attitude of trade unions. General and craft unions are often presented as motivated by a gender ideology shared with employers which leads them to exclude women or restrict them to the least skilled work. But male trade unionists and employers did not share a single 'gender ideology' which controlled women's work, pay and union membership. The attitude of the general unions to women's recruitment was shaped by a growing sense of fairness and equity as well as by a desire to protect male jobs and pay. Such unions also began to put forward claims for wage increases that challenged employers' criteria for women's pay. Their outlook was thus more complicated than their apparent adherence to a gender-based wages structure suggests. Craft unions like the ASE did try to resist the extension of women's work but they were motivated by a need to control entry to their trades and protect standards of living for their members during a period of fragmentation of skilled work, unemployment and wage cuts.

Similarly, closer examination of the role of both craft and general trade unions in negotiating dilution reveals that it was not an unambiguous gender struggle in which the interests of women were sacrificed to those of men. In the First World War, the approach of the ASE to dilution and equal pay was part of a defensive response in the face of cheap, unskilled labour. It opposed the withdrawal of customary rights against the encroachment of the unskilled of either gender. In the Second World War, both skilled and general unions aimed to protect themselves against competition from rival workforces. The AEU's concern with women's work and pay under dilution was part of its broader strategy to control recruitment and rewards among the growing body of semi-skilled workers – male and female – over whom it had no control. General unions negotiated dilution on behalf of female as well as male members and wanted to ensure fair treatment of their female members as well as to protect the position of the latter. They also made positive attempts to deliver wage increases to the industry's female workers and to bring their pay more in line with the nature and value of their work.[2]

Theories which stress the role of beliefs about gender differences, then, leave out other factors which affect labour markets and employers' choice of labour. As this book has shown, the boundaries of women's work were also decided by the historical interaction between employers, unions and male and female workers within particular product and labour markets. Such theories also confine trade unions to a restrictive gender ideology, while evidence shows that alternative viewpoints competed for attention and held support. As we saw, these were reflected in changes towards the recruitment of women members, and in challenges unions made to the criteria for women's pay.

This book has deliberately chosen to explore the perspectives of employers and trade unions rather than those of women workers themselves. However, women's involvement with unions in the industry's collective bargaining procedure has revealed some of their own attitudes to work, pay and unionism, challenging the uninterest and passivity often attributed to them. They had distinct priorities – reductions in working hours, for example – and shorter horizons, with greater emphasis on immediate pay increases and less willingness to tolerate lengthy official procedures.

General unions learned from their experience of disputes between the wars that women, as well as men, had ideas of tolerable levels of effort, pay and working conditions and that, even if not expected to have a lifetime in industry, they were prepared to defend their interest in work and the conditions in which it was carried out. This did not necessarily translate into unionism, however. Chapter 6 showed that the circumstances in which women worked and their experience of collective bargaining were more likely to encourage spontaneous and unofficial industrial action than trade union membership. A more rounded depiction of women's experience of wartime engineering also confirmed that women were not passive or uninterested about the issues trade unions existed to defend, like pay and working conditions – nor even about union membership itself. But their attitudes were shaped by a perception that trade unions were irrelevant to them as temporary war workers or that unions failed to serve women's interests. Where pay was at issue, women could and did seek union membership and take

2. See also Richard Croucher, *Engineers at War* (1982).

industrial action or, alternatively, pursue unofficial action or transfer their membership to another union. The evidence of chapters 6 and 8 revealed more complex attitudes than the apathy contemporaries attributed to women workers. Instead a picture emerges of women as more astute buyers of trade-union services than men, their expectations of unions sharpened rather than lowered by their shorter industrial life. Through the fears and complaints of engineering employers negotiating dilution and equal pay in the Second World War, 'trained' and 'skilful' women are revealed as likely to feel aggrieved and to cause trouble and disruption as they left 'women's work' for better paid jobs or threatened to leave the industry if better rates for 'women's work' were not conceded. These are not the images of women workers typically portrayed by historians or theorists of women's work.

How widespread or significant these images might be would require a new and different study. It might also examine not factory work but factory life, most studies of which are either contemporary and sociological or concern the world wars. If this study has revealed, even unintentionally, unexpected attitudes to work, pay and unionism, much more must remain to be uncovered about habits and customs at work, group behaviour, and relationships with each other and with men. What this book has demonstrated is the value of probing beyond the simplistic messages of ideology to a more complex but wider world of women workers on the engineering shopfloor.

Bibliography

BOOKS AND ARTICLES

The place of publication, unless otherwise stated, is London.

Histories and theories of women's work

COCKBURN, CYNTHIA, 'The gendering of jobs', in S. WALBY (ed.), *Gender Segregation at Work* (1988).

FISHER, C.C., 'Towards a more complex understanding of occupational sex discrimination', *Journal of Economic Issues*, 21 (1987).

GALES, K. and MARKS, P., 'Twentieth century trends in the work of women in England and Wales', *Journal of the Royal Statistical Society*, 137 (1974).

HAKIM, CATHERINE, 'Grateful slaves and self-made women: fact and fiction in women's work orientations', *European Sociological Review*, 7. 2 (Sept. 1991).

HARTMANN, H., 'Capitalism, patriarchy and job segregation by sex', in M. BLAXALL and B. KEGAN (eds), *Women and the Workplace* (1976).

HATTON, T.J. and BAILEY, R.E., 'Female labour force participation in interwar Britain', *Oxford Economic Papers*, 40 (1988).

HUNT, FELICITY, 'Opportunities lost and gained: mechanisation and women's work in the London bookbinding and printing trades', in A.V. JOHN, *Unequal Opportunities. Women's Employment in England 1800–1918* (1986).

JORDAN, ELLEN, 'The exclusion of women from industry in nineteenth century Britain', *Comparative Studies in Society and History*, 31. 2 (Apr. 1989).

MINCER, J., 'Labor force participation of married women: a study of labor supply', in A.H. AMSDEN (ed.), *The Economics of Women and Work* (1980).

OSTERUD, N.G., 'Gender divisions and the organisation of work in the Leicester hosiery industry', in A.V. JOHN, *Unequal Opportunities. Women's Employment in England 1800–1918* (1986).

PHILLIPS, A. and TAYLOR, B., 'Sex and skill: notes towards a feminist economics', *Feminist Review*, 6 (1980).

ROSE, SONYA, 'Gender antagonism and class conflict: exclusionary strategies of male trade unionists in nineteenth century Britain', *Social History*, 13. 2 (May 1988).

THANE, PAT, 'The social, economic and political status of women', in PAUL JOHNSON (ed.), *Twentieth Century Britain. Economic, Social and Cultural Change* (1994).

WALBY, SYLVIA, 'Theorising patriarchy', *Sociology*, 23. 2 (May 1989).

ZEITLIN, JONATHAN, 'Social theory and the history of work', *Social History*, 8 (1983).

—— , 'Theories of women's work and occupational segregation', *Bulletin of the Society for the Study of Labour History* (1989).

AMSDEN A.H. (ed.), *The Economics of Women and Work* (1980).

BARKER, D.L. and ALLEN, S. (eds), *Dependence and Exploitation in Work and Marriage* (1976).

BEAUCHAMP, J., *Women Who Work* (1937).

BEECHEY, VERONICA, *Unequal Work* (1987).

BRADLEY, HARRIET, *Men's Work, Women's Work. A Sociological History of the Sexual Division of Labour in Employment* (1989).

COCKBURN, CYNTHIA, *Machinery of Dominance. Women, Men and Technical Know-How* (1985).

FINE, BEN, *Women's Employment and the Capitalist Family* (1992).

HAKIM, CATHERINE, *Key Issues in Women's Work. Female Heterogeneity and the Polarisation of Women's Employment* (1996).

JOHN, A.V., *Unequal Opportunities. Women's Employment in England 1800–1918* (1986).

JOSEPH, GEORGE, *Women at Work. The British Experience* (1983).

LEWIS, JANE, *Women in England 1870–1950. Sexual Divisions and Social Change* (1984).

MALLIER, A.T. and ROSSER, M.J., *Women and the Economy. A Comparative Study of Britain and the USA* (1987).

MCBRIDE, THERESA, *The Domestic Revolution. The Modernisation of Household Service in England and France, 1820–1920* (1976).

PAHL, R.E. (ed.), *On Work. Historical, Comparative and Theoretical Approaches* (1988).

PUGH, MARTIN, *Women and the Women's Movement in Britain 1914–1959* (1992).

PURVIS, J. (ed.), *Women's History. Britain 1850–1945. An Introduction* (1995).

ROBERTS, ELIZABETH, *Women's Work 1840–1940* (1995 edn).

ROSE, SONYA O., *Limited Livelihoods. Gender and Class in Nineteenth Century England* (1992).

TILLY, LOUISE and JOAN, SCOTT, *Women, Work and Family* (1978).

WALBY, SYLVIA, *Theorising Patriarchy* (1990).

—— (ed.), *Gender Segregation at Work* (1988).

——, *Patriarchy at Work* (1986).

New industries and women's employment

APPLEBAUM, EILEEN, 'Technology and the redesigning of work in the insurance industry', in BARBARA DRYGULSKI et al. (eds), *Women, Work and Technology* (1987).

CASTLE, J., 'Factory work for women: Courtauld's and GEC between the wars', in B. LANCASTER and T. MASON (eds), *Life and Labour in a Twentieth Century City: The Experience of Coventry* (1986).

COOPER, PATRICIA, 'The faces of gender: sex segregation and work relations at Philco 1928–38', in AVA BARON (ed.), *Work Engendered. Toward a New History of American Labor* (1991).

FERGUSON, NEAL A., 'Women's work: employment opportunities and economic roles, 1918–1939', *Albion*, 7 (Spring 1975).

GREEN, VENUS, 'Goodbye Central: automation and the decline of personal service in the Bell System, 1878–1921', *Technology and Culture*, 36 (1995).

DE GROOT, GERTJAN and SCHROVER, MARLOU, 'Between men and machines: women workers in new industries 1870–1940', *Social History*, 20. 3 (Oct. 1995).

JORDAN, ELLEN, 'The lady clerks at the Prudential: the beginning of vertical segregation by sex in clerical work in nineteenth-century Britain', *Gender and History*, 8. 1 (Apr. 1996).

LIPARTITO, KENNETH, 'When women were switches: technology, work and gender in the telephone industry, 1890–1920', *American Historical Review* (Oct. 1994).

MILKMAN, RUTH, 'Female factory labor and industrial structure: control and conflict over "Woman's Place" in automobile and electrical manufacturing', *Politics and Society*, 12. 2 (1983).

SAVAGE, MIKE, 'Trade unionism, sex segregation and the State: women's employment in new industries in inter-war Britain', *Social History*, 13. 2 (May 1988).

SCHROVER, MARLOU, 'Cooking up women's work: women workers in the Dutch food industries 1889–1960', in GERTJAN DE GROOT and MARLOU SCHROVER (eds), *Women Workers and Technological Change in Europe in the Nineteenth and Twentieth Centuries* (1995).

ANDERSON, G. (ed.), *The White Blouse Revolution. Female Office Workers since 1870* (1988).

COHN, SAMUEL, *The Process of Occupational Sex-typing. The Feminization of Clerical Labour in Great Britain* (1985).

GLUCKSMANN, MIRIAM, *Women Assemble. Women Workers and the New Industries in Inter-war Britain* (1990).

DE GROOT, GERTJAN and SCHROVER, MARLOU (eds), *Women Workers and Technological Change in Europe in the Nineteenth and Twentieth Centuries* (1995).

SMITH, H. LLEWELYN, *The New Survey of London Life and Labour* (2 vols, 1931).

STROM, SHARON HARTMAN, *Beyond the Typewriter. Gender, Class and the Origins of Modern American Office Work 1900–1930* (1992).

War and women's employment

CARRUTHERS, S.L., 'Manning the factories: propaganda and policy on the employment of women 1939–1947', *History*, 75. 244 (Jun. 1990).

MORGAN, BEN, 'The efficient utilisation of labour in engineering factories (with special reference to women's work)', *Proceedings of the Institution of Mechanical Engineers*, May 1918.

REID, A., 'Dilution, trade unionism and the State in Britain during the First World War', in S. TOLLIDAY and J. ZEITLIN (eds), *Shopfloor Bargaining and the State. Historical and Comparative Perspectives* (1985).

PARKER, R.A.C., 'British rearmament, 1936–39: Treasury, trade unions and skilled labour', *English Historical Review*, 96 (1981).

SMITH, HAROLD L., 'The problem of equal pay for equal work in Great Britain during World War II', *Journal of Modern History*, 53 (Dec. 1981).

—— 'The effect of the war on the status of women', in H.L. SMITH (ed.), *War and Social Change. British Society in the Second World War* (1986).

SUMMERFIELD, PENNY, 'Women, war and social change: women in Britain in World War II', in A. MARWICK (ed.), *Total War and Social Change* (1988).

——, 'What women learned from the Second World War', *History of Education*, 18. 3 (1989).

——, 'The patriarchal discourse of Human Capital: training women for war work, 1939–45', *Journal of Gender Studies*, 2. 2 (Nov. 1993).

——, *Reconstructing Women's Wartime Lives. Discourse and Subjectivity in Oral Histories of the Second World War* (1998).

——, 'Women and war in the twentieth century', in J. PURVIS (ed.), *Women's History. Britain 1850–1945. An Introduction* (1995).

——, '"They didn't want women back in that job": the Second World War and the construction of gendered work histories', *Labour History Review*, 63. 1 (Spring 1998).

THOM, DEBORAH, 'A revolution in the workplace? Women's work in munitions factories and technological change 1914–1918', in GERTJAN DE GROOT and MARLOU SCHROVER (eds), *Women Workers and Technological Change in Europe in the Nineteenth and Twentieth Centuries* (1995).

BRAYBON, GAIL, *Women Workers in the First World War* (1989).

BRAYBON, GAIL and SUMMERFIELD, PENNY, *Out of the Cage. Women's Experiences in Two World Wars* (1987).

CALDER, ANGUS, *The People's War, Britain 1939–45* (1971).

COLE, G.D.H., *Trade Unionism in the Munitions Industries* (1923).

CROUCHER, RICHARD, *Engineers at War* (1982).

DOUIE, VERA, *Daughters of Britain. An Account of the Work of British Women during the Second World War* (1950).

GOLDSMITH, MARGARET, *Women at War* (1943).

——, *Women and the Future* (1946).

INMAN, PEGGY, *Labour in the Munitions Industries* (1957).

MARWICK, ARTHUR, *War and Social Change in the Twentieth Century* (1974).

MASS-OBSERVATION, *People in Production. An Enquiry into British War Production, Part I. A Report prepared by Mass-Observation for the Advertising Service Guild* (1942).

——, *War Factory* (1943; Cresset Library edn, 1987).

——, *The Journey Home. A Report prepared by Mass-Observation for the Advertising Service Guild* (1944).

PARKER, H.M.D., *Manpower. A Study of War-time Policy and Administration* (1957).

PEDERSON, SUSAN, *Family, Dependence and the Origins of the Welfare State. Britain and France 1914–1945* (1993).

SUMMERFIELD, PENNY, *Women Workers in the Second World War. Production and Patriarchy in Conflict* (1984).

THOM, DEBORAH, *Nice Girls and Rude Girls. Women Workers in World War One* (1997).

THOMAS, GEOFFREY, *Women at Work. Wartime Social Survey. An Enquiry made for the Office of the Ministry of Reconstruction* (Jun. 1944).

TOMLINSON, JIM, *Democratic Socialism and Economic Policy* (1997).
WILLIAMS-ELLIS, AMABEL, *Women in Wartime Factories* (1943).
WOOLLACOTT, ANGELA, *On Her their Lives Depend. Munition Workers and the Great War* (1994).

Women and trade unions

NICKELL, S.J., 'Trade unions and the position of women in the industrial wage structure', *British Journal of Industrial Relations*, 15 (1977).
TOLLIDAY, STEVEN, 'Militancy and organisation: women workers and trade unions in the motor trades in the 1930s', *Oral History*, 11. 2 (Autumn 1983).

BAIN, G.S. and PRICE, R., *Profiles of Union Growth. A Comparative Statistical Portrait of Eight Countries* (1980).
BLACKMAN, JANET, *Economic History of Women in England 1870– 1980* (1992).
BOSTON, SARAH, *Women Workers and Trade Unions* (1987).
BURMAN, S. (ed.), *Fit Work for Women* (1979).
JOHN, A.V. (ed.), *Unequal Opportunities. Women's Employment in England 1800–1918* (1986).
LEWENHAK, SHEILA, *Women and Trade Unions. An Outline History of Women in the British Trade Union Movement* (1977).
SOLON, N.C., *Women in the Trade Unions 1874–1976* (1978).
VOYDANOFF, P. (ed.), *Work and Family. Changing Roles of Men and Women* (1984).

Company and industrial histories

CATTERALL, R.E., 'Electrical engineering', in N. BUXTON and D.H. ALDCROFT (eds), *British Industry between the Wars. Instability and Industrial Development 1919–1939* (1979).
CHURCH, R.A., 'Innovation, monopoly and supply of vehicle components in Britain, 1880–1930: the growth of Joseph Lucas Ltd.', *Business History Review*, 52. 2 (Summer 1978).
CHURCH, ROY and MILLER, MICHAEL, 'The Big Three: competition, management and marketing in the British motor industry, 1922–1939', in BARRY SUPPLE (ed.), *Essays in British Business History* (1977).
COLEMAN, D.C., *Courtauld's. An Economic and Social History* (3 vols, 1969, 1977).

MILLER, M. and CHURCH, R.A., 'Motor manufacturing' in N. BUXTON and D.H. ALDCROFT (eds), *British Industry between the Wars. Instability and Industrial Development 1919–1939* (1979).

CORLEY, T.A.B., *Domestic Electrical Appliances* (1966).

HANNAH, LESLIE, *Electricity before Nationalisation. A Study of the Development of the Electricity Supply Industry in Britain to 1948* (1979).

JONES, ROBERT and MARRIOTT, OLIVER, *Anatomy of a Merger. A History of GEC, AEI and English Electric* (1970).

KAHN, A.E., *Great Britain in the World Economy* (1946).

NOCKOLDS, HAROLD, *Lucas: The First 100 Years* (2 vols, 1976 and 1978).

ODDY D. and MILLER, D., *The Making of the Modern British Diet* (1976).

POLLARD, SIDNEY, *The Development of the British Economy 1914–1967* (1969).

SUPPLE, B., *Essays in British Business History* (1977).

WILSON, JOHN F., *Ferranti and the British Electrical Industry 1864–1930* (1988).

Engineering industry

CANEL, ANNIE and ZACHMANN, KARIN, 'Gaining access, crossing boundaries: women in engineering. A comparative perspective', *History and Technology* special issue, 14 (1997).

PURSER, CARROLL, ' "Am I a lady or an engineer?" The origins of the Women's Engineering Society in Britain, 1918–1940', *Technology and Culture*, 34 (1993).

TOLLIDAY, STEVEN, 'Management and labour in Britain 1896–1939', in J. ZEITLIN and S. TOLLIDAY (eds), *The Automobile Industry and its Workers* (1986).

ZEITLIN, JONATHAN, 'The labour strategies of British engineering employers, 1890–1922', in H.F. GOSPEL and C.R. LITTLER (eds), *Managerial Strategies and Industrial Relations. An Historical and Comparative Study* (1983).

——, 'The internal politics of employer organisation: the Engineering Employers' Federation 1896–1939', in J. ZEITLIN and S. TOLLIDAY (eds), *The Power to Manage? Employers and Industrial Relations in Comparative Historical Perspective* (1990).

ZEITLIN, JONATHAN, 'The triumph of adversarial bargaining: industrial relations in British engineering 1880–1939', *Politics and Society*, 18. 3 (1990).

ZEITLIN, JONATHAN and MCKINLAY, A.,'The meanings of managerial prerogative: industrial relations and the organisation of work in British engineering, 1880–1939', *Business History*, 31. 2 (Apr. 1989).

DOWNS, LAURA LEE, *Manufacturing Inequality. Gender Division in the French and British Metal-working Industries, 1914–1939* (1995).

DRAKE, BARBARA, *Women in the Engineering Trades. A Problem, a Solution and Some Criticism: Being a Report based on an Enquiry by a Joint Committee of the Labour Research Department and the Fabian Women's Group* (1918).

JEFFERYS, J.B., *The Story of the Engineers 1800–1945* (1945).

MARSH, ARTHUR, *Industrial Relations in Engineering* (1965).

WIGHAM, ERIC, *The Power to Manage. A History of the Engineering Employers' Federation* (1973).

YATES, M.L., *Wages and Labour in British Engineering* (1937).

ZEITLIN, JONATHAN, *Between Flexibility and Mass Production. Strategic Debate and Industrial Reorganisation in British Engineering 1830–1990* (forthcoming).

——, *The Sinews of Flexibility. Skills, Training and Technical Education in British Engineering, 1850–1980* (book manuscript in progress).

Labour market theories

BEECHEY, VERONICA, 'Women and production: a critical analysis of some sociological theories of women's work', in A. KUHN and A. WOLPE (eds), *Feminism and Materialism* (1978).

HARRISON, BENNETT and SUM, A., 'The theory of dual or segmented labour markets', *Journal of Economic Issues* (1979).

RUBERY, J., 'Structured labour markets, worker organisation, and low pay', in A.H. AMSDEN (ed.), *The Economics of Women and Work* (1980).

BECKER, G., *The Economics of Discrimination* (1957).

CRAIG, C., RUBERY, J., TARLING, R. and WILKINSON, F., *Labour Market Structure, Industrial Organisation and Low Pay* (1982).

DOERINGER, P. and PIORE, M.J., *Internal Labor Markets in Manpower Analysis* (1971).

MARSDEN, D., *The End of Economic Man? Custom and Competition in Labour Markets* (1986).

PIORE, M.J., *Birds of Passage. Migrant Labor and Industrial Societies* (1979).

PIORE, M.J. and BERGER, S., *Dualism and Discontinuity in Industrial Societies* (1980).

PIORE, M.J. and SABEL, C.F., *The Second Industrial Divide. Possibilities for Prosperity* (1984.)

SABEL, C.F., *Work and Politics. The Division of Labor in Industry* (1982).

Labour process debate

ARMSTRONG, P., 'Labour and monopoly capital, the degradation of debate', in R. HYMAN and W. STREECK (eds), *New Technology and Industrial Relations* (1988).

BEECHEY, VERONICA, 'The sexual division of labour and the labour process', in S. WOOD (ed.), *The Degradation of Work? Deskilling and the Labour Process* (1982).

KELLY, J., 'Management's redesign of work: labour process, labour markets and product markets', in D. KNIGHTS, H. WILMOTT and D. COLLINSON (eds), *Job Redesign: Critical Perspectives on the Labour Market* (1985).

LAZONICK, WILLIAM, 'Industrial relations and technical change: the case of the self-acting mule', *Cambridge Journal of Economics*, 3. 3 (1979).

LIFF, SONIA, 'Technical change and occupational sex-typing', in D. KNIGHTS and H. WILMOTT (eds), *Gender and the Labour Process* (1986).

MARX, KARL, 'The results of the immediate process of production', unpublished paper appended to *Capital*, vol. 1 (Pelican edn, 1982).

BRAVERMAN, HARRY, *Labor and Monopoly Capital* (1974).

KNIGHTS, D., WILMOTT, H. and COLLINSON, D. (eds), *Job Redesign: Critical Perspectives on the Labour Market* (1985).

STURDY, A., KNIGHTS, D. and WILMOTT, H. (eds), *Skill and Consent. Contemporary Studies in the Labour Process* (1992).

THOMPSON, P., *The Nature of Work. An Introduction to Debates on the Labour Process* (1993).

WOOD, S. (ed.), *The Degradation of Work? Deskilling and the Labour Process* (1982).

——, *The Transformation of Work? Skill, Flexibility, and the Labour Process* (1989).

Manufacturing practice

ARMITAGE, H.C., 'Jigs, tools and special machines with their relation to the production of standardised parts', *Proceedings of the Institution of Mechanical Engineers*, Mar. 1919.

——, 'Machine tools from the manufacturing user's point of view', *Proceedings of the Institution of Automobile Engineers*, Dec. 1930.

AUSTIN, SIR HERBERT, 'The influence of mass production on design', *Proceedings of the Institute of Production Engineers*, 14. 8 (Aug. 1935).

ENGELBACH, C.R.F., 'Problems in manufacture', Presidential Address, *Proceedings of the Institution of Automobile Engineers*, 1933–4.

HURFORD, G., 'Mechanisation in a works', *Proceedings of the Institute of Production Engineers*, 11. 8 (Nov. 1932).

LYDDON, DAVE, 'The myth of mass production and the mass production of myth', *Historical Studies in Industrial Relations*, 1 (Mar. 1996).

WHITSON, KEVIN, 'Scientific management and production management practice in Britain between the wars', *Historical Studies in Industrial Relations*, 1 (Mar. 1996).

MANUSCRIPT SOURCES

Engineering Employers' Federation, Broadway House, London

'Part-time workers', undated file [1942–50].

Modern Records Centre, University of Warwick

Amalgamated Engineering Union

Executive Council minutes 1900–1950.
National Committee reports of proceedings 1920–1950.
Monthly Report/Monthly Journal 1900–1950.
East Midlands Joint Standing Committee of Engineering Employers minute books 1920–1940.

Engineering Employers' Federation

Main series of minute books 1900–1950.
Minutes of the Administration Committee 1924–1936.
Misc. series of minute books 1920–1949.
Minutes of negotiating conferences held with trade unions and union federations 1897–1927.
Minutes of special and central conferences held with trade unions 1919–1950.

Microfilms of subject and correspondence files (the 'disputes' files) 1900–1950.
Wage rates data 1897–1961.
Wages items 1862–1965.
Wage and other enquiries 1926–1949.
Workforce statistics 1910–1950.

National Union of General and Municipal Workers

National Executive Council minutes 1920–1950.
Reports of the biennial congress 1920–1950.
General and Municipal Workers' Journal 1931–1950 (incomplete).

Transport and General Workers' Union

General Executive Council minutes 1924–1950.
Minutes and records of biennial delegate conferences 1925–1949.
Annual reports 1922–1950.
The Record 1921–1940.
File of correspondence concerning 'poaching' and relations with AEU 1942–3.

Trades Unions Congress

Engineering industry 1927–60.

Public Record Office, London

Board of Trade Departmental Committees 1916–1928, BT 55.
Board of Trade Chief Industrial Adviser 1929–1932, BT 56.
Minister of Reconstruction, Secretariat Files 1943–1951, CAB 124.
War Cabinet Committees on Reconstruction 1941–1945, CAB 87.
Department of Employment and predecessors: industrial relations registered files 1924–1950, LAB 10.
Welfare Department 1940–1950, LAB 26.
Official Histories: correspondence and papers 1940–1950, LAB 76.
Ministry of Supply files 1946–1950, SUPP 14.

Company archives

GEC-Alsthom, formerly Metropolitan-Vickers, Trafford Park, Manchester: AEI personnel department files 1918–1960.

The General Electric Company, London: English Electric, annual reports 1919–1930, GEC annual reports 1925–51.

Company magazine, *The Loudspeaker,* 1924–38, Local Studies Dept., Coventry City Library.

GEC-Plessey Telecommunications Plc., Coventry: *A Brief History of GEC Telecommunications Ltd* produced by the Company (1981).

Joseph Lucas Ltd, file titled 'Women – historical', n.d., British Motor Industry Heritage Trust, Studley, Warks.

Lucas Industries Plc., Brueton House, Solihull: Joseph Lucas Ltd, minutes of the board of directors, including managing director's reports to the board of directors, 1928–1950, annual reports 1912–1950.

Company magazine, *Lucas Reflections,* 1921–1950, Birmingham Central Library.

Professional bodies

The Women's Engineering Society, Institute of Electrical Engineers, London

Council minutes 1919–1944.
Correspondence 1919–1945.
The Woman Engineer 1920–50.

NEWSPAPERS AND PERIODICALS

Coventry Chamber of Commerce, *Annual Report.*
Coventry Herald.
The Engineer.
Engineering.
Engineering World News and Views.
The Midland Daily Telegraph.
Proceedings of the Institute of Automobile Engineers.
Proceedings of the Institute of Mechanical Engineers.
Proceedings of the Institute of Production Engineers.
Times Engineering Supplement.
Wolverhampton Express and Star.

PRINTED GOVERNMENT REPORTS

A Study of the Factors which have Operated in the Past and those which are Operating Now to Determine the Distribution of Women in Industry, Cmnd 3508 (1929).
British Labour Statistics Historical Abstract 1886–1968 (1971).

Final Report on the Third Census of Production of the UK (1924), The Iron and Steel Trades, the Engineering Trades and the Non-Ferrous Metals Trades (1931).

Final Report of the Fourth Census of Production of the UK (1930) Part II, The Iron and Steel Trades, the Engineering and Shipbuilding and Vehicle Trades, the Non-Ferrous Metals Trades (1934).

Final Report of the Fifth Census of Production and the Import Duties Act Inquiry (1935) Part II, The Iron and Steel Trades, the Engineering and Shipbuilding and Vehicle Trades, the Non-Ferrous Metals Trades (1939).

The Report on the Census of Production for 1954.

The Committee on Industry and Trade, Iron and Steels Trades. Engineering, Electrical Manufacture, Shipbuilding, Being Part IV of a Survey of Industry, Cmnd 3282 (1928).

Official History of the Ministry of Munitions.

Report of the Committee on Women in Industry, Cmnd 167 (1919). Appendices: Summaries of Evidence.

Royal Commission on Equal Pay, *Minutes of Evidence* (1945–6).

UNPUBLISHED THESES

CARR, F.W., 'Engineering Workers and the Rise of Labour in Coventry 1914–1939' (Ph.D. thesis, University of Warwick, 1979).

CASTLE, J., 'Factory Work for Women in Inter-war Britain: the Experience of Women Workers at GEC and Courtauld's in Coventry 1919–39' (MA thesis, University of Warwick, 1984).

CLAYDON, T.J., 'The Development of Trade Unionism among British Automobile and Aircraft Workers, c.1914–1946.' (Ph.D. thesis, University of Kent, 1981).

DOWNS, LAURA LEE, 'Women in Industry, 1914–39: the Employers' Perspective. A Comparative Study of the French and British Metals Industry' (Ph.D. thesis, University of Columbia, 1987).

HOWARD, GARY, 'Trade Unions and Dilution: the Coventry Engineering Industry during World War II' (MA thesis, University of Warwick, 1994).

KOZAK, MARION, 'Women Munitions Workers During the First World War' (Ph.D. thesis, Hull University, 1976).

KREIS, STEVEN, 'The Diffusion of an Idea. The History of Scientific Management in Britain 1890–1945' (Ph.D. thesis, University of Missouri, Columbia, 1987).

WIGHTMAN, CLARE, 'Key Girls. The Engineering Industry and Women's Employment 1900–50. (Ph.D. thesis, University of London, 1997).

Index

References to tables and figures are in **bold**.